206

God, Church, and Flag

God, Church, and Flag

Senator Joseph R. McCarthy
and the Catholic Church
1950–1957

by
Donald F. Crosby, S.J.

Library of Congress Cataloging in Publication Data

Crosby, Donald F   1933–
    God, church, and flag

    Bibliography: p.
    Includes index.
    1. McCarthy, Joseph Raymond, 1908–1957.
2. Catholics—United States History.   3. United
States—Politics and government—1945–1953.
4. United States—Politics and government—1953–
1961.   5. Legislators—United States—Biography.
I. Title.
E748.M143 C76   973.918'092'4   77–14064
ISBN 0-8078-1312-5

To
John Bernard McGloin, S.J.

Table of Contents

Preface

I suppose it is a sign of the changing times that hardly anyone noticed how Catholics voted in the presidential election of 1972. Yet it was an epochal event in American religious history, for it signaled the first time that Catholics had voted for a Republican candidate for president. That no one seemed to care how Catholics voted is also of great moment, especially when one contrasts it to the intensive scrutiny given to the Catholic vote for Senator Joe McCarthy. Although no one takes more than a passing interest in what Catholics thought in 1972 of Richard Nixon, many political commentators in the fifties seemed obsessed with the question of what *Catholics* thought about McCarthy.

Between 1952 (the year of McCarthy's reelection to the Senate) and 1972 most observers stopped thinking about the Catholic vote as a solid bloc. Rather, they began to believe that Catholics vote according to their social status, their occupation, their region, their suburb, their background, their prejudices, or any of the other factors that motivate the typical American voter.

But in times past Catholics formed their own monolithic entity —standing apart, living apart, and voting apart (or at least that is the way the conventional wisdom usually had it). To be sure, one could find solid reasons for thinking that Catholics were somehow "different" from the rest of American society. Many Catholics did in fact view themselves as an embattled minority, struggling to maintain the purity of their religion and striving above all to prove their patriotism. In days gone by, it took little imagination to see Catholics as a society unto themselves, protecting peculiar beliefs and acting in a manner that seemed more "foreign" than truly "American." Above all, Catholics seemed to be one of the most combative sectors of American society, always ready to do battle with the Protestants and Other Americans United for Separation of Church and State, the American Association of University Professors, the Civil Liberties Union, or even the *New York Times*—as the occasion demanded.

The Catholic reaction to Senator Joseph Raymond McCarthy of Wisconsin was one of the most controversial chapters in the continuing story of Catholic confrontation with the rest of American society. To many observers of the American scene, it seemed as if Catholics had gone out of their way to defend their fellow Catholic, Joe McCarthy. Dissident Catholic voices often seemed few and enfeebled, and Catholic McCarthyites appeared to form a large and inflammatory majority. To many a frustrated American liberal engaged in the angry battle with McCarthy and the McCarthyites, it seemed that Neanderthals had captured the American Catholic church. The "Catholic bloc" was overwhelmingly for McCarthy—or so the liberals believed. In addition, many Catholic liberals and intellectuals felt themselves isolated and outshouted and wondered if McCarthyism had not taken over the whole Catholic community.

Did McCarthy really capture the loyalty of the nation's Catholics? Or was this just another myth in a controversy that had more than its share of myths? This essay will attempt to determine the true extent, the fluctuations, and the intensity of McCarthy's Catholic following (especially as compared to Protestant and Jewish opinion of McCarthy). At the same time, of course, we will want to find answers to the same questions for McCarthy's none-too-loyal Catholic opposition. It will not do, however, simply to describe the limits of McCarthy's Catholic strength: we will need to determine the ideological sources of both Catholic McCarthyism and anti-McCarthyism. Did they lie in the church's teachings, in the American political tradition (both liberal and conservative), or in other areas? Finally, we will try to see what part the bishops, the lower clergy, the laity, the Catholic press, and the many Catholic charitable and social organizations played in the story. Did the Catholic lay people go their own way, or did they blindly follow the lead of the hierarchy?

Preface

Catholic response to McCarthy did not happen in a vacuum, of course. In reacting to McCarthy, Catholics found themselves thrown into painful and sometimes even violent contact with other Americans—with Protestant liberals and conservatives, with Jewish Americans who had their own divisions, and with liberal pundits in search of a story. This interaction of Catholics with the rest of American society forms another large area of our story. Did the struggle cause an eruption of ill feeling between Protestants and Catholics, or did it bring them closer together? How did the liberal and intellectual journals like the *Nation* and the *New Republic* react to the Catholics as they took the measure of their fellow Catholic, Joe McCarthy? And finally, what did the professional politicians, both Democratic and Republican, think of all this? Did the Democrats simply continue to take the "Catholic vote" for granted, even in the face of a highly publicized Catholic politician who somehow had ended up in the camp of the enemy? We will try to find solutions to these problems as well.

Finally, a set of larger interpretative questions will occupy our attention. What does the McCarthy story say about the historical role of American Catholicism? What was the church's position in American society? What was the extent of its assimilation into that society? What is the impact of religion on one's politics? What is the impact of politics on one's religion? We will try to answer all of these questions in the course of our investigations.

The problem of communism is, of course, the larger question with which this book must deal. It has also formed the background for much Catholic history in the past one hundred years, both that of American Catholics and that of Catholics across the globe. Indeed, one wonders if anything has so mesmerized Catholicism in the past century as the continuing problem of Marxism. Long before the cold-war years, Catholics stood in the vanguard of those dedicated to the eradication of communism. In the McCarthy era this impulse reached its zenith, for true Americanism and true Catholicism both found a common base in the drive against the Communists, and

Preface

what was more verifiably anti-Communist than McCarthyism? The McCarthy controversy illuminated the problem of Catholic anti-communism as never before, throwing into full light both the ideological conflict between the Catholic left and right and the struggle for power within the Catholic community.

If this study focuses more on Catholic elites than on the masses of Catholics, it is because the elites took a much more active part in the controversy. This is not to say, however, that the masses of Catholics failed to react to McCarthy. Unquestionably they did respond to him, and the author has been at pains to describe that reaction by analyzing the results of opinion polls and of certain key elections in which McCarthyism seemed to be a factor.

A word now about terminology. Throughout this work the reader will find references to Catholic "leaders." This does not mean that the leaders in fact led the rest of the Catholic community in the sense that a general leads an army or even that a mayor leads a city council. Rather, we have used the word in the sense in which it was widely used in the days of McCarthy and which is still fashionable to some extent: the leaders were the elite in the Catholic church. They were the Catholics who held the most important, responsible, and prestigious positions—the bishops, the editors of the more important journals and diocesan newspapers, the heads of religious orders, the presidents or chairmen of the large Catholic fraternal and charitable associations, and some of the politicians whom one naturally and without fear of correction would label "Catholic politicians."

The terms *Catholic conservative* and *Catholic liberal* also occur repeatedly in the pages that follow. The author has used the word *conservative* to describe the McCarthyites and the word *liberal* to define the anti-McCarthy forces. The writers of the period used the words in that way, and the terms accurately described what in fact was true: the Catholic McCarthyites generally took a conservative stand on domestic issues, following the Republicans in their opposition to such programs as legislation to aid labor unions, to expand social security, to provide public housing for the needy, and to assist with health and educational schemes. The Catholic conservatives also tended to oppose the extension of civil rights and took a dim view of the liberals who placed such heavy emphasis on the preservation of civil liberties. In foreign policy they gravitated to the Taft-Knowland-Jenner forces who favored isolationism and found the security programs of the Democrats radically deficient. By and large, the Catholic conservatives gathered around the McCarthy standard—and we do them no injustice by calling them conservatives. This is not to deny that a few Catholic conservatives opposed McCarthy, or that a small number of Catholic McCarthyites favored more liberal programs of domestic and foreign policy. They formed rare exceptions, however, and we have so noted them in the text. By contrast, the Catholic liberals favored the New Deal–Fair Deal programs of social legislation as well as the cold-war foreign policies of the Truman administration. In the growing debate over security, they tended to join the other Democrats who defended the Truman-Acheson policies. Not unexpectedly, they rejected the McCarthyite approach to the problem of subversion in government. Again, a few Catholic liberals favored McCarthy and a smaller number of anti-McCarthy Catholics opposed the social welfare schemes of the New Deal and Fair Deal. They also constituted an exception, however, and we have described them as such in the pages that follow.

This essay represents an attempt to describe a most crucial chapter in the history of American religious life. The author's purpose has been to make a coherent statement about the role of religion in American culture and about the impact of American society, in turn, on the churches. If in the course of the following pages a better picture emerges of both McCarthy and McCarthyism, then so much the better, but that is not the primary focus of the piece. The literature on McCarthyism is voluminous and still growing, but the works on contemporary American Catholicism are neither. This book aims to strengthen that body of writing.

A word now about sources. This study relies not only on the abundant printed works that flow from this period (newspapers, magazines, memoirs, etc.) but on a large mass of archival materials as well. Some of these collections, such as the Benton Papers at the State Historical Society of Wisconsin and the Jesuit Archives at Fordham University, proved to be enormously valuable. Others, among them the presidential papers of Harry S Truman and Dwight David Eisenhower, were considerably less so. Neither president paid much attention to the question of McCarthy and the Catholics; each chose instead to let the professional politicians in his party handle the issue at a lower level. None of this should occasion surprise. Since Eisenhower preferred at all times to pretend that McCarthy did not exist, he naturally tended to ignore the topic this book discusses. With Truman the case was different: although he battled long and hard with McCarthy, he took little interest in the religious dimensions of the McCarthy issue and treated McCarthyism simply as a partisan political question. It does not seem to have occurred to him (as it did to others in his party) that Catholic votes might be at stake. The author's careful canvass of both the Eisenhower and Truman papers yielded no surprises and few real "finds" that earlier scholars had failed to uncover.

Equally disappointing were the recently opened papers of Bishop G. Bromley Oxnam, the prominent Methodist divine who played a key role in the church-state issues of the period. Although Oxnam was deeply embroiled in most of the battles between Protestants and Catholics that arose over the question of Communists in government, he paid little attention either to the McCarthy squabble or to its religious aspects. Again, the reasons are not hard to find: the McCarthy years saw Oxnam deeply involved in his own battles with congressional investigating committees—most of all with the House Un-American Activities Committee, which believed that his liberal views on social questions showed softness on communism. In private he condemned McCarthy with vehemence, seeing McCarthy's brand of antiintellectualism as a mortal threat to civil liberties in America. In public he said little about McCarthy and nothing at all about the senator's personal Catholicism or his Catholic following.

Preface

The papers of Senator McCarthy are closed to scholars; they probably will remain so for years to come, thanks to the unrelenting efforts of his widow to protect his manuscripts from the eyes of prying historians. It is highly unlikely, however, that the collection contains anything of relevance for this study, since the senator took such little interest in the religious dimensions of his politics. Furthermore, it was his annoying habit to conduct most of his business through personal conversation (usually over the telephone), leaving as little as possible in writing.

A list of all the people who helped with the preparation of this work would rival the Boston telephone book in length. Suffice it to say that it would not have appeared at all without the help of John P. Roche, who suggested the topic in the first place. The author is also indebted to Morton Keller and Marvin Meyers, who gave the preliminary drafts an enormously helpful critical reading, as did David O'Brien at a later stage. Others whose suggestions and comments proved helpful were James MacGregor Burns, Moreau B. C. Chambers, John C. Cort, John F. Cronin, Vincent DeSantis, James E. Doyle, Robert F. Drinan, Monsignor John Egan, Monsignor John Tracy Ellis, Steven Gelber, Robert Griffith, Monsignor George Higgins, Charles Kersten, Monsignor Francis Lally, William Liebman, Norman F. Martin, John B. McGloin, Gerald McKevitt, Miles McMillin, Francis Maloney, Edward A. Marciniak, James O'Gara, Maurice Rosenblatt, Morris Rubin, Patrick F. Scanlan, George N. Shuster, and Athan Theoharis. Finally, the author gratefully acknowledges the generosity of his superiors at the University of Santa Clara, who gave him a leave of absence for one quarter in order to write this study.

To all of the above, the deepest thanks. To the author alone belongs the responsibility for what follows.

God, Church, and Flag

Chapter 1

The Anti-Communist Impulse in American Catholic Life, 1850–1950

"PUT UP OR SHUT UP," screamed the title of the front-page editorial in the *Brooklyn Tablet*. Long known as one of the most vehemently anti-Communist newspapers in the country, the weekly organ of the Brooklyn Catholics was in especially high dudgeon in June 1950 because opposition seemed to be rising against its newest anti-Communist hero, the junior senator from Wisconsin, Joseph Raymond McCarthy. "The time for being naive about the substance of the McCarthy charges is long past," it proclaimed. "The presence of close to a hundred perverts in the State Department—even though [Alger] Hiss has been forced out and convicted and the perverts fired—justify [sic] a complete and thorough search for further evidences of the Communist conspiracy within the departments of our government. That is the avowed objective of Senator McCarthy's efforts." The *Tablet* exhorted its Catholic readers to write their congressmen or senators at once: "It is time to put the direct question to each Congressman and Senator: 'What are YOU doing about getting rid of Communists in our government? It is YOUR job as well as Senator McCarthy's. What are YOU doing about it?" Concluded the *Tablet*: "It is time for every Congressman and Senator to put up or shut up. If he (or she) cannot offer any better way of reaching and destroying the Communist conspiracy in our government than is being offered by Senator McCarthy, then at least, for the welfare of the United States, let him hold his peace and be silent!"[1]

How had the question of Joe McCarthy and the Communists

brought the nation's largest Catholic paper near the point of hysteria? The church itself had prepared its members to take up arms against the Marxist infidel by conditioning its followers to believe that communism represented the very Antichrist himself. The anti-Communist stance of the church was, of course, part of its larger struggle with the secular liberalisms of the eighteenth and nineteenth centuries, a struggle that received its earliest expression in the papal encyclicals *Nostis et Nobiscum* (1848), *Quanta Cura* (1864), and *Diuturnum Illud* (1881). The popes taught that communism was essentially atheistic and irreligious; they objected to its elimination of private property on the grounds that property was an essential ingredient for an orderly society; they regarded the Communists as anarchistic, violent, and opposed to what was best for man; finally, they believed that the relentless materialism of the Communists struck at the heart of what the church was about, namely the world of God and of the spirit.[2]

The popes of the nineteenth century made little attempt to discriminate communism from Marxism, socialism, anarchism, or even such traditional papal *bêtes noires* as secularism and materialism. The popes believed them all radical-leftist movements, and they condemned them all as destructive of religion and degrading to human nature. In the twentieth century much happened to communism: new and highly nationalistic forms of the system developed, and communism adopted new strategies to fit new circumstances. In the eyes of the popes, however, communism was always communism, no matter when or where one found it. As a result, papal thought on communism remained frozen until the time of Pope John XXIII, who dared to suggest that Catholics and Communists might be able to engage in fruitful dialogue. Until his time, however, dialogue was totally out of the question. One need hardly emphasize that in a church as centralized, as hierarchical, and as tightly structured as Roman Catholicism, what the popes believed was usually the norm for what most Catholics believed.

The clash between communism and Catholicism first hit American shores in the 1870s and 1880s during the debate over the Knights of Labor. A late nineteenth-century worker's movement with a strong following among lower-class Catholics, the Knights frightened many conservative American Catholics because their constitution contained phrases that seemed to smack of socialism and communism. The American Catholic conservatives, convinced that the Knights represented the work of the devil himself, took the matter to Rome and nearly succeeded in securing a papal condemnation of the group. Their liberal opponents or "Americanizers," however, believed that the Knights represented a step in the right direction, since they were helping Catholics take a greater part in secular affairs. After intensive politicking on both sides of the Atlantic, the liberals succeeded in blocking the move of the conservatives. The Holy Office (the executive arm of the papacy) issued a directive saying that Catholics could indeed maintain membership in the Knights, provided that the union dropped the offensive phrases from its constitution.[3] Ironically enough, the statements stood as they were, but the problem of Catholic membership disappeared as the Knights went into a long decline from which they never recovered. The incident is important, nevertheless, because it shows the continued concern of the church over Communist influence on Catholics in America.

The Bolshevik Revolution in Russia and the savage persecution of Russian Catholics that followed intensified the church's hostility to communism. Watching helplessly as the Roman Catholic church in Russia fell to pieces was Pope Pius XI, who excoriated the Communists for waging an "atheistic" war on the church and mounted a worldwide campaign of prayer for the Catholics in Russia.[4] From that time on, prayers for the "conversion of Russia" and sermons on the theme of the "sorrows of the Russian people" became the staples of American Catholic piety, resounding monotonously in Catholic parishes from Boston to San Diego.

During the early 1930s the reform programs of Franklin D. Roosevelt's New Deal attracted many leading Catholic liberals, among them reformers such as Monsignor John A. Ryan and Dorothy Day.[5] Catholic voters, meanwhile, played a major role in the electoral triumphs of Roosevelt and the Democratic party. By the late thirties, however, many Catholic leaders had become increasingly worried about the threat of domestic radicalism, which they associated with the Roosevelt administration. Although few went as far as Father Charles Coughlin or the *Brooklyn Tablet*, both of whom denounced the New Deal as the precursor to a Communist takeover, many of the church's leaders were anxious over the emergence of depression-bred radicalism. In 1938 the American bishops warned of the "spread of subversive teachings" in the United States and called for a "Crusade for Christian Democracy" to instill civic and social virtues in American youth. Though Catholic liberals continued to dispute the conservative equation of the New Deal with communism, it was nevertheless true, as the leading student of New Deal Catholicism has concluded, that the issue of communism, "more than anything else, inhibited further progress in Catholic social thought after 1936."[6]

Catholic leaders also took deep offense at the Roosevelt administration's recognition of the Soviet Union in 1933. Besides seeming to bestow the administration's blessing on Marxism, Roosevelt appeared to be ignoring the profound distress the church's leaders felt over the persecution of the Russian church. Even *Commonweal*, the most liberal and pro-Roosevelt of all Catholic publications, opposed the president's action, arguing that it was useless to recognize a government opposed to international law and morality. Not unexpectedly, the *Brooklyn Tablet* outdid all Catholic publications in vituperation; it also organized mass meetings, petition drives, and public demonstrations protesting the government's action.[7] Not until its campaign on behalf of Senator McCarthy in the 1950s did the *Tablet* pursue a cause with such unremitting dedication and with such cold scorn for the opposition.

What the recognition of Russia had begun, the Spanish Civil War brought to a climax. Much as Catholics disliked Roosevelt's Russian policy, they found the Spanish Civil War even more difficult to contemplate, for it seemed clear to many American Catholics that the Loyalist, or leftist, side was directing a savage persecution against the Spanish church. In July 1937 Generalissimo Francisco Franco precipitated a revolt of the army against the leftist government of Spain, thereby beginning the most vicious civil war in this century. A devout Catholic as well as a shrewd militarist and politician, Franco trumpeted his movement as a Christian crusade against the forces of atheistic communism and barbarism. The government in power—a shaky leftist coalition of Socialists, Communists, Anarchists, and anticlericalists—meanwhile assembled its own forces to do battle with the Generalissimo. For Spanish Catholics the choice between Franco's Nationalists and the government's Loyalists soon became no choice at all, for anticlerical factions in the government began to attack the church in the areas still under government domination. Not surprisingly, the Spanish Catholic bishops lined up solidly behind Franco, choosing to ignore reports of his wholesale execution of political enemies and his plain indifference to personal freedoms.[8]

With the war simplistically depicted as a struggle between the forces of God and the Antichrist, Catholics in America grew even more alarmed over the dangers, both real and imaginary, of atheistic communism. (Significantly enough, Catholic laymen were far more divided over the war than the church's leaders, with large minorities either opposing Franco or remaining neutral.)[9] In the eyes of conservative Catholics, however, the support that many American liberals gave so unhesitatingly to the Loyalists simply reinforced the conservative belief that liberalism and communism were the same. Pope Pius XI gave still another pretext for this line of thinking when in March 1937 he issued his encyclical *Atheistic Communism*, which stated that the church's strongest objection to communism was its militant atheism.[10]

Thus it happened that by the late thirties many Catholics had discovered in anticommunism a means of identifying themselves with the greater American society. As David O'Brien has concluded: "In fighting the red peril the Catholic could dedicate himself to action which was both Catholic and American. Few would disagree that he was proving his worth as an American and demonstrating the compatibility of faith and patriotism."[11] Thus Catholic anticommunism was reinforced by the secular anticommunism of the American political culture. Anticommunism had become a common denominator, the bulwark of both true Americanism and authentic Catholicism. The Catholic leadership, in combining these explosive elements, had mixed a heady brew that fired the blood of American Catholics for at least two decades.

The zeal of the church's leaders for the cause of anticommunism diminished only slightly during World War II. In November 1941, on the eve of America's entry into the war, the American bishops condemned communism and nazism as "subversive" forces, both bent on world dominance. "Neither system," the bishops concluded, "understands or permits freedom in its true Christian sense."[12] Throughout the war the news releases emanating from the National Catholic Welfare Conference, an agency of the Catholic bishops that provided "Catholic" news for diocesan newspapers, maintained a steady barrage of anti-Russian and anti-Communist propaganda. When Warner Brothers released the pro-Soviet film *Mission to Moscow* in 1943, the Knights of Columbus condemned the work as an attempt to "spread propaganda on behalf of the atheistic, Communistic minority in control of Russia."[13]

In the final year of the war, Catholic anticommunism entered a new phase; what had previously been only one of a large number of concerns became virtually a way of life. American Catholics had only one thought on their minds—the preservation of their church from the Marxist marauder. For the next ten years all other issues tended to fade into the background as Catholics in America launched an all-out campaign against communism, both overseas and at home. American Catholics had a new obsession, and they would receive nothing but encouragement from a large part of the American press and electorate, which shared the same obsession.

Anti-Communist Impulse

As the war drew to a close and the Soviet Union moved deep into Eastern Europe, Catholic leaders across the world became increasingly apprehensive about the fate of Catholics in the occupied countries. The rise of Communist regimes in Eastern Europe and in China, and the subsequent persecution of the church in those lands, raised American Catholic anxiety to a fever pitch. Between 1945 and 1950 diocesan weekly newspapers carried articles in nearly every issue detailing the sufferings of Catholics in Soviet-occupied countries. Church leaders were especially critical of the results of the wartime conferences at Teheran and Yalta. Father James Gillis of the *Catholic World*, a Paulist journal, called upon Americans to "remember that since the beginning of our alliance with Stalin, or at the latest since our 'compromise' with him at Yalta, the crimes of Russia are on our soul." The American bishops issued a strong statement declaring that the agreement was not consistent with the "sovereign equality of peace-loving nations. . . . We are struck," the prelates lamented, "by the silence of the three great powers on Lithuania, Estonia and Latvia." Still other Catholics worried about what the Yalta agreements would mean for the church in Eastern Germany and the Balkans.[14]

Yet the most vivid symbol of the church's struggle was Poland: throughout 1945 Polish American Catholics thronged to their cathedrals and even took to the streets to protest the Soviet occupation of their homeland. Solemn Masses in which church leaders lauded Poland as a "Christian Democracy" and called for its "spiritual liberation" were held in Milwaukee, Chicago, and New York. In San Francisco, Archbishop John J. Mitty led a "Mass for the Cause of Poland," timed to coincide with the deliberations over the United Nations Charter.[15] Prominent Catholic clergymen urged President Truman to press for Soviet withdrawal and free elections, and the Knights of Columbus repeatedly denounced the "conspiracy of silence" surrounding news of Poland.[16] United States recognition of the Soviet-sponsored Polish government in the summer of 1945 was, according to Charles Rozmarek of the Polish-American Congress, "a tragic historical blunder," the result of a "shortsighted policy of appeasement" that was "paving the way for world chaos."[17]

With Catholics becoming increasingly bitter over the fate of Poland, they needed only a martyr to galvanize their feelings into determined action. The arrest and imprisonment of Archbishop Aloysius Stepinac of Yugoslavia provided them the one they needed. Defiantly opposed to Marshall Josef Tito's Communist regime in that country, Stepinac came under arrest in September 1946 and was subsequently tried on trumped-up charges of having collaborated with the Germans and Italians during the war; in October 1946 he received a sentence of sixteen years in prison. Catholics in America were shocked at the Communists' cavalier treatment of the archbishop, widely regarded as one of the leading spokesmen for world Catholicism. The National Council of Catholic Women, the official Catholic women's organization in America, broke its policy of avoiding controversial topics when shortly after Stepinac's imprisonment it sent a message to Secretary of State James F. Byrnes, urging him to intercede personally with the Yugoslav government. Calling the bishop a "saintly" man, they dubbed the Tito regime the "atheistic communistic forces" of Yugoslavia.[18]

In December 1946 forty thousand people massed at a huge rally in Philadelphia, again objecting to the persecution of the church in Yugoslavia and demanding the archbishop's release. The crowd jammed the city's Convention Hall and spilled onto the streets outside. Conspicuously present at the gathering were the mayor of the city, leaders of the Catholic War Veterans who had staged the spectacle, and the senator from Pennsylvania, Francis J. Myers.[19] Other Catholic politicians, including Congressmen John McCormack (D., Mass.) and John J. Rooney (D., N. Y.), soon joined the crusade to save Stepinac. McCormack called on the secretary of state to lodge a formal protest with the Yugoslavs, and Rooney sought, unsuccessfully, to push through the House of Representatives a resolution demanding such a protest.[20]

Inspired perhaps by the leadership of Francis Cardinal Spellman, the most passionate outbursts came from New York City. Speaking at a World Peace Rally in New York on 6 October 1946, Spellman asked the prayers of the Catholic faithful for Stepinac, "whose only crime is fidelity to God and country. . . . The confidence and conscience of the American people . . . have again been outraged by this latest infamy and affront to human dignity and decency."[21] To show that his words were not empty, he announced a drive to pay for an "Archbishop Stepinac High School" in New York. Responding eagerly to his call, the Catholics of New York raised $4,000,000— some $2,000,000 more than needed—in less than a year.[22] At about the same time that the cardinal was happily dedicating the new school, a group of fifty Catholic students from St. John's University in Brooklyn picketed the Yugoslav consulate in New York City; they were acting under the auspices of the Committee for the Liberation of Archbishop Stepinac, which claimed to represent thirty-seven organizations of Catholic laymen in New York City.[23]

Adding impetus to the cardinal's efforts in New York were the Catholic War Veterans, whose national leadership came largely from New York and whose membership was greatest in that area (it numbered over 200,000 nationally). Repeatedly the Veterans demanded that Truman and the State Department take firm action against the Yugoslav Communists, bitterly assailing "the silence of President Truman" and even protesting the sending of foreign aid to Yugoslavia. (The National Commander of the CWV told the leaders of the local units to oppose such aid until "these ignoble puppets of the Kremlin" showed a willingness to "render to God the things that are God's.")[24] Protests continued for the rest of the decade, even after other Communist crimes began to catch the attention of the American Catholic public.[25]

The greatest of all Catholic martyrs to communism was Joseph Cardinal Mindszenty, whose tortured and emaciated body came to symbolize the sufferings of Catholics behind the iron curtain. The cardinal had fiercely opposed the attempts of the Hungarian regime to reduce the church; when it became obvious to the authorities that he would not be intimidated into silence, they arrested him on 26 December 1948 and tried him on grounds of treason, subversion, and spying. At the height of the trial, he appeared before the court—a gaunt, broken, and dreadfully sick man. Though he meekly "confessed" his guilt on all counts, a shocked world concluded (probably rightly) that his confession had been extorted. The court sentenced him to death but later commuted the sentence to life imprisonment.[26]

America's Catholics were appalled at Mindszenty's fate, but none more so than Cardinal Spellman, who knew him and admired him deeply. On 6 February 1949 the cardinal, speaking from the pulpit of St. Patrick's Cathedral in New York for the first time since V-E Day, called on the leaders of the American government to "raise their voices as one and cry out against" the "Satan-inspired Communist crimes."[27] On another occasion he told a group of Catholic boys belonging to the Catholic Youth Organization that Mindszenty was the victim of "Christ-hating Communists" with "anti-Christian minds drenched and drugged in the devil's cauldron of hatreds and iniquities."[28] Not surprisingly, New York City's millions of Catholics rallied to the cause. When the cardinal declared 6 February 1949 a day of prayer for Mindszenty, four thousand Catholic Boy Scouts marched down Fifth Avenue to St. Patrick's Cathedral as part of a public demonstration. That same day three thousand students at Fordham University, the Jesuit college in the Bronx, recited the rosary together on behalf of Mindszenty and affirmed their support for a group of student leaders who had sent a telegram of protest to President Truman.[29] Later that year twenty thousand Catholics gathered at Ebbets Field in Brooklyn, where they recited prayers for the cardinal and heard speeches condemning the Communists. The principal speaker of the day said that Mindszenty had been put in jail because "he dared to defend Catholic interests against Red tyrants."[30]

The legacy of the Mindszenty crisis was not only a renewal of Catholic protests against communism but a new form of Catholic anticommunism as well. Extreme right-wing Catholics began to form "Mindszenty Circles" and "Freedom Foundations" dedicated to the destruction of communism everywhere and modeled along the lines of Communist cells. Meeting in small groups and acting often in secret, they studied Communist literature, plotted political action, kept the memory of the cardinal alive, and looked for the influence of communism everywhere (usually they found it). Though small in numbers, they bulked large in influence, thanks to the impressive number of priests they succeeded in attracting to their ranks. Because of their secretive nature little is known about their organization, though they appear to have flourished especially well in southern California and seem to have attracted Catholics whose political views were extremely right wing.

By 1950 the worst part of the Communist attacks on the church was over. Catholicism in most of the iron-curtain countries lay crushed; in a few others, such as Poland, only an uneasy detente with the Communists allowed the church to function. The American Catholic press, however, continued to act as if the persecutions were continuing unabated, and it reported even small incidents as if they were major crises in the life of the church. The News Service of the National Catholic Welfare Conference (NCWC) still continued to pour out an unending stream of dispatches, sensationally reporting Communistic acts of barbarism against the church. Without question this contributed to the continuing hatred of Catholics for communism and may well have helped create a climate conducive to McCarthyism among Catholics.

The political leader of American Catholic anticommunism was unquestionably Francis Cardinal Spellman of New York City. His was basically a simple faith: communism was evil; Catholicism and America were good; therefore Catholicism and America must join together to combat atheistic communism. Although he worried much over the fate of the church in the iron-curtain countries, he was concerned also about the problem of Communist subversion in the United States, and his concern sometimes reached the point of obsession. As early as October 1946 he warned that the Communists "are today digging deep inroads into our own nation" and are "tirelessly trying to grind into dust the blessed freedoms for which our sons have fought, sacrificed and died."[31] Later that same year he urged the Catholic chaplains of the army and navy to "protect America against aggression of enemies within her borders."[32] Unimpressed by the Communist hunt then sweeping the country, he said in 1947 that "once again while Rome burns . . . the world continues to fiddle. The strings of the fiddle are committees, conferences, conversations, appeasements—to the tune of no action today."[33] Again and again in the years that followed, he repeated monotonously the same themes: Communist subversion is making "fools and tools" of Americans, anti-Catholic bigotry in America comes from the Communists, and America will be unsafe until every Communist is removed from influence in American life.[34] Without question the nation's best known Catholic prelate, Spellman took every opportunity to pound home the gospel of anticommunism, exhorting the practice of a brand of anti-Marxism that was both truly Catholic and fully American. His language may have been clumsy and repetitive, but no one could claim that his message was obscure.

One does not have to look very hard to find the roots of Spellman's passionate anticommunism. In the late 1930s and the early war years he had enjoyed frequent meetings with President Roosevelt, whom he seemed to admire greatly. Near the end of the war, however, he had seen Roosevelt "give in," so he thought, to the Communists by letting them have concessions disastrous both to the security of the United States and to the Catholics unfortunate enough to live behind the iron curtain. Spellman was dumbfounded: if Roosevelt was openly cooperating with the Communists (as he believed), what did this say about the other liberals? Spellman came to distrust them too, thus placing himself firmly in the conservative camp on the issue of internal security, though not so far to the right as the *Brooklyn Tablet*. Although far too shrewd a churchman to side openly with either political party, or even to endorse a political candidate, his constant harpings on the threat of subversion led many to conclude that he was conservatively Republican and anti-Fair Deal in his beliefs. His private papers, however, yield no evidence to support such a conclusion but simply give further basis for the thesis that he was a superpatriot who pursued a rather thoughtless anticommunism because he believed it to be the purest possible expression of true Americanism as well as of authentic Catholicism.[35]

If Spellman was the political leader of Catholic anticommunism, then its prophet and philosopher was Bishop Fulton J. Sheen, Spellman's assistant in New York City. For nearly twenty years before McCarthy ever appeared on the scene, Sheen poured forth a gushing stream of books, articles, pamphlets, sermons, and speeches detailing the theory and dynamics of Communism, and emphasizing its relation to Roman Catholicism. For Sheen as for Spellman, communism was the epitome of both irreligion and un-Americanism. The good Catholic, it followed, was one who gave his unstinting support to the efforts of both the church and the nation to the destruction of the Communist peril.[36] Though his Catholic followers may have used his prodigious mass of works as a pretext for Communist hunting, Sheen himself showed little interest in the subject. It was just as well, perhaps, since his one foray into the area was conspicuously unsuccessful. In a speech before a group of Catholic journalists in March 1946, he said that a congressional committee had just uncovered a "full-fledged Soviet agent." When reporters pressed him for details, he refused to give either the man's name or his position in the government, saying, "I am not here to give information, but to stimulate members of the press." One of those so stimulated was the reporter from the *New York Times* who found that neither the FBI nor the House Un-American Activities Committee knew anything about Sheen's Soviet spy.[37] No one ever found out who the alleged spy was, or if he even existed.

During the McCarthy years Sheen continued to remain detached from the political crises that shook the nation over the issue of domestic communism. One could not fairly say the same, however, about some of his well-known converts to Catholicism who had once been Communists. The most famous of these was Louis F. Budenz, the former editor of the *Daily Worker* and one-time Catholic, who returned to the faith of his fathers in 1945 and subsequently carried on a fanatical crusade against his former Marxist comrades. Not surprisingly, he became one of Senator McCarthy's warmest supporters.[38]

The militant anticommunism preached by Spellman and Sheen was perhaps best exemplified by the zealous, though sometimes crude, activities of the Catholic War Veterans and the Knights of Columbus. As early as 1946, for example, the Catholic War Veterans, whose greatest strength lay in New York City and its suburbs, demanded that the United States take firm action against Communist regimes in Eastern Europe. Again and again in the years that followed, they protested the federal government's failure to take decisive action against the Communist dictators behind the iron curtain and demanded that the Kremlin leaders be brought to their knees forthwith.[39]

In March 1948 the Veterans picketed the Russian freighter *Chukotka*, then moored at a New Jersey dock, on the grounds that it was carrying materials to Russia that could be used to make war against the United States. They carried signs saying, "Hitler and Mussolini were amateurs compared to Pal Joey" (a reference to a Broadway musical called *Pal Joey* and to the Soviet Premier Joseph Stalin) and "American goods for American defense." After halting the loading of the vessel for a short period, they picketed a second Russian vessel and ended their efforts only when assured that the shippers would undergo investigation.[40] A year later—when a group of fourteen leftist intellectuals from Russia, Poland, and Czechoslovakia came to New York for a Cultural and Scientific Conference for World Peace —the CWV announced that it would picket the meeting, and a Catholic group dedicated to the freeing of Cardinal Mindszenty declared that it would muster fifty thousand demonstrators. The picketers carried crepe-draped flags of the nations behind the iron curtain as well as placards proclaiming, "Communists are not welcome here. We don't want you. Get out!"[41]

Always a potent force in New York City, the Veterans took special pains to oppose the presence of Communists and their "sympathizers," especially in the city's governmental and educational systems. In mid-1947 they pressured Mayor William O'Dwyer to "purge" the city's payroll of all Communists and "fellow travelers." Later that year they demanded that the Board of Education state why it permitted "subversive" groups, such as the American Youth for Democracy, to use school facilities for their meetings. Other New York Catholic groups also demanded the removal of Communists from the city payroll. The Holy Name Society of the city's police force complained that New York City had more Communists than any other city of comparable size "outside Moscow." Meanwhile, Brooklyn Catholics successfully stopped a local bank from publishing a series of articles on Russia in its monthly publication for school children.[42]

As alert as the Veterans were to the problem of Communist subversion, the Knights of Columbus, the largest Catholic fraternal organization in the country, matched them in vigilance, energy, and political resourcefulness. Numbering over 600,000 active members, the Knights declared war on subversion almost as soon as World War II ended. In June 1946 its New York State chapters called on Americans everywhere to reject candidates for office who supported communism or acted as "fellow travelers." The national convention of the Knights later that year proclaimed a four-point program of action designed to combat communism, insisting especially on an all-out effort against the "infiltration of atheistic communism into our American life and economy." Not even the entertainment world was safe from subversives: a New York Knights group urged the boycotting of stage and screen entertainment with which Communists or their "sympathizers" had any connection.[43]

All this anti-Communist activity demanded an appropriate

system of education, since Communists, clever as they were at hiding their real work and assuming misleading disguises, were often hard to identify. Catholic groups therefore drew up detailed and complex programs designed to educate their fellow Catholics about the wiles and machinations of the Communists. The CWV in July 1948 announced the formation of an Officer Candidate School, which trained two men from each state in the workings of subversive groups as well as in the methods most appropriate to combating them. After completing the course, each man returned to his state and set up similar schools.[44] The next year the Veterans heralded a nationwide campaign to expose the Communist fifth column in America. The drive featured courses in the detection of Communist subversives, films demonstrating the dangers of communism, and newspaper advertisements publicizing the domestic communist menace.[45]

The Knights of Columbus, following a slightly different scenario, built their educational programs around the use of the radio and town-hall meeting. In 1947 they began a series of six broadcasts, carried over 226 stations, entitled "Safeguards for America." Its purpose was to provide "the truth" about the Communists in America. When the *Daily Worker* called the series the "biggest and most vicious scare hoax in the history of radio," a spokesman for the Knights replied confidently that they could not have had better proof that they were "hitting the Commies where it hurts." "Communism is a lie and a lie hates the truth. The six powerful doses of truth about Communism . . . are giving the comrades a headache."[46] In 1948 the Knights initiated a series of town-hall meetings in Washington, D.C. J. Edgar Hoover sent his congratulations, claiming that there was a "definite need" to arouse the citizenry "to those forces which menace the future security of America."[47] The Knights could not have asked for higher praise.

The News Service of the National Catholic Welfare Conference further contributed to the public clamor over communism by supplying diocesan papers with a seemingly interminable list of dispatches, meticulously and dramatically chronicling every investigation, trial, or suspected act of disloyalty. Equally important were the many pamphlets on communism produced by Catholic instructional groups in the late forties. Some of the most widely read came from the Catholic Information Society of New York, which printed a series of twenty-six pamphlets on communism written by such notable conservatives as William H. Chamberlain, Eugene Lyons, Suzanne LaFollette, and the recent convert from communism to Catholicism, Freda Utley.[48] One of the more lurid of such publications was a comic book entitled *Is This Tomorrow?* that showed a Communist mob attacking St. Patrick's Cathedral in New York and nailing Cardinal Spellman to the door.[49]

Catholic anticommunism was not restricted to the zealous fundamentalism of Cardinal Spellman or the Catholic War Veterans, however. Liberal Catholics, too, sought to expunge communism from American life, though they differed sharply with conservatives over the means to this end. Probably the most outstanding example of the liberal attitude was the thesis found in the pages of the *Commonweal*, the weekly journal of political opinion edited by reformist-minded Catholic laymen. The editors stood second to none in their defiant opposition to communism, finding it anti-democratic, monolithic, and maliciously conspiratorial. Like their conservative counterparts, they too worried frequently about the presence of Communists in the government and other institutions; at least one of them, James O'Gara, was personally convinced that Alger Hiss was guilty.[50] Yet unlike many of the conservatives who thought that foreign aid was a waste of money, the liberals at the *Commonweal* supported the Marshall Plan and President Truman's programs of aid to countries like Greece and Turkey because they believed that with the elimination of the poverty and suffering that spawned communism, the Communists would have nowhere to go. Indeed, they believed that the answer to communism was not an extension of Red hunts and repressive legislation but an expansion of social programs designed to end hunger, disease, deficient housing, and the other social and economic ills that drove men into the hands of the Marxists. The editors derived much of their inspiration from the so-called social encyclicals of the popes, among them *Rerum Novarum* (1891) of Pope Leo XIII and *Quadragesimo Anno* (1931) of Pope Pius XI. The pontiffs had advocated strong programs of social action to achieve what they called "human dignity," a condition of human living that disappeared when men lived in grinding poverty. Communism thrived in this atmosphere, the popes noted, though tragically enough both communism and un-bridled capitalism robbed men of the dignity to which they had a right. Catholic liberals and intellectuals of the *Commonweal* stripe showed a close familiarity with these teachings, as well as with the broad streams of liberal European and American Catholic thought. If social action was the answer to communism, then repressive legislation was no help at all, they believed. On the contrary, proposals such as the Mundt-Nixon Bill and other "Communist-control" legislation frustrated the war on communism, because they created a totalitarian atmosphere that was little different from communism itself.[51] This concept was yet another manifestation of the profound belief of the *Commonweal* school that civil liberties were the mainstay of American democracy. The *Commonweal* editors most fervently believed that if due process and personal freedoms were taken away, America as we know it would wither up and die away.

Finally, the *Commonweal* carried on intermittent warfare with the conservative Catholics over the problem of Catholic attitudes toward communism. If the *Brooklyn Tablet* and its followers believed the *Commonweal* "fuzzy" and "weak" on communism, then the *Commonweal* staff was ready with a handful of charges all its own. Far too much of Catholic anticommunism was mindless, hyper-emotional, and superpatriotic, they lamented. They too wanted to fight communism and drive the subversives out of American life, but they believed that there was a right way to do it. The right way was what they called "the democratic way," which meant that those accused of subversion or "softness on communism" ought to receive every legal right, that they should not be treated as guilty until so proven, and that their accusers ought to show respect for those with contrary opinions. It became a dogma of the Catholic liberal ethic (one best expressed by the *Commonweal*) to believe that right-wingers in general, and Catholic right-wingers in particular, often violated the democratic way. They believed further that the Catholic conservatives showed tendencies toward fanaticism and hysteria, and they pointed to the front-page editorials of the *Brooklyn Tablet* as example and proof. The liberals on the *Commonweal* bitterly denounced the conservative brand of anticommunism as "shrill hyper-patriotism," seeing in it the specter of the dreaded yahoo. They insisted that impassioned declarations of patriotism, beclouding the issue with emotionalism and windy rhetoric, had nothing to do with the hunt for Communists. Finally, they believed that Catholics were all too ready to write off criticism of the church as "Communist-inspired." It simply was not true, as some Catholics believed, that every critic of the church was somehow under the influence of the Kremlin. Nor was it true that people who criticized the church were anti-Catholic; sometimes the church deserved criticism, the *Commonweal* believed, and at those times Catholics would do well to listen.[52]

Liberal Catholics were especially active in the drive to purge Communists from the American labor movement. By 1945 the church's leaders had organized nearly one hundred "labor schools," which annually trained more than seven thousand Catholic trade unionists. Originally formed as part of the church's labor ministry, they rapidly became focal points in the fight against communism. Although most of these schools were operated by the Jesuits or by local diocesan authorities, their spirit and purpose was best typified by the Association of Catholic Trade Unionists (ACTU). Organized in 1937 as an offshoot of the Catholic Worker movement, the ACTU was a voluntary association of Catholics interested in the problems of unions. Almost from the very beginning it had directed much of its energy toward the fight against communism. The ACTU helped train anti-Communist labor leaders, sponsored conferences on anti-Communist strategy and tactics, provided legal aid to those seeking to expel Communists from leadership positions in the unions, and published two widely circulated newspapers, *The Labor Leader* and *The Wage Earner*. By 1949, at least in part as a result of ACTU activities, Communist influence had been virtually eliminated from organized labor.[53]

A symbol of the church's war against Communists in the unions was the colorful "waterfront priest." Often tough-talking and hard-fisted, the waterfront priest worked with the men in the plants and on the docks, gaining their friendship and respect and often exhorting them to repel Communists and racketeers. In many cases the men grew to love the priests, who for their part went about their work with a pragmatic hardheadedness and a quiet fervor that seemed to epitomize the best in American Catholicism. In the popular Marlon Brando movie, *On the Waterfront* (1954), the Hollywood actor Karl Malden skillfully portrayed one such waterfront priest, thus giving many Americans a vivid image of these men who seemed remarkably gifted at fighting unionized communism.

For all their differences, however, both Catholic liberals and conservatives shared a core of common values and beliefs. Both were passionately, even obsessively, opposed to communism, profoundly convinced that it represented the greatest of all possible dangers to both church and Republic. Both shared a brand of patriotism that one can only describe as strident, though the conservatives outdid the liberals in this department. Both liberals and conservatives found inspiration in the teachings of the church, though they selected different traditions. Liberals looked to the social encyclicals; the conservatives limited themselves to the church's anti-Communist polemics. For that matter, the bulk of conservative inspiration came not from the church's teachings but from conservative American politics. Neither, finally, doubted the gravity of the church's confrontation with communism, though the liberals were quicker to perceive the reduction in tensions that came in the early 1950s.

Though firm empirical evidence is largely missing, it appears that the conservatives captured a larger part of the Catholic audience than the liberals. Certainly more of the Catholic leadership belonged to the conservative camp and more Catholic organizations favored that persuasion. In addition to this, most Catholic periodicals and newspapers tended to follow the conservative line. We might well ask ourselves why the liberals seemed to form a smaller group than their conservative counterparts. One reason was that the posture of the liberal Catholics at times seemed (to the uninitiated at least) alarmingly similar to the Communist position. Both liberals and Communists favored strong governmental programs aimed at solving problems of inequality and injustice, and both harped repeatedly on themes such as "the needs of the poor," the "sufferings of the disadvantaged," etc. Both groups detested fascism, or anything that even smacked of fascism. Both the Communists and the liberals often criticized the Catholic church, though for different reasons: the Communists viewed it as a fascist organization designed to exploit the workers of the world and the poor; the Catholic liberals, in turn, disliked what they called the church's "authoritarianism," which they defined as its tendencies toward intolerance and conformism, and its dogmatizing of nonreligious opinions. The Catholic liberals also formed a smaller and weaker body because liberalism had become almost a synonym for "softness on communism" in the supercharged atmosphere of the late 1940s. Thus if one maintained a liberal political posture, one also had to take great pains to defend one's anti-Communist credentials. In an interview James O'Gara ruefully recalled the many times he had to say publicly that he was not a Marxist.[54] Finally, the liberal position was a tangled and sophisticated one, demanding a knowledge not only of the theory and tactics of communism but of the church's teachings on society and economics and of the American civil libertarian tradition as well. It did not lend itself easily to catch phrases, sensationalizing, mass demonstrations, or any of the other techniques that seemed to be very much a part of the conservatives' stock in trade.

At the same time, however, it would be wrong to assume that the conservatives took the American Catholic community completely by storm. If they had succeeded in doing so, this would certainly have shown up in the attitude of Catholics toward the Democrats, for the conservative cry of "Communists in the government" often turned into an attack on the Democratic party and the reigning Truman administration. As a matter of fact, however, Catholics stood steadfastly by the Democrats and Truman: surveys of Catholic college graduates showed that Democrats still outnumbered Republicans and that support for the New Deal still remained strong.[55] Nor did the Republican rise to power in the cold-war years put the Catholics into the Republican camp: Catholics voted 2 to 1 for Truman in 1948, and not even the Eisenhower landslide of 1952 could make the Catholics vote for a Republican president (43 percent of them went for Stevenson and 41 percent for Eisenhower).[56] The Catholic members of Congress also stayed firmly in the liberal camp, at least on the issue of subversion. A *Commonweal* study (based on an earlier analysis by the *New Republic*) showed that the votes of Catholic congressmen on both the Mundt-Nixon Bill and on legislation supporting the House Un-American Activities Committee were far more liberal than those of the House of Representatives taken as a whole.[57]

Finally, one has to question whether Catholics were vastly more concerned over the threat of Communism to their religion than the rest of the populace. National opinion polls showed that an overwhelming majority of both Catholics and non-Catholics believed that the Communists would certainly destroy Christianity if given a chance to do so.[58] Huge majorities of both groups also believed that it was impossible for one to be a good Christian and a Communist at the same time.[59] In sum, though the Catholic population felt a deep concern over the problem of communism, so did the rest of America, and if the Catholic anxiety was the greater, it was not overwhelmingly so. More to the point, the worry that Catholics felt over communism was never strong enough to push them into supporting a massive, hysterical Red hunt. Indeed, the battle between the conservatives, who wanted liberal heads to roll, and the liberals, who wanted a search for subversives but wanted it carefully circumscribed by the protections of the law, seems to have taken place on an elite level. Editors, authors, political leaders, directors of fraternal organizations, and leading clergymen all fought out the battle among themselves, and the masses of lay Catholics participated sporadically or watched in a largely passive manner.

By 1950, then, the conservatives in the Catholic leadership were predisposed to respond favorably to the call of Senator McCarthy to take up arms in the struggle between "our western Christian world and the atheistic Communistic world," as he put it in the speech that opened his campaign against the subversives.[60] A smaller group of liberal Catholic leaders, however, could be counted on to stand defiantly against such a posture. And what of the masses of Catholics who made up the body of believers? They might well have been more predisposed toward McCarthyism than the rest of the population, but many of them remained indifferent, neutral, or passive. It would not be easy to whip up a popular crusade either in favor of McCarthyism or against it.

Chapter 2

Joseph Raymond McCarthy: The Man, the Catholic, and the Catholic Issue

Joseph Raymond McCarthy came into the world on a small farm in the village of Grand Chute, Wisconsin, in 1908. His father, Timothy, seems to have been a humorless, hardworking Irishman who demanded that his sons become successful farmers and "respected churchgoers."[1] His mother, Bridget, was a kindly woman, devoutly religious and protective of young Joe. The boy seems to have been insecure, ill at ease with his environment, and given to clinging timidly to his mother. The McCarthys were faithful Catholics, showing up every Sunday at St. Mary's Catholic Church in the nearby town of Appleton. (St. Mary's was the "Irish" church, catering to the minority of Irish-American Catholics in the area.) There the parish priest baptized young Joe, and there McCarthy made his First Communion and received the fundamental instructions in religion customarily given to young Catholics. The religious life of the McCarthys seems to have been regular, strict, unquestioning, complicated neither by theological argument nor by a searching crisis of faith. And for the rest of young Joe's life, religion was a "Sunday thing," scrupulously if unthinkingly observed. He would no more question his religion than he would miss Mass on Sunday. If the Senator McCarthy of the 1950s showed an acute embarrassment at public discussion of his religion, the roots of it were probably in his early home life. Religious practice also had an ethnic dimension for the McCarthys, since they lived in a small Irish Catholic enclave, surrounded by Dutch and German farmers. It would be wrong to place undue emphasis on this fact, however, since the senator seems to have made little out of his Irishness; nor does his Irish background seem to have been one of the more important influences on his career.

After he graduated from the Underhill County School at the age of 14, he began working on the family farm, since further education had no appeal for him. By the time he was 20, however, he was ready to go back to school, and in the year that followed he made a lightning dash through the local high school, finishing the normal four-year curriculum in one year.[2] Immediately after, in the fall of 1930, he entered Marquette University, the Jesuit college in Milwaukee. Registering first in engineering but changing later to law, he carved a wide path through Marquette, making a name for himself as a "big man on campus." The Jesuit fathers at Marquette who remember McCarthy describe him as fun-loving, possessed of a winning personality, faithful in his religious duties, and always deferential to the clergy.[3] He had a distinctive talent for attracting attention and for building a campus following (he was president of his class). His principal extracurricular activity was boxing, a sport in which he showed uncommon aggressiveness if little real skill. One of his college friends, Arlo McKinnon, recalls the "sheer guts" and fierce determination to win that he showed whenever he stepped into the ring.[4] His work in the law school was neither distinguished nor poor; he graduated on schedule in 1935 and was soon admitted to the Wisconsin bar.

Viewed in retrospect, his Marquette experience seems less an exercise in formation at the hands of the Jesuits than simply a stop on the way up the ladder to political success. Although Marquette gave him the legal background he needed to advance in politics, he did not seem to undergo any kind of transformation as a result of his stay there. As a student in the law school, he certainly would have heard something about the church's position on communism (and the related issue of social justice), but it seems to have made little impression on him. In sum, the Marquette Jesuits seem to have had little impact on either McCarthy's character or his system of values.

After a brief career as a small-town lawyer, McCarthy ran for the judgeship of the tenth circuit court of Wisconsin. He gave an example of the kind of "dirty tricks" he would use in his later campaigns when he accused his opponent, the incumbent judge, of being "too old" for the job; McCarthy said repeatedly that the judge was seventy-three, when in fact he was only sixty-six. Elected to office, he handled his duties on the bench in such a cavalier fashion that he soon became one of the most hotly controversial judges in the history of the state. In one celebrated incident (the Quaker Dairy Case) he actually destroyed some of the evidence that the lawyers had brought before the court. This action earned him an official reprimand from the Wisconsin Supreme Court.[5]

Of special interest was his reputation as the most popular "divorce judge" in Wisconsin. The source of his popularity was clearly the speed with which he processed the divorce cases that came before his court; Richard Rovere, in his unfriendly biography of McCarthy, says that Judge McCarthy became known for his "five-minute" divorce judgments.[6] Although no one knows the exact number of marriages he annulled, it was clearly enough to earn him statewide repute. The adamant opposition of his church to divorce seems not to have troubled him in the slightest, nor did it bother two of his friends from Milwaukee, Arlo McKinnon and Charles J. Kersten, also Catholics, who represented many of the divorce petitions brought before his court.[7]

When World War II broke out, McCarthy left the bench and joined the marines. Life in the Marine Corps did not prevent him from continuing his political career, though military statute expressly forbade servicemen from engaging in political activity of any kind. The climax of his wartime politicking came in 1944, when he ran unsuccessfully for the Republican senatorial nomination against the incumbent Alexander Wiley. Although religion seems to have played no part in the campaign, Jack Anderson and Ronald May (the authors of a popular study of McCarthy) reported that he attended a "different Catholic Church almost every Sunday."[8] The story, if true, shows a sorely misguided candidate, for Wisconsin was no more than one-third Catholic, and so obvious a political gambit would have cost him votes in the long run. The Anderson-May story is worth mentioning only because it shows how hard McCarthy's critics sometimes strained to find evidence that he was using his Catholicism to snare the Catholic vote. In fact, he carefully avoided this tactic in 1944 and in every other campaign he waged. Yet he did not ignore the Catholic vote; like every shrewd candidate he did everything he could to win it, but he never paraded his own identity as a Catholic to get Catholics to vote for him.

With the war over, McCarthy returned to Wisconsin, undaunted by his loss to Wiley in 1944. Running as "Tail Gunner Joe," he entered the 1946 Republican primary against Wisconsin's renowned senior senator, Robert M. LaFollette, Jr. LaFollette apparently thought that the young upstart from Appleton posed no threat at all to his seat, and he hardly bothered to campaign. McCarthy, by contrast, waged a furious campaign, attacking LaFollette's liberalism and parading his own reputation as a "marine war hero." The result was one of the most shocking upsets in Wisconsin history, with the supposedly unbeatable LaFollette losing to McCarthy by three thousand votes.[9]

During the campaign against LaFollette, McCarthy addressed the usual Catholic clubs, but with his own Catholicism so well known, his talks attracted a flurry of attention. At the conclusion of a speech he gave to a Catholic audience in Neva, Wisconsin, he recalled that one day during his stay with the marines in the South Pacific the senior commander had asked the chaplain to address the marine flying squadron because "we know [that] many of these men shall die today." The chaplain then told the men that if they remembered "two fundamental truths taught by all religious groups . . . first, there is a God, who is eternal and second, that each of you has a soul, which is immortal, then you will acquit yourselves as men."[10] It was vintage McCarthy, designed to tug at the heart if not the head.

Although religious in tone, the story was the kind he might have told to any similar group in Wisconsin—the Boy Scouts, the PTA, or the ladies aid society of the local Methodist church.

With LaFollette definitively out of the way, McCarthy took aim at his Democratic opponent in the general election, Professor Howard McMurray of the University of Wisconsin. A mild and thoughtful liberal, McMurray had to run against one of the most aggressive campaigners the Republicans fielded in that harvest year of 1946, when they took both houses of Congress. McCarthy was off at a furious pace from the start, getting financial backing from the wealthy boss of the conservative Wisconsin Republicans, Thomas Coleman (a Catholic), and putting his old friends Kersten and McKinnon in charge of the campaign in the critical Milwaukee area.[11] McCarthy succeeded in waging the campaign on his own terms and was not above using the Communist issue against McMurray. (He told one audience that the professor was "Communistically inclined.") The main thrust of his attack, however, was against the New Deal and the Truman administration, whose lapses and defects he pinned effectively on McMurray.[12] The "Catholic issue" arose briefly during the campaign, when the Wisconsin newspapers printed a report that the priest in McCarthy's home church in Appleton had told his parishoners to "vote against the Communist candidate." McMurray was furious: "I am ashamed of the fact that men in their pulpits have used the epithet 'Communist candidate.' I am ashamed because I am a Christian."[13]

When McCarthy continued to insinuate that McMurray had Communistic associations, the Democrats in Appleton decided to use the Catholic church against the Catholic Joe McCarthy. They talked a Catholic bishop, Bernard J. Sheil of Chicago, into making a public statement condemning political candidates who smeared their opponents by calling them "Communists" when they could not meet the issues head-on.[14] A bishop with a national reputation as a friend of labor unions and an advocate of social justice, Sheil's declaration (entitled "Spike the Communist Smear") was designed

to appeal to both the Catholic and non-Catholic workers in the
Appleton area. It was the first time the anti-McCarthy forces had
used Sheil against the senator, but it was by no means the last.

Whether because of his roughhouse methods or in spite of
them, McCarthy scored an overwhelming victory over his bland
opponent. Thus ensconced in the Senate, McCarthy built himself a
reputation as one of that chamber's most brash and bellicose members. Less noticed (but perhaps more important) was his relentless
conservatism. Time after time he opposed public housing, lobbied
on behalf of the sugar interests, joined the conservatives in opposing
the Fair Deal's welfare legislation, and voted against the many
foreign-aid bills that the Truman administration proposed to the
Senate. One Catholic political scientist, studying the voting habits of
the Catholic senators in the 80th Congress (in session from 1947 to
1949), concluded that of the six Catholics then sitting in the Senate,
McCarthy was by far the most conservative. His study showed that
of the fifteen key bills that the Congress had considered, McCarthy
had voted with the conservatives in all but one. By contrast, the other
five Catholic senators had voted consistently with the liberals.[15]

By the time McCarthy was ready to launch his crusade against
communism in February 1950, he had established an undeniable
reputation as one of Washington's most colorful characters. He had a
personality that one never forgot, even if one disliked it (as many
did). In his personal appearance he was either "ruggedly handsome"
or "had the look of the bully," depending on one's point of view. He
was a stocky and thickset man: to some he came across as well built
but to others he was simply overweight. Though his voice was set in
the lower register, his friends described it as a "resonant baritone."
But his critics heard the "rantings of the demagogue." Even his
heavy beard brought a division to the ranks—to the believers it was a
sign of his undoubted masculinity, but to the doubters it was a five
o'clock shadow that mirrored the unkempt and disheveled nature of
his politics.[16]

McCarthy seemed strangely divided between the public and the private man. The public McCarthy could be relentlessly aggressive, ruthless, stubborn, and totally unforgiving. In private, however, he could be disarmingly engaging, gentle, and deeply loyal. Most remarkably, he could attack someone in public (for example, a witness in a congressional hearing) then afterward he could put his arms around the same person and ask that no offense be taken.[17] His easy friendliness impressed not only his friends but even some of his convinced critics like Father Theodore Hesburgh (president of the University of Notre Dame). Hesburgh, who met him once during a vacation, recalls that the senator was "just a hell of a nice guy. We split a can of beer together."[18]

McCarthy, it seemed, would split a can of beer with anyone, be he friend or enemy. He seemed most at ease, however, while playing the role of the "man's man"—frying steaks ("I like it cremated," he would say), playing poker, or hunting in the north woods—far away from Washington and the pressures of paperwork at the office. On such occasions he would revel in the bawdy humor he so carefully screened from the public. A friend recalls one example of the earthy McCarthy wit: it seems that Dean Acheson died and went down to hell. There he stood, up to his armpits in fecal matter. With deep resignation he sighed, "Well, I guess I'm safe, so long as I can keep my head and shoulders above all this stuff." Suddenly a voice from heaven said, "Wait until Joe McCarthy comes by in his speedboat."[19] Dean Acheson, it seems safe to assume, would not have been amused.

In truth, McCarthy was an almost totally unreflective man, given to frenetic bursts of activity as well as loud and boisterous speech making. None of his friends recalls that he did much reading, or that it had an impact of any kind on his thought. Even his most faithful admirers freely admit that McCarthy had little of the intellectual in him. (His detractors were equally ready to concede the same point.) If the intellectual life was not his forte, neither was a sense of organization. The McCarthy office presented a jumbled scene of chaos almost without rival in Washington. On a typical afternoon the senator would be talking on the telephone (sometimes speaking into two phones at once), aides would be scurrying in and out, and two or three reporters would be trying at the same time to conduct an interview with the senator. He was the despair of his close friend and admirer Clarence Manion (one-time dean of the University of Notre Dame Law School), who tried repeatedly to make him prepare his speeches in advance, especially the ones for television. Manion complains that he never succeeded.[20]

June was an exception [handwritten annotation]

The senator's political style flowed naturally enough from his personality. It is probably not surprising that one who rushed so thoughtlessly into action, seldom prepared in advance for what he had to say, habitually took a cavalier attitude toward what more scrupulous mortals would term "a careful regard for the truth." He told stories which later turned out to be quite false. For instance, he liked to say that the limp in his leg was due to the "ten pounds of shrapnel" that he carried around as a result of a "war wound." In fact, he had suffered no "war wound" at all, but had merely banged up his leg in a wartime prank with his fellow marines.[21] He testified under oath that during the war he had flown thirty-one "combat missions." The truth is that he flew no "combat missions" at all but served instead as a briefing officer for marine pilots.[22] Is it any wonder, then, that McCarthy repeatedly changed his famous list of 205 "members of the Communist party" working in the State Department, first to 205 "bad risks" in the department, then to 57 "card-carrying Communists," and finally to 81 "cases" of espionage and treason?[23] Richard Rovere perhaps summed it up best when he wrote that the McCarthy style was based on what he called the "multiple untruth." This was a long series of loosely related falsehoods that, repeated in rapid-fire order, seemed to lead to a logical conclusion.[24] Of course they did no such thing because they were all false, but McCarthy made a career out of this kind of advanced illogic.

With his arguments so open to rebuke, McCarthy took the only course that made sense to him: he attacked and attacked and then attacked some more. If his assaults on his enemies answered few questions, they at least garnered headlines, and the resulting publicity kept him at the top of the American political scene for nearly five years. The McCarthy family coat of arms is a stag rampant. Perhaps it is a fitting symbol for this obstreperous and psychologically violent man who seemed to bring chaos and disorder to everything he touched, and who came to such an untimely end at the age of forty-nine.

It is surely one of the great ironies of McCarthy's story that as much as he tried to direct the glare of publicity onto himself and his career, he tried equally hard to keep his religion quietly to himself. Yet he failed in the latter completely, probably because he had succeeded very well in the former. Nevertheless, it seems clear that few Catholic politicians ever made less public display of their religion than did Joe McCarthy. Whatever the reasons, his religious life was a strictly private concern, limited largely to going to Mass on Sunday. His private religious feelings were affairs that he carefully avoided discussing in public, and he never used them as a political lever. Yet the senator's whole career was built on the fight against the Communists; with anticommunism such an important part of Catholicism, his religion inevitably became a public topic, subject to incessant discussion and debate. All of this must have come as something of a surprise to Joseph Raymond McCarthy, who apparently gave hardly a passing thought to the more philosophical and political aspects of his religion and who asked only that he be known as an enemy of subversives, not as a Roman Catholic senator.

Almost all of those who knew the senator have attested to the regularity of his religious practice. If McCarthy thought that going to Sunday Mass (as well as getting baptized, married, and buried in the church) was all that Catholicism stood for, it was nevertheless true that he observed these functions with a fidelity that would have brought joy to the heart of many a Catholic pastor. His Jesuit teachers at Marquette noted his careful observance of his religious duties, as did his wartime companions in the Marine Corps. His close friend Charles Kersten remembers hearing that while McCarthy was in the South Pacific he sometimes made strenuous efforts to get to Sunday Mass.[25] It was the same story for the rest of his life; his Wisconsin Catholic friends the Van Susterens and the Wyngaards all remember seeing him interrupt weekends of fishing and driving in order to get to church on Sunday.[26]

If his religious life was unfailing in its fidelity, it was interior and secretive as well. Charles Kersten insists that while McCarthy refused to "Wear his religion on his sleeve," he "certainly had it in his heart."[27] Another good friend, Patrick F. Scanlan (editor of the *Brooklyn Tablet*), recalls that he did not find out that the senator was a Catholic until some time *after* the *Tablet* had declared its war in favor of McCarthy.[28] McCarthy prided himself on this interior dimension of his religion, once telling his fellow Catholic Clement Zablocki, when both men were freshmen members of Congress, "I'm a good Catholic, but not one of your 'candle-lighting' Catholics."[29]

As a typical Catholic of his times, McCarthy was especially attentive to priests, giving them a deference and courtesy that the clergymen seldom forgot. One Wisconsin priest who was studying in Washington while McCarthy was in the Senate recalls that when the senator happened to see a priest around the Capitol, he would go out of his way to greet the man, to find out where he was from, and to make him feel at home in Washington. He remembers that this stood in marked contrast to the behavior of young John F. Kennedy, who never went out of his way to greet the clergy and who even seemed embarrassed by the presence of priests.[30] McCarthy plainly believed that the good Catholic was one who kept all the rules, including the one that forbade Catholics to serve as godparents or sponsors at the baptism of a non-Catholic child. A priest who knew McCarthy well, recalls that when some good friends of the senator who were Episcopalians asked him to act as godfather for their child, he quietly but firmly refused, saying that his religion would not allow him.[31]

McCarthy's insistence on confining his religion to the prescribed duties and his apparent lack of interest in the intellectual aspects of his faith separated him decisively from the Catholic liberals and intellectuals of his time. The liberals of the 1940s and 1950s scorned the "Sunday Catholics" like McCarthy who showed up faithfully for Sunday Mass but made not the slightest attempt to apply their religion to their business affairs, their politics, or their personal life. Furthermore, intellectual Catholics like Congressman Eugene McCarthy of Minnesota (who wrote articles for the *Commonweal* and lectured to liberal Catholic groups about the popes' social encyclicals) believed that Catholics should make a searching, probing examination into their religion, keeping up with the latest interpretations of Catholic belief and looking always for new ways to apply one's religion to one's whole way of life. None of these considerations, however, occupied his fellow Catholic Joe McCarthy, whose approach to politics was relentlessly secular and pragmatic.

As firm as McCarthy's religious feelings seemed to be, they appeared to have little to do with his friendships. If his friends Charles Kersten and Arlo McKinnon were Catholics, it was more a result of accident and of common politics than of sharing the same religion. They were all conservatives, all Republicans, and all anti-Communist crusaders; they might as easily have been Presbyterians or Methodists instead of Roman Catholics.

If McCarthy's religion had been anything more than matter-of-fact, the Catholic McCarthyites would undoubtedly have made the most of it, but their failure to do so simply gives further proof to the thesis that he kept it mostly to himself. When he died, his admiring eulogists spoke of his "deep faith" and his "profound devotion to the Church," but their words had the distinct ring of perfunctory praise and did not seem to come from deep-felt conviction. At the memorial service held in the Senate shortly after his death, only four of the thirty-six senators who spoke on the occasion even bothered to mention his religion.[32]

Since Catholic regulations obliged the Catholics of the 1950s to abstain from eating meat on Friday, *Time* magazine created a stir in October 1951 when it reported that "Joe seldom misses Sunday Mass, although he cannot pass up a steak on Friday."[33] McCarthy himself never commented publicly on *Time's* allegation, but his defenders did. Prominent among these was the columnist Father James Gillis, who wondered why *Time's* "little army of 'researchers' " was going around "spying, snooping, tattling" on the senator. Gillis also asked, "What business is it of *Time* whether Joe McCarthy is or is not a strict Catholic? Talk about 'hitting low blow after low blow.' "[34] Charles Kersten unequivocally denies that McCarthy ever broke the no-meat rule, since "he took his religion seriously."[35] One of the senator's Catholic critics, on the other hand, insists that one Friday he saw McCarthy eating meat right in the middle of the Senate restaurant.[36] Perhaps the dispute said more about the senator's friends and enemies (and his own controversial nature) than it did about his eating habits.

Both his admirers and his detractors admitted that McCarthy made few, if any, attempts to exploit his religion for political purposes. Three of his staunchest critics—Miles McMillin of the *Madison Capital-Times* and two of the editors of the *Commonweal*, John Cogley and James O'Gara—are all emphatic on this point. McMillin is especially insistent about this. He remembers the "Eastern hotshot intellectuals" who came "piling into Wisconsin," looking for a "nativist, fascist movement" and expecting to find McCarthy acting like a religious bigot in search of the Catholic vote. "The point is that there was very little . . . religionism in Joe. He never felt comfortable with that kind of stuff."[37] The only dissenting opinion comes from Anderson and May, who wrote that soon after he started his crusade against communism, he began deliberately bringing religion into his speeches in an attempt to build a "religious campaign" on his behalf. An examination of their evidence shows that they based their whole case on the speech in which he said that the two "fundamental truths of religion" were the "God who is eternal" and the "soul which is immortal." From this single statement they concluded firmly that

McCarthy was waging a religious campaign.[38] The blunt fact of the matter is that Catholicism had precious little to do with the senator's hunt for subversives. His designs were political and practical, as his friends William F. Buckley, Jr., and Roy Cohn readily concede. Charles Kersten cannot recall a single occasion when McCarthy mentioned Catholicism in connection with his anti-Communist crusade.[39]

One of the reasons why it was so risky to accuse McCarthy of carrying on a "religious campaign" was that he seemed so totally ignorant of his own church's teaching, both on communism and on the related issue of social justice. The Catholic church possesses a large body of thought on both topics; yet McCarthy gave no indication at all that he had even a nodding familiarity with it. William Shannon and Oliver Pilat, in their series of articles on McCarthy published in the *Washington Post*, concluded that he did not have "even a foggy knowledge of Catholic social and economic theory."[40] Their judgment may have seemed harsh at the time, but it is not unthinkable in view of the evidence.

The most serious charge of all, however, was that McCarthy was "uncharitable," an accusation that Catholic critics leveled at him with anger and even bitterness. One priest wrote the *New York Times* that "from an objectively moral standpoint, Senator McCarthy is without doubt the most uncharitable, vituperative and insulting anti-intellectual I have ever heard."[41]

What was the basis for this charge? The senator's critics objected chiefly to his rough handling of his opponents (his habit of calling them "Communist sympathizers," for example) and his often violent assaults on the witnesses he called before his committee. His opponents charged that he was violating the most important canons of Christianity, the rules of charity. This accusation was a widespread one, coming even from so mild a McCarthy observer as Congressman Clement Zablocki of Milwaukee, who accused him of "character assassination" and of drawing "innocent people into false charges."[42]

Everything that touched McCarthy's religion somehow seemed to turn into a major controversy. Unlike other Catholics he could not even give money to Catholic charities without rousing a political debate. Drew Pearson's attorney, for instance, accused him of making donations to Catholic seminaries and parishes "for political purposes with a large group of voters in Wisconsin."[43] (This was undoubtedly a veiled reference to the state's Catholic voters.) In fact, his benefactions usually went to a Catholic seminary in Burma, where he stood little chance of improving his political position.[44]

Even McCarthy's Catholic wedding became a political topic. His marriage in September 1953 to Jean Kerr (his former assistant) took place at St. Matthew's Catholic Cathedral in Washington, D.C. The McCarthyite *Brooklyn Tablet* reported exultantly that a huge crowd had come to the cathedral, giving a "magnificent tribute to Senator McCarthy and an answer to his detractors. It showed some of those who were proud to be counted as his friends."[45]

Although the wedding and the reception passed without incident, the newspapers headlined the "special papal blessing" that the couple had received at the end of the ceremony. "Couple Gets Pope's Blessing" headlined the *Washington Star*, which reported that the wedding had been "especially blessed by Pope Pius." The *Washington Post* stated in a front-page story that the officiating priest had "read a cablegram from the Vatican declaring that Pope Pius XII cordially imparted his 'paternal apostolic blessing' to the couple."[46] Did this mean that the pope himself had put his solemn imprimatur on McCarthy's career? Many liberals in Washington wondered about the meaning of the "special blessing" from Rome. They need not have worried, however. A detailed investigation by the National Committee for an Effective Congress, an anti-McCarthy lobby in Washington, revealed that the blessing was "a routine thing," implying no papal approval of McCarthy's political activities.[47]

Arguments such as these, however, had little effect on those conservative Catholics who favored McCarthy precisely because he was a Catholic. To this embattled faction he had always been a "loyal

Catholic," one whose fidelity to the church matched his loyalty to the marines and to the nation. Though few Catholic McCarthyites would say that he was a "saint," many regarded him as a "good Catholic man" who had tried to do his best for his church and his country and had received only abuse in return.[48] Dr. David Goldstein of Boston, a convert from Judaism to Catholicism, wrote a poem that summed up what many of the Catholic McCarthyites felt:

> McCarthy is a man to be honored!
> McCarthy is a name to revere!
> McCarthy stands firm for America!
> Our Homeland! Our Country so dear!
>
> They persecute, slander, harass him,
> And pour out their venom and smear,
> But he stands with his God and his Country,
> That makes him a man that they fear.
>
> So we bless [him] and love him and trust him,
> We'll stand with him right to the end,
> When his foes have faded and perished
> For he is America's friend.[49]

To McCarthy's critics, of course, the Catholicism of the senator was often a painful embarrassment. After a speech in which McCarthy insinuated that Adlai Stevenson was just like Alger Hiss, a liberal Catholic wrote that McCarthy "deserves nothing but complete, utter contempt. That McCarthy is a Catholic only intensifies the shame which I feel."[50] Many liberals felt the same feeling of shame, especially the kind who read the *Commonweal* or who voted for reformist causes.

Occasionally, a liberal anti-McCarthyite not of the Catholic faith complained that McCarthy was "playing up" to the Catholics to get their support. Richard Rovere seemed especially convinced of this, writing in one place that although McCarthy usually acted like a "vulgarian," he would "get a shave, perfume his breath, scrub up his language . . . and lay on the particular kind of charm" of a "nice

Catholic boy"[51] if he found himself scheduled to speak before the Gold Star Mothers or the Catholic Youth Organization. This is an intriguing thesis, but Rovere cites no specific occasions when McCarthy did this, nor is it likely that there were many such. "Catering to the Catholics" was not his stock in trade.

Nor was "playing up to the Protestants" part of his bag of tricks. The Protestant fundamentalists, however, found it immensely profitable to support McCarthy's campaign against subversives. This decision marked a turning point in the history of the fundamentalist movement in America, for it had long been a vehemently anti-Catholic force in American life. In effect, the fundamentalists decided to ignore McCarthy's "wrong ideology" in favor of his "right politics." Right-wing ministers like Carl McIntyre suddenly found themselves supporting the Roman Catholic Joe McCarthy because they, too, believed that liberal Communist sympathizers and even Communists themselves had wormed their way into the government.[52] It is important to note, however, that the softening of the fundamentalists toward McCarthy failed to bring about either a reduction in tensions between fundamentalists and Catholics or a political union between Catholic McCarthyites and Protestant McCarthyites. The old wounds remained unhealed, as the presidential election of 1960 soon revealed: Protestant right-wingers openly attacked John Kennedy for his Catholicism, accusing him of being the unwitting tool of the papacy. (Know-Nothingism was not yet dead, it was only on vacation.) In short, McCarthyism did nothing to bring the Protestant Bible Belt and Roman Catholicism together. If Carl McIntyre and Cardinal Spellman happened to agree on Joe McCarthy, they disagreed on nearly everything else.

McCarthy's Catholicism was an inescapable political fact, no matter how much both the McCarthyites and the anti-McCarthyites insisted that McCarthyism was a political issue and not a religious one. With the church's adamant stand against communism so firmly etched into the national consciousness, no one could realistically ignore the Catholicism of the nation's most publicized Red hunter. As he charged from sensation to headline to exposé, his Catholicism stubbornly followed him, bringing with it a confused legacy of dismay, anger, hope, and consolation. At no moment in his crusade was the religious dimension very far from the surface—not even when he began it all at Wheeling, West Virginia, on 9 February 1950.

Chapter 3

The McCarthy Crusade Begins

When the ladies of the Republican Women's Club of Wheeling, West Virginia, asked Senator Joseph McCarthy to address them, they probably had little idea that they were about to witness one of the landmark events in the history of the cold-war era. Indeed, nothing about the speaker, the speaker's history, or the circumstances surrounding the speech seemed to presage anything newsworthy or arresting. The orator for the evening had compiled a conservative political record marked in no way by a consistent program or a coherent political philosophy. If he was distinguished at all, it was for his reputation as a roughhouse politician and a rude destroyer of the solemn "club rules" of the United States Senate. None of this bothered the junior senator from Wisconsin, either before or after the Wheeling address.

The senator's precise words to the ladies that evening have become a matter of considerable dispute.[1] No one, however, would ever debate the import of his message, which was plain enough: Communists and their dupes have infiltrated the State Department, much to the danger of America's foreign policy and to its security against Marxist marauders. Nor would anyone ever debate the impact of his words on the nation's political system. The speech attracted instant and national attention, bringing the senator almost overnight from obscurity to renown. What accounts for his sudden and unprecedented success, one that came so quickly it seems to have startled even the senator himself? It was, of course, a major statement on foreign policy by a United States senator and as such was bound to attract a reporter or two. But other senators spoke the same day on other topics, and within the same week other senators joined McCarthy in talking about communism; yet none of them became celebrities like McCarthy. Why not? The answer seems to be that McCarthy's effort succeeded in exploiting a climate of fear that surrounded the cold war and everything that had to do with domestic subversion. In such an atmosphere it was inevitable that McCarthy's sensational charges would find a ready (even fanatical) audience.

"I always felt afraid" is a statement that might well sum up the temper of the cold-war era. Liberals working in the government, the press, higher education, and many professions often feared for their reputations and even their jobs if their credentials as American patriots became tarnished or questionable. A brief flirtation with Communist front organizations in the thirties, a record as a conscientious objector in World War II, a run with the Catholic Workers for three or four years, or a series of public statements denouncing the loyalty oaths of the period—any of these could be enough to send a leftist-leaning American to the political gallows. It was not an easy time to be a liberal, especially if such liberalism impelled one to defend civil liberties (somehow the ACLU had taken on a pinkish hue), to vote Socialist (only grammarians recognized a difference between socialism and communism), or to say publicly that raving demagogues had infiltrated the ranks of the anti-Communists. But for that matter it was not easy to be a conservative either. A clammy pall of fear hung over the ranks of rightist-leaning Americans in both major parties. A series of unnerving events had convinced them that the security of the Republic was no longer beyond question and that subversive persons had indeed "wormed their way into the federal government" (to use the cliché born of the period).[2]

Before World War II had ended, government agents announced in February 1945 that they had found more than a thousand highly classified documents in the offices of *Amerasia*, a magazine with alleged pro-Communist connections. Though the government's lengthy investigations into the publication failed to turn up any Communist spies, the extensive publicity given to the case intensified public fears that Communists had indeed undermined the federal agencies charged with the nation's security.

Stung by charges that he was not doing enough to combat domestic communism, President Truman soon launched a rigorous loyalty-review program designed to remove employees of questionable loyalty from the government.[3] Though the Truman program failed to produce a single bona fide Communist spy, it did have two results. First (and this was probably good for the administration and the Democrats), it drastically reduced the number of security violations occurring in the federal government. Second (and this was in no way good for Truman and his party), it focused national attention myopically on the problem of Communists in the government. No matter that of the 4,722,278 names checked by the FBI, only 575 had to be denied employment on grounds of loyalty. (Most were deemed "security risks"; only a few were dismissed because they were found to be "loyalty risks," a far more serious charge.) No matter at all, because 3,634 government workers had quit before the government finished investigating them.[4] Had they resigned because they were guilty of following the Marxist-Stalinist line? In a world where communism seemed to be marching inexorably around the globe, no one could be sure.

Fears intensified in 1949 when the Department of Justice brought indictments against the eleven members of the Communist party's national board, charging them with violations of the Smith Act of 1940, which had made it a federal crime to advocate the violent overthrow of the government. After a tumultuous trial that in many ways foreshadowed the histrionics of the McCarthy hearings, the court found the eleven members guilty and packed them off to jail.

In spite of the Communist party's undoubted decline in numbers and influence, a celebrated ex-Communist succeeded in deepening even more the nation's worries over communism. Whittaker Chambers, repentant of his sins against religion and capitalism, dramatically accused Alger Hiss (a former State Department official) of espionage at the highest level. It somehow seemed significant that the Harvard-educated Hiss had been present at Yalta, though few took the trouble to find out precisely what he had done at that fateful conference. Of far deeper significance was Chambers's declaration that Hiss, while working at State, had clandestinely given Chambers highly classified government documents. If the charges were true, then Hiss was undoubtedly guilty of treason. Challenged to produce the evidence or retire in silence, Chambers sensationally brought forth a packet of microfilm rolls containing photographs of the documents that he claimed he had received from Hiss. With Hiss unable to explain why some of the microfilmed documents were typed on a typewriter he had once had in his own home, the jury on 21 January 1950 found Alger Hiss guilty of perjury. (The statute of limitations prevented the government from returning a charge of espionage.) Intensifying the political debate surrounding the two Hiss trials was the insistence of the Truman administration officials that Hiss's character was beyond reproach. No other event did more to strengthen the Republican party's charge that the Democrats were the "party of treason," as McCarthy later put it. No other event did more to convince the nation that Communist spies had once lurked in the marbled halls of the Department of State. It is no accident that Senator McCarthy would say later on, "We got Alger Hiss," thus claiming partial credit for a conviction in which he played no role whatever.

As frightening as the domestic scene appeared in 1949, the advance of Asian communism seemed even more ominous. In spite of $400 million in foreign aid for China, the Nationalist Chinese government of Chiang Kai-shek fell in late 1949 to the victorious Communist forces of Mao Tse-tung. For the Republican party the fall of China was both a tragedy and an opportunity. Even if China could not be reclaimed from the Communists, at least the Democratic politicians who made the tragedy possible could be run out of office, they reasoned. The next two years witnessed a withering assault on the Democrats that climaxed in the Republican sweep of the White House and the Congress in 1952.

The McCarthy Crusade Begins

The times had thus mixed the ingredients for a witch hunt of enormous proportions. It is ironic indeed that the McCarthy crusade occurred at a time when the fortunes of the Communist party in America were at a low ebb, when further efforts to find Communists were producing almost nothing at all, and when the government's own loyalty-check programs were becoming so stringent that they called forth the wrath of liberals and the ACLU. The Alger Hiss episode, followed in rapid order by the discovery of a Communist spy (Klaus Fuchs) in the ranks of the British atomic scientists and the subsequent implication of two American scientists (Julius and Ethel Rosenberg) in the Fuchs scandal, seemed to make such a crusade inevitable. It was McCarthy's supreme fortune (and his opponents' decided bad luck) that he was able to capitalize on this remarkable series of reverses and apparent treacheries against the security of the nation. Seldom has a campaign born and nurtured on fear seen such a spectacular birth. Many a Democrat and liberal went down to defeat in the ensuing struggle and so did at least one famous Republican —Joseph Raymond McCarthy himself.

McCarthy would never have launched his anti-Communist crusade at all had he not heard from a Catholic priest that the anti-Communist trail was the one to follow if he wanted reelection in 1952 and a major career in American politics (or at least that is the way the story usually goes). The conventional wisdom has it that on 7 January 1950 McCarthy met for dinner at Washington's Colony restaurant with a prominent Washington attorney, William A. Roberts, Professor Charles Kraus of the Department of Political Science at Georgetown University, and Father Edmund Walsh of the same university's School of Foreign Service. (Father Walsh had a formidable reputation in Catholic circles as an expert on international communism.) During the meal McCarthy remarked that he was looking for an issue to get him the publicity he needed to win reelection in 1952. One of the dinner companions suggested the St. Lawrence Seaway Project, but McCarthy rejected it as too unexciting. When McCarthy himself proposed a large-scale pension plan for the aged, the others condemned it as economically unsound. Finally, Father Walsh suggested that McCarthy try the issue of Communist subversion; not only was the country in real danger from the threat of Communist spies, but the voters were ready to support a good Red hunt. McCarthy leaped at the idea, saying he was sure that this was the issue he needed for his campaign. When the other three warned him to be careful to "get the facts," insisting that the public was tired of Red scares, McCarthy replied absentmindedly that he would follow their advice. McCarthy's companions then left, thinking that they had done a great service both to him and to the country. (Less than a month later, McCarthy gave his famous speech in Wheeling, announcing that he had a list of Communists actually working in the State Department.) Though the Colony incident has many variants, these elements seem to be common to all of them.

How did the tale get its start? Almost certainly it first appeared in the columns of Drew Pearson, at that time the scourge of Washington politicians and socialites. Pearson's column in the *Washington Post* for 14 March 1950 contained an item about the "likable [sic] young Senator Joe McCarthy" who had asked his friends for a winning issue and had learned that "any Senator who consistently attacked communism would have a great appeal for the voters." Pearson wrote that today "the man who urged this latter advice, Father Edmund A. Walsh of Georgetown University, is not happy at the outcome."[5] A month later Pearson repeated his charges, saying that McCarthy's campaign had been "encouraged by some of the clergy at Georgetown university [sic] acting unofficially and as individuals."[6] Pearson did not name Walsh, but by that time almost everyone in Washington knew whom he meant. Thanks to Pearson's subsequent repetitions of the story, the Colony dinner soon became an accepted part of McCarthy lore.[7]

Two years later the story, somewhat embellished, appeared in the popular biography of the senator by Jack Anderson and Ronald

May. Their version contained snatches of conversation designed to make it interesting reading. Thus, when the St. Lawrence Seaway proposal came up, McCarthy is supposed to have said, "That hasn't enough sex." To Walsh's idea of the Communist hunt, McCarthy reportedly replied, "The Government is full of Communists. The thing to do is hammer at them."[8] Frustratingly enough, Anderson and May failed to tell where they got their information. The Anderson and May volume, an immediate commercial hit, gave the story a currency it had not enjoyed before. In June 1953 I. F. Stone wrote that McCarthy "has had the guidance of Father Edmund A. Walsh," and in the same month the *Nation* said that Father Walsh had "selected" the "emotion-filled issue of communism" for McCarthy's attention.[9] Subsequent versions of the story by Richard Rovere and Eric Goldman added further (and highly imaginative) details to the account.[10] Goldman was the first to suggest that McCarthy's Irish blood may have had something to do with the event. He noted that Walsh's intervention "cut deep" into McCarthy's Irish background: "The Irish Catholics of his area, while New Dealers, had always suspected Easterners."[11] Like his predecessors Goldman also failed to provide supporting evidence. Once the story had received the imprimatur of Rovere and Goldman, it became firmly fixed in the McCarthy legend, enduring to the present day.[12]

For all the monotonous repetitions of the story, the incident has received only one systematic critique. Michael O'Brien has noted that fully three months before the Wheeling speech McCarthy had successfully attacked a leftist reporter for the *Madison* (Wis.) *Capital-Times*, charging that he had Communistic leanings. Though McCarthy was unable to uncover enough incriminating evidence to make the charges stick, he reaped a harvest of hometown publicity for his efforts. For the next three months (all *before* Wheeling) communism was the principal and repeated theme of his political speeches. O'Brien concludes plausibly that the senator "needed no suggestion from Father Walsh to realize the political value of the Communist issue."[13]

The author's own research into the story casts further doubt on it. When Pearson wrote in March 1950 that Father Walsh was "not happy at the outcome" of the dinner, he was quite right, but not in the way that he suggested. No one knows what Walsh personally thought about McCarthy, since he wrote nothing about him, said nothing in public, and did not even discuss the senator with his Jesuit confreres at Georgetown University. (Nor do his personal papers give us any indication at all of his reactions to either McCarthy or the Colony controversy.)[14] Nevertheless, Walsh made his feelings about the Pearson article abundantly clear to anyone around the university who cared to listen. Normally a restrained and self-possessed man, Walsh angrily told his fellow Jesuits that Pearson was a "liar." He said that he had even offered Pearson $1,000 for the columnist's favorite charity if Pearson could prove his accusations. If Pearson could not prove them, then he challenged Pearson to pay $1,000 to Walsh's own pet philanthropy. To Walsh's intense disgust, Pearson ignored the challenge.[15]

The president of the university, Father Hunter Guthrie, stoutly defended Walsh's side of the controversy, but did so only in private.[16] Unfortunately, Guthrie never denounced the story publicly, nor did Walsh himself ever publish a denial of Pearson's allegations. Hence the rumors and the popular belief that Walsh had instigated McCarthy's Red hunt.

What can one say about the most famous dinner party McCarthy ever attended? Clearly it all began with Drew Pearson; it is not impossible that he made up a good part of the story. His associate Jack Anderson, who embellished it most imaginatively, refused to answer the writer's letters of inquiry, as did Richard Rovere, who claims that he received his information from "one of the participants." Since three of the principals—McCarthy, Walsh, and Roberts —are all dead, and the remaining witness, Professor Kraus, has dropped out of sight, it is impossible to acquire firsthand information about the event. It is essential to note, however, that no documentary evidence of any kind exists to prove that Walsh ever exhorted McCarthy to go on his political crusade. If the story now seems suspect, why did it gain such currency? The answers are not hard to find. It made sense, of course, to say that a *priest* had given the idea to McCarthy because Catholicism was known to have a special argument with communism. Secondly, everyone in Washington knew of Walsh's long-standing interest in communism; indeed, one careful observer has described him as "almost the symbol of clerical anticommunism in Washington." Especially noteworthy were Walsh's popular Washington lectures on the subject of "world communism," in which Walsh dramatized the worldwide threat of communism before a hugely admiring audience of Washington conservatives and interested politicians.[17]

An alert critic, however, would have noted two flaws in the argument-from-the-priesthood: first, Walsh never said a word in public or in private about McCarthy, and second, Walsh almost never discussed the problem of Communists in government. Long known as a popular authority on the geopolitics of Russian expansionism, Walsh spent all of his time on the problem of external communism. His concerns were defense, security, and preparedness; his scholarly interests were Russian and Communist history, and his deepest anxiety was what he called "the godless and materialistic" nature of Marxism. The result was that he almost never talked about the question of subversion. For instance, the entire 293 pages of his best known work, *Total Empire* (1951), show only two passing references to the issue of Communists in government.[18] His other books and articles, as well as his many speeches, show a surpassing concern (one might almost say an "obsession") with the menace of external communism. But if Walsh ever exhorted McCarthy to take up arms against Communist spies in Washington, then he acted in a way that was completely out of character for him.

One might suggest the following, by way of ringing down the curtain on *l'affaire Colony*: the meeting almost certainly took place, and the participants may well have discussed communism. Given the senator's growing interest in domestic communism and Walsh's constant preoccupation with what he called "international Marxism," it is also possible that they had an exchange on the politics of anticommunism. It is highly improbable, however, that Walsh urged McCarthy to go on a crusade against subversives on the ground that it would bring him instant political stardom.

The only possible basis for this story was Walsh's failure to make a public denial, despite the potentially damaging effects to himself and to the university. To Walsh's close friends at Georgetown, the reasons for his silence seem obvious: he probably believed that a reply would glorify Pearson's story. To others, however, it has not been so obvious. Given this one qualification, it should be apparent by now that the story's foundations are extremely shaky and completely bereft of documentary support. Future historians would do well to consign it to the oblivion it has long deserved.

With or without the help of Edmund Walsh, Joseph Raymond McCarthy was soon off and running. On 9 February 1950 he told the Republican ladies in Wheeling, "I have here in my hand a list of 205—a list of names that were made known to the Secretary of State as being members of the Communist party and who nevertheless are still working and shaping policy in the State Department."[19] The Democrats immediately attacked McCarthy, accusing him of specious reasoning and of failing to prove his charges against the State Department. As McCarthy's Republican allies took up his cause, it became increasingly obvious that an angry party battle was brewing in the Senate. Sensing a rare opportunity to embarrass the Democratic administration, Republican senators maneuvered the Senate into passing a resolution calling for a complete investigation of McCarthy's charges. From that time until the Senate began its hearings on 8 March, McCarthy and his staff busied themselves with research on the "cases" the senator intended to present to the investigating committee.

The committee that McCarthy faced was tough and aggressive, and it was made up of a majority of Democrats, since they controlled both houses of Congress. The Democratic chairman was Millard E.

Tydings of Maryland, a skilled partisan who immediately challenged McCarthy to prove his accusations. For the next week the Tydings committee (a subcommittee of the Foreign Relations Committee), wrangled bitterly with McCarthy, reaching ultimate agreement on nothing. Meanwhile, McCarthy continued to build a national reputation as the country's number-one Communist hunter.

What did the nation's Catholics think about McCarthy's performance? One of the first to speak out was the liberal Catholic congressman from St. Paul, Minnesota, who happened to have the same last name as the Wisconsin senator. The hero of the Catholic intellectuals and reform-minded liberals, Congressman Eugene McCarthy came from a thoroughly Catholic background, beginning with a stay in a seminary and continuing with a professorship at a Catholic college in St. Paul, where he lectured on Catholic principles of government and politics. His idols were the Catholic liberals of European and American history, and his ideals were the principles of justice and equity that he found in the popes' social encyclicals. Shortly after the Wheeling speech, Congressman McCarthy spoke before a Catholic group in suburban Washington. Bitterly he criticized the senator, claiming that his methods directly contradicted Catholic social and political principles. Since that time Eugene McCarthy has claimed, "I was the first to challenge Senator McCarthy," though the impossibility of establishing the exact date of his speech makes it difficult to prove his claim.[20] Regardless of this problem, it is a fact that the forces of American Catholic liberalism, aptly symbolized by Eugene McCarthy, wasted no time coming to the conclusion that the junior senator was a menace both to the church and to the nation.

If the Gallup poll was any indication, however, Eugene McCarthy's voice represented only a minority of the nation's Catholics. A survey conducted in March 1950 (a month after the Wheeling address) showed that nearly half (49 percent) of the Catholics believed McCarthy when he said that Communists still worked in the State Department, and only 28 percent thought that he was just playing politics. (The figures for non-Catholics were virtually the same as for Catholics.)[21] At that time the advantage seemed to lie with the Catholic McCarthyites, because of their greater numbers. The leadership of this band came from the *Brooklyn Tablet*, which lost no time in climbing on the McCarthy bandwagon. Reflecting as always the archconservative views of its editor, the *Tablet* described McCarthy's speech to the Senate of 20 February as "a straightforward American address," one prepared with great skill, and truly an "A-1 patriotic effort." As good as McCarthy's effort was, however, he needed help, because time was running out for America: "Every American is burdened with the obligation of saving his country before it is too late. Write your support of Senator McCarthy NOW!"[22] This was only the first of many times that it called on its readers to exert public pressure in favor of McCarthy.

Although some Catholic publications shared the *Tablet*'s warm enthusiasm for McCarthy, a number agreed with the *Boston Pilot* (the Catholic paper for that city), which said that a prudent caution was in order; "patience, sincerity, and a scrupulous regard for factual information" ought to govern the debate over McCarthy's charges, the *Pilot* argued.[23]

Virtually alone in condemning McCarthy was the *Commonweal*, the leading voice for Catholic liberal and intellectual opinion. The magazine's editors found the senator an ignorant and irresponsible man, one who made a "moderate and constructive approach" to the problem of loyalty quite impossible.[24] "With a trail of unresolved accusations behind him," McCarthy lunges from one indictment to the next, mixing "mere assertion" with evidence, it said. It suggested that the Chief Justice of the Supreme Court be asked to appoint a distinguished panel of public figures charged with the task of looking impartially into McCarthy's charges. Such a panel would surely have the public confidence, as the present "scandal-screaming investigations just as surely do not."[25] The *Commonweal* thus sounded the opening blast in its five-year war against Joe McCarthy. From that moment until his censure in December 1954, hardly a week went by without an editorial or article detailing the senator's latest crimes against the Republic.

Before the debate over McCarthy had hardly begun, it was evident that the Catholic press had torn itself apart over the issue surrounding him. The large number of vehement articles written on McCarthy showed how deeply both liberals and conservatives felt about the question. Only a small group of Catholic publications tried to find a middle-of-the-road approach—one somewhere between the *Brooklyn Tablet*, which wanted the administration run out of office, and the *Commonweal*, which wanted McCarthy denounced roundly and definitively. Eventually even the "moderates," few as they were, had to choose sides over McCarthy.

The position that each publication took on McCarthy depended on whether its political policy was generically liberal or conservative. Thus the liberal papers and magazines, which tended to look favorably on the Truman administration's foreign and domestic policies, predictably took a hard line against McCarthy, inveighing against his methods and defending the administration's right to keep national-security affairs secret from his investigation. Conservative organs, on the other hand, which had long feared that the administration was becoming "Socialistic," wanted a tough stand taken against "liberal thinkers" whom they believed were sympathetic toward the Communists; not unexpectedly, they jumped to McCarthy's defense and taunted the administration for hiding behind executive privilege.

The McCarthy question, in sum, mirrored the greater division within American Catholicism, the split between the left and the right. The Catholic liberals, most of whom favored the Democrats, wanted an open and changing church and looked on the intellectual life with unabashed approval. McCarthyism smacked all too much of the Catholic ghetto and Catholic power politics. The Catholic conservatives, meanwhile, generally took the Republican side in political questions. In church affairs their primary concern was the defense of the church, and they had little patience either with non-

Catholics or with intellectuals, believing that both groups were hostile to the church and were tinged with the heresies of secularism, Protestantism, and liberalism.

In the early weeks of the Tydings investigation, a prominent Catholic priest in Washington tried to steer McCarthy in a more cautious and less erratic direction, but with no success at all. The clergyman was Father John Cronin, who worked in the Social Action Department of the National Catholic Welfare Conference, acting as the bishops' resident expert on communism. In the early cold-war years, he had made a detailed study of domestic communism for the Catholic bishops, in the process compiling one of the most complete files on Communist subversion ever assembled in the country. When McCarthy came on the scene, Cronin thought that perhaps he could get McCarthy to take a less sensationalistic approach if he supplied the senator with the kind of precise information on subversion that was needed to conduct a proper investigation. Cronin believed that a restrained and scholarly approach would impress the senator, but he was due for a rough surprise. Once or twice a month during the Tydings hearings, Cronin and his aides delivered to McCarthy a packet of information about people in the government whom they believed worthy of investigation. To their acute disappointment, however, McCarthy completely ignored their information and continued to churn out wild accusations and garbled pieces of misinformation. McCarthy failed even to glance at their materials, and "when he showed no improvement we gave up on him," Cronin recalls.[26]

Word of Cronin's attempt to redirect McCarthy reached the Washington rumor factory, with the usual confused results. In February 1951 Drew Pearson's attorney reported that Cronin had been "working very closely" with McCarthy (which was quite inaccurate) and that Cronin had given McCarthy "considerable financial support" (which was completely false).[27] The Pearson report (fortunately never made public) contained no supporting evidence, and indeed there was none to find. Cronin had given McCarthy no money at all, either his or the bishops'.[28] More important, by the time that the Pearson report was completed, Cronin had publicly stated his objections to McCarthy, saying that McCarthy had repeatedly made charges that he would never be able to prove.[29] Though the incident may seem of small significance (since the report remained confidential), it is nevertheless of considerable importance because it illustrated vividly the tendency of many Washington liberals (Pearson in particular) to see connections between McCarthy and the Catholic church, connections that never existed.

The turning point in the Tydings committee hearings came when McCarthy dramatically announced on 21 March 1950 that he had the name of the "top Russian espionage agent" in the United States. The "agent" turned out to be Professor Owen Lattimore of the Walter Hines Page School of International Relations at Johns Hopkins University in Baltimore. A recognized expert on Mongolia, Lattimore had never been a regular member of the State Department but had served several times as a consultant to the government. As a specialist in Far Eastern affairs, he had been active in the Institute of Pacific Relations, a private organization concerned with political events in the Pacific area. In the years since the war had ended, his thoughts on China policy had earned him the undying ire of General Chiang Kai-shek's supporters in the United States, usually known as the "China lobby." Once favorable toward Chiang, Lattimore had become increasingly critical of him in the mid-1940s; to the China lobby he seemed much less hostile toward the Communists. Right-wing journalists and politicians took ever sharper aim at the professor as the decade neared its end, and they were especially upset at the suggestion he made in 1949 that the United States withdraw from South Korea.[30] McCarthy quickly decided that he would let his case against the State Department "stand or fall" on Owen Lattimore.

In preparing his charges against Lattimore, McCarthy had the help of an old friend, former Congressman Charles Kersten of Wisconsin. (Defeated for reelection in 1948, Kersten was temporarily "free" to help McCarthy.) McCarthy called him to Washington and asked him if he knew anything about Owen Lattimore. Kersten replied that at least he knew Louis F. Budenz, who perhaps might know something about the professor. Kersten immediately called Budenz and asked him if he knew anything about Lattimore. Budenz replied confidently, "Of course I do. He was a member of the party, assigned to Far Eastern matters." Budenz had learned all about Lattimore's Communist connections during his days as editor of the *Daily Worker*. When he brought back this startling piece of news, "Joe kind of danced in the office there, saying, 'Gee, this is wonderful,'" Kersten recalls. Kersten then went up to New Rochelle, New York, to see Budenz. He found the former Communist more than willing to cooperate; Budenz was sure that Lattimore was a Communist because he remembered that Lattimore's reports for the party often came into the *Worker*'s office. He felt more confident than ever in describing Lattimore as the "true purveyor of Moscow's line on the Far East."[31]

Budenz appeared before the Tydings committee on 20 April 1950. With intense publicity heralding his appearance, a huge crowd, anxious to hear what Budenz had to say about Owen Lattimore, packed into the committee room. The professor later recalled that the audience included a "strong representation" of priests whose "black garb made them stand out conspicuously."[32] Briefly summed up, Budenz's testimony went as follows: Lattimore had been a member of a Communist cell within the Institute of Pacific Relations; in 1943 party leaders had told him to change his "line" on Chiang Kai-shek to one of opposition and hostility; in 1944 instructions had come to Budenz telling him to "consider Owen Lattimore a Communist." Finally, the party had told Budenz that Lattimore had been "of service" in the *Amerasia* case.[33]

McCarthy's Republican supporters in the Senate rejoiced at Budenz's testimony, believing that at last they had found the damning evidence against Lattimore that they needed to finish his career. In time, however, certain weaknesses in Budenz's testimony began to show up: first, most of what Budenz had said was based on oral report—he had been informed of this, or told of that, and so on. When pressed for specific details, he failed to produce anything more convincing. Secondly, Budenz had spent many hours with the FBI, following his defection from communism in 1945, testifying voluminously about Communist activity in America. Yet he had never mentioned Owen Lattimore in all the hours of testimony he had given to the bureau. (When asked twenty-two years later about this discrepancy, Budenz replied defensively that "it wasn't pertinent to discuss it."[34] He refused to explain why it was not "pertinent.") Finally, he was always careful to say he "had been informed" that Lattimore was a Communist, but he never stated flatly that Lattimore had been a party member. When the author asked Budenz about this, he insisted that he "could not say" the professor was a Communist because he was "giving testimony." That is to say, "I couldn't swear to it." There were other people whom he knew to be Communists, and he was able to list them by name, but with Lattimore his information "wasn't as firm," Budenz said.[35]

Catholicism became an issue in Budenz's testimony, largely because he made it so. Budenz declared confidently that he was "a different man than five years ago" because the Catholic sacrament of "confession" had given him redemption from his past sins. Apparently he hoped that this would convince his listeners of the reliability of his testimony. Indeed, his return to Catholicism had been in the back of his mind all during his appearance before the Tydings committee. When asked if he had been thinking about the church during his appearance on the witness stand, he answered emphatically that it was "overwhelmingly my thought."[36] It seems clear, in retrospect, that Budenz's traumatic departure from communism, his abrupt return to Catholicism, and his highly conservative political posture all converged to produce a man whose religion and politics centered on anticommunism. It remained that way until he died in 1972.

How did Catholics react to their coreligionist, Louis F. Budenz? Without doubt he posed a special problem for some of them because of his status as a convert from communism, his popularity as a Catholic lecturer and author, and his use of the Catholic argument against Communist subversives. For a number of Catholics, however, Budenz was no problem at all. Typical of the pro-Budenz faction was the University of Notre Dame publication called *Ave Maria*, which argued that Budenz's status as a former Communist was reason enough to believe him.[37] Argued *Ave Maria* with passion: "He was himself tangled in the meshes of communism for a while, but the heartcalls of Faith and motherland won him back to his earlier loyalties."[38]

For anti-McCarthy liberals across the country, the picture of Budenz using his Catholicism to denounce suspected Communists was utterly beyond endurance. Elmer Davis complained that certain ex-Communists, finding that "final truth" does not reside in Moscow, have "sought and found it in Rome." A few have even become "their own Popes and are just as sure of their own infallibility as they were in the days when they parroted the resolutions of the Comintern."[39] The *Washington Post* wondered whether it was really necessary for converts to Roman Catholicism to *lead* the movement away from communism.[40]

Budenz's most potent adversary, however, was a Catholic senator, Dennis Chavez of New Mexico. With a growing sense of frustration, he watched Budenz deliver his lengthy story to the Tydings committee. By the time Budenz was finished, he was hot with anger, telling a friend, "One of us Catholics ought to challenge this man— one of us should do it—I should do it!"[41] Having decided that he was the one to express liberal Catholicism's indignation with Budenz, Chavez rose on the Senate floor on 12 May 1950 delivering an impassioned attack on the ex-Communist. His voice trembling with emotion, Chavez said that in all his nineteen years in the Congress, he had never referred publicly to his religion. Now, however, "I speak as a Roman Catholic." He accused Budenz of using "the Church which I revere" as a "shield and a cloak" to protect testimony that was clearly unfair and untrue. Budenz has not been talking merely as a private citizen, Chavez insisted. Rather, he has been "speaking with special emphasis as a Catholic, investing his appearances and utterances with an added sanctity" by virtue of his recent conversion. "My ancestors brought the cross to this hemisphere," Chavez shouted. "Louis Budenz has been using this cross as a club."[42]

Chavez's passionate outburst on the "Catholic issue" brought tempers to the flash point, as always happened during the McCarthy controversy. To the Jesuit president of Fordham University, Lawrence J. McGinley, Chavez was a "modern Pharisee," the kind who is "always ready to point a self-righteous finger at their fellow man."[43] Other Catholic publications shared McGinley's sense of outrage.[44] Probably the most vehement attack on Chavez came from a columnist in the *Los Angeles Tidings* (the Catholic paper for that city) who said that if the attack on Budenz had come from a Communist, it might have made sense. But "for a Catholic to do this to one of our Prodigal Sons—amid the joyous howls of all the atheist conspirators against God and mankind—is in my view unspeakably low."[45]

Meanwhile, the source of all the contention, Louis F. Budenz, was saying nothing. When asked shortly before his death about the Chavez episode, he simply repeated all the charges that his supporters had levelled against the senator some twenty years before. "Truman was back of the whole thing," he insisted, repeating the rumor common around Washington that the president had somehow maneuvered Chavez into doing a dirty job he wanted to avoid doing himself. Most of Budenz's advocates, and Budenz himself, believed that Chavez had always been a bad Catholic anyway and that this somehow accounted for his attack on Budenz. All the while that the argument was raging over Chavez's address, the story circulated that a "Communist lawyer" had written Chavez's speech, though the name of the lawyer somehow remained a secret. Many conservative Catholics believed this curious story. Chief among them was Louis F. Budenz himself, who believed it until the day he died.[46] When told about the rumor, Chavez replied, "Neither a

Communist lawyer nor any other kind of a lawyer helped me prepare that speech."[47] Chavez was right, but a bit misleading, since he had received extensive help on the speech from a man who was neither a Communist nor a lawyer, but an energetic political activist in Washington. The gentleman in question, Maurice Rosenblatt, was one of the founders of the National Committee for an Effective Congress, a liberal political lobby that eventually spearheaded the drive to censure McCarthy.[48] Rosenblatt was also extremely sensitive to the religious dimensions of the McCarthy debate and was one of the first people in Washington to attempt the mobilization of Catholic forces against the senator.

Both Catholic and Protestant liberals, meanwhile, had begun to take Chavez's side in the dispute.[49] His most important ally by far was Monsignor George Higgins, head of the Social Action Department of the National Catholic Welfare Conference. Higgins saw Budenz as a serious threat both to the reputation of the Catholic church and to its work. Nothing irked him more than the preposterous notion that Catholics ought to support Budenz because he was a member of their church. Catholics were free, absolutely and unqualifiedly free, to make up their minds about Budenz, about Chavez, or about anyone else, he wrote. Nor was it true that Louis F. Budenz ever "speaks for the Catholic Church," nor does Chavez, nor McCarthy, nor even George Higgins, he added. He hoped that someday Budenz would make it "unmistakably clear to the American public that the Church . . . is not a sort of international FBI." Most important of all, he hoped that Budenz would make it equally clear that the anticommunism of the church "goes hand in hand with a radical program of social justice," one that some of the "patriots" who were so enthusiastic about Budenz seemed unwilling to honor.[50] Higgins's words carried considerable weight, both because of his position in Washington and because of his reputation as perhaps the leading exponent of Catholic liberalism in America. As the McCarthy era dragged on, Higgins continued to press for social action as the proper antidote to communism; Budenz and McCarthy moved in another direction entirely.

If McCarthy was becoming more and more identified with the Catholics, part of the reason may have been that he gave some of his most important speeches before Catholic audiences. The first of these came on 25 May 1950, just three months after Wheeling, when he addressed the annual convention of the Catholic Press Association in Rochester, New York. Always a struggling and impoverished organization, the association wanted a famous speaker for the keynote address who would bring the group national headlines and the attention it thought it deserved. The CPA leaders had tried to engage President Truman but when he proved unavailable they managed to snare Senator McCarthy, who was on a speaking tour at the time. The negotiations with the senator were long and painstaking, since some of the Catholic bishops were plainly upset that McCarthy was scheduled to speak under Catholic auspices. Anxious to avoid unpleasantness, the editor in charge of arrangements, Monsignor John Randall of the *Rochester Courier-Journal*, kept in almost daily telephone contact with McCarthy, reminding him that he would be coming into hostile territory and warning him that he had better be able to document whatever he said.[51] McCarthy clearly understood this and responded by giving a speech that was not only prepared well in advance and read exactly as prepared but accompanied by extensive documentation. (Though many of the Catholic auditors would later find his documentation unconvincing, the Rochester speech at least represented a rare departure from McCarthy's usual off-the-cuff and unprepared style.)

Randall had not exaggerated when he told McCarthy that there were unhappy "rumblings," as he called them, from the hierarchy. At a CPA luncheon on the day of McCarthy's address, Bishop Matthew Ready of the Press Department of the National Catholic Welfare Conference angrily denounced McCarthy before 250 Catholic editors and publishers. He said that it was time for the Catholic press to begin paying more attention to those Catholics who devoted themselves to the "essential interests of God and country" instead of giving so much publicity to "those who lately and hysterically identify themselves as the sole defenders of the nation." Though he avoided mentioning McCarthy by name, none of his shocked listeners doubted whom he meant. Immediately afterward he left the convention, obviously upset that McCarthy was going to speak that night.[52]

That evening McCarthy gave his speech to a sellout audience. He had not come as a spokesman for the Catholic church, he said, nor for any Catholic organization, but was "just speaking for Joe McCarthy."[53] And what did Joe McCarthy have to say? He began by defending his star witness, Louis Budenz, saying that he was happy to note that "Protestants, Jews, and Catholics" have "spontaneously" come to Budenz's defense, thus repudiating "this stupidly vile attack on him, his wife and his family." The large number of good Americans who supported Budenz showed that the Communist party would never be successful "in its attempts to inject religious bigotry into this fight."[54] In an attempt to appeal to the anticommunist impulse in the Catholic editors, McCarthy praised them warmly for their fight against the "Communist menace." He said that communism was a force that sought to destroy "all the honesty and decency that every Protestant, Jew and Catholic . . . [had] been taught at his mother's knee." The Catholic editors of America, however, had been engaged in this battle with communism "long before I came on the scene. You have been engaged in what may well be that final Armageddon foretold in the Bible—that struggle between light and darkness, between good and evil, between life and death, if you please."[55]

It was then time for McCarthy's *pièce de résistance*. Brandishing the inevitable fistful of documents, he announced that the photostatic copies he held in his hand proved unmistakably that Owen Lattimore had intervened in the State Department to secure employment for two men who were known Communists. He also accused the State Department of a "fraudulent cover-up" of the Communists, saying that it had tried to sell a "calculated, vicious fraud" to the American people.[56] As he was speaking, McCarthy's assistants handed out copies of the documents to the editors. Those who took the trouble to examine them with care subsequently concluded that they demonstrated none of the things that McCarthy had said they proved. The editors of the *Commonweal*, for instance, found that his "secret files" had "proved to be something less than was expected."[57]

Most of the Catholic editors, however, were highly enthusiastic about the speech, cheering the senator when he finished and eagerly perusing the photostatic copies of the documents he had given them. Only a small minority of dissenters refused to join the accolade that followed the end of the speech. They were, of course, the *Commonweal* editors, who found McCarthy's performance disgusting and demagogic, and the contingent from the Catholic newspaper in Milwaukee, the *Milwaukee Herald-Citizen*. The Milwaukee delegates (the only Wisconsin group at the convention) felt constantly on the spot, since the other editors kept asking them what they thought about the famous senator from their state. They thought that McCarthy was a "phony," in the words of one of their number. They found that his "documents" contained nothing of substance, even though they had examined them with meticulous care. So distressed were they by his antics that after the speech they met together to decide whether they should "blow the whistle" on him. In all likelihood they would have done precisely that, had they not met a stern veto from the publisher of the paper, a convinced follower of the senator.[58]

Even more convinced was the editor of the *Brooklyn Tablet*, Patrick F. Scanlan, whose warm support for McCarthy turned into unrestrained hero worship after the speech. McCarthy's address had an "intellectual and patriotic appeal," he wrote afterward and added that the senator had delivered it with "sincerity" and in a "temperate vein." The audience listened with "rapt attention" and gave McCarthy a "tremendous ovation" when he finished. For Scanlan the occasion had also been personally rewarding, since he had been given the high honor of introducing the senator to the audience. In the course of the evening, he had a chance to talk with McCarthy, and their warm friendship dated from that time.[59]

The editors' unreserved enthusiasm for McCarthy earned them a slicing rebuke from a noted Protestant minister and educator, Dean Walter G. Muelder of the Boston University School of Theology. He told a conference of eastern and midwestern Methodists, meeting in Boston, that the Catholic editors' invitation to McCarthy only "confuses the issue" and encourages "rumor and gossip regarding Catholic power tactics and irresponsible expressions of freedom."[60] Catholics, in other words, were reinforcing their reputation for antiintellectualism and intolerance by supporting McCarthy.

Seen in retrospect, McCarthy's address to the Catholic journalists looms as one of the most revealing incidents in the whole story of Catholics and McCarthy, for it throws light on all of the elements essential to the controversy that followed. The senator himself came as close as he ever did to using a specifically "Catholic" argument against communism when he praised the editors for fighting the "atheistic" leaders of communism, as well as for engaging in that "final Armageddon foretold in the Bible." At the same time, however, he was careful to insist that he was speaking for himself, not for the Catholic church.

Instructive here was McCarthy's use of the "Protestant-Catholic-Jew" theme, one that he mentioned twice in his remarks. One suspects that he was trying to rise above the "Catholic issue" and his Catholic audience by attempting to appeal to all of American society. The familiar refrain of "Protestant-Catholic-Jew" had become a virtual synonym for the "American way of life," and in repeating it here McCarthy could legitimately claim that he was speaking to all of America, not just Catholics alone.

It also became painfully apparent that the cleavage in the Catholic press between the senator's supporters and his detractors had deepened considerably. Conservatives such as Pat Scanlan of the

Tablet had found common ground with such conservative Catholic columnists as Richard Ginder and James Gillis, as well as with publications like the *Wanderer* and *Ave Maria*. Though neither the liberals nor the conservatives entered into formal alliances with the other editors who shared their views, two distinct camps had formed, with tension between the two groups escalating perceptibly. The "moderates" and the "middle-of-the-roaders" who might have been able to prevent a definitive split in the ranks of Catholic journalists were almost too few to count.

It turned out to be a torrid summer, both for McCarthy and for his colleagues on the Tydings committee. As May passed into a steamy June and July, charges met countercharges, tempers flared, and agreement seemed as hard to find as a cool spot along the sweltering Potomac. At the heart of the dispute was the stubborn refusal of the Truman administration to let the committee examine its security files. "Evasion," cried McCarthy and his supporters, both Catholic and non-Catholic alike. "Smear-tactics," answered his liberal critics, among them the *Commonweal*, which was now unalterably opposed to McCarthy and all his works.

After four months of partisan wrangling, the Tydings committee issued a report on 17 July 1950 concluding its investigations. It announced to the surprise of no one at all that it had found no truth whatever in McCarthy's indictments against the administration and called him a "fraud" as well.[61] Although the committee's findings were fully predictable, the response of the Catholic press to the report contained a few surprises. Even the *Commonweal*, which previously had seen nothing good in McCarthy, found that the committee's inquiries had been "inconclusive and unsatisfactory" because they left the question of Communist espionage still unanswered. It continued to believe, of course, that McCarthy had failed to prove his charges and kept up its demands for an impartial investigation by a bipartisan commission.[62] Far more strenuous in its criticism was the *Brooklyn Tablet*, which characterized the committee members as the "stooges" of the administration, accusing them of examining, not "the Reds in the Government, as they were supposed to do," but the "one senator who made the public aware of the perilous situation."[63] The rest of the Catholic press agreed that the administration had tried to cover up its mistakes by investigating McCarthy himself instead of McCarthy's charges against the administration.[64]

By the time the Tydings report hit the front pages, the essential outlines of the Catholic struggle over McCarthy had become clear. Yet in spite of the obvious division within Catholic ranks over the senator, a number of observers outside the church continued to presume that McCarthy had massive support in the Catholic community. Not even the bitter feuding of the next four and one-half years convinced all of them that they might be wrong. Even at an early stage, however, they ought to have had second thoughts about the "Catholics-for-McCarthy" thesis, not only because of the abundant evidence of a split among Catholics, but because strong points of convergence were appearing between Catholics and non-Catholics over McCarthyism and its related issues. Thus Catholic McCarthyites tended to share the same political and cultural views as did the non-Catholic followers of the senator. By the same token, McCarthy's enemies in the Catholic church seemed to veer in the same liberal direction as did his non-Catholic opponents.

Complicating this seeming harmony, however, was the growing tension between Catholics and Protestants, a strain that deepened because of the McCarthy issue. Catholic and Protestant liberals agreed in their support of the Fair Deal, but they were quick to protest when they heard their own church coming under criticism from the other side. At the same time, both Catholic and Protestant conservatives condemned the Truman foreign policy—often at the same time and with the same words. But no real conversations were taking place between these two conservative factions, and none came about as a result of McCarthy. On the contrary, even the mildest comments from Protestants about McCarthy stirred up deep Catholic hostilities, just as Catholic statements about him angered Protestants. The religious conflicts of the fifties, in turn, mirrored the deeper divisions in American society—tensions between north and south, city and suburb, WASP and ethnic, educated and uninstructed, liberal and conservative. The war over McCarthyism exacerbated all of these antagonisms, and Catholics participated intimately in each phase of the struggle.

Meanwhile, the Truman administration clearly had a problem on its hands. Having failed to rout McCarthy in its first skirmish, what should it do? If it chose to dismiss him as a fraud and a charlatan, it still had to watch him with great care because he had become a major political figure with a growing national following (six months of front page publicity had seen to that). The Truman Democrats had to deal not only with McCarthy himself but with his political entourage as well. Prominently placed on the McCarthy bandwagon were his Catholic followers, whom no political party could safely ignore since Catholics constituted roughly a fifth of the nation's population. The Democrats might well worry about McCarthy's impact on Catholics in the congressional elections of 1950. True, Catholics had voted heavily for Truman in 1948, but would they continue to vote Democratic, especially if the McCarthy forces tried to capture the Catholic vote?

The congressional elections of 1950 might well provide an indication of what the Catholic electorate thought about McCarthy. The senator had vowed to work for the defeat of Millard Tydings in Maryland, and since that state was thought to be a "heavily Catholic" one, perhaps the contest there would show whether McCarthyism had any charms for the nation's Catholics. McCarthy would be watching the Maryland election carefully, and so would his Republican supporters and his Democratic detractors.

Chapter 4

The Congressional Elections of 1950 and Their Aftermath

The *New York Times* was worried. With the congressional elections only six months away, it was so concerned about McCarthy's popular support that it sent its crack political analyst into Wisconsin to find out what McCarthy's constituents thought about him. What James Reston learned was ominous indeed. He reported that McCarthy was receiving "effective support from leaders of the Roman Catholic Church in Wisconsin."[1] With roughly one-third of the state's voters calling themselves Catholics, this was a dark portent, if true. Fortunately for the forces of anti-McCarthyism, the senator was receiving "effective support" in the elections from no sector of Wisconsin Catholicism—not from the bishops (who pretended he did not exist), not from the lower clergy (who had only passing interest in political affairs), and not from the laity (who voted their party affiliation with little thought for McCarthy). Reston's observation demonstrated most clearly the continuing fear of many East Coast liberals that McCarthy was building a right-wing Catholic following in Wisconsin. Subsequent events showed that if such a following existed anywhere, it was right under Reston's nose along the East Coast, not in Wisconsin.

In none of the 1950 congressional elections in Wisconsin did McCarthyism emerge as an important issue. If Communist subversion was a theme (though a minor one), McCarthyism certainly was not. Rather, the candidates and the voters looked hard at the dominant issues of 1950: the Korean War, inflation, charges of corruption in the Truman administration, and a vague feeling of discontent with the Democrats resulting from their long tenure in the White House.

If Wisconsin Catholics had taken any interest at all in Joe McCarthy, they would have done so in the fourth congressional district, a heavily Polish Catholic area located on Milwaukee's south side. The race in the fourth district, however, saw the incumbent, Congressman Clement Zablocki, swamp his Republican opponent by 82,000 votes to 53,000.[2] The Catholic Zablocki took no notice of McCarthy because he had no need to do so; his Polish Catholic constituents liked his support of the Fair Deal's social justice programs, and they repeatedly rewarded him with their votes. Zablocki won reelection year after year (he has been in the House since 1947) with what he calls the "bread and butter" issues of employment, welfare, housing, and education.[3] In no other campaign did McCarthyism emerge as a usable issue, not even when McCarthy's friend Charles Kersten ran successfully for his old seat in the fifth district.[4]

Seen in retrospect, the 1950 elections were clearly no test of McCarthy or McCarthyism at all. By the same token they were no test for Catholic support of McCarthy either. Oddly enough, McCarthyism had yet to become a burning issue in Wisconsin, probably because most of McCarthy's activities took place in far-off Washington. In addition to that, the senator's own contest for reelection was still two years away, and few Wisconsinites seemed inclined to view the 1950 contests in terms of the upcoming 1952 campaign.

The Democrats were far more apprehensive about the contest in Maryland, where McCarthy's arch-critic Millard Tydings had to face a McCarthyite candidate, John Marshall Butler. Since McCarthy had sworn to drive Tydings out of the Senate, all eyes focused on the Old Line State to see what the Catholics there would do. Adding tension to the fight was the common belief that Maryland was a heavily "Catholic" state, one where the traditional Catholic "ethnic minorities" made up a formidable part of the population. A more critical look at the religious makeup of the state, however, would have revealed that the Catholics made up less than 20 percent of the state's population, with most of them packed into the urban Baltimore area.[5]

Though the Catholic vote was relatively small, the Butler forces did make one clumsy attempt during the campaign to capture the Catholic electorate: they sent out a letter bearing Butler's signature to the state's Catholic clergy, promising to defend the United States against "atheistic Russia overseas" and from "Communists and their friends within our government."[6]

McCarthy himself spoke only three times in the Maryland campaign (on one occasion accusing Tydings of shielding traitors "at a time when the survival of western non-atheistic civilization hangs in the balance."[7] Nevertheless, his was clearly the guiding hand behind the Butler forces, as a subsequent congressional investigation revealed. McCarthy sent his personal staff into the state, where they proceeded to conduct "a despicable 'back-street' type of campaign,"[8] as congressional investigators later described it. The McCarthy staffers collected campaign funds that they somehow failed to report; they mailed out hundreds of thousands of postcards claiming to be signed "personally" by John Marshall Butler, but which in fact were signed for him by paid campaign workers. Most serious of all, they produced a scurrilous piece of campaign literature called "From the Record" that purported to prove Tydings's pro-Communist leanings. The most sensational item in the "Record" was a photograph showing Tydings in animated conversation with Earl Browder, the prominent Communist party leader.[9] Though this famous "doctored photo" was later shown to be a composite of two separate pictures and therefore an undoubted fake, the discovery came too late to affect the outcome of the election. The *Commonweal* expressed the indignation of liberals and Democrats everywhere when it asserted that McCarthy's Maryland campaign had debased the "integrity and honor of our national life." McCarthy's method was not the "American way"; rather it was the method of a "man who runs along the back streets to do his cheating when he hasn't the stuff to do things the straight and open way."[10]

The results of the election came as a shock to anti-McCarthy forces across the nation. Tydings lost his Senate seat by more than

40,000 votes, but more importantly, many people believed that it was Joe McCarthy, and not John Marshall Butler, who had defeated him. The Democrats in the Senate who pondered Tydings's fate may also have trembled.[11]

Louis Bean, the noted political analyst and pollster, soon afterward examined the Catholic vote in Maryland and concluded that Tydings's "greater losses" were "associated with the greater Catholic concentrations." Thus in rural Carroll County, with a Catholic index of only 6 percent, Tydings's vote dropped by four points from his position in the 1944 election, but in the city of Baltimore, with a Catholic index of fifty, he dropped by nineteen points. In other counties he found that the larger the Catholic population, the larger Tydings's losses were. Bean concluded that although the Catholic vote did more damage to Tydings in some areas of the state than it did in others, the "direction of its influence appears to have been consistent, against Tydings."[12]

Bean's analysis abounds with difficulties. First of all, the percentage of Catholics in the areas of "greater Catholic concentration" that he studied is too small to prove that it was the *Catholic* vote that defected from Tydings. The city of Baltimore was the most solidly Catholic area he analyzed, but it showed a Catholic population of no more than 50 percent, and Baltimore County (another area he selected for special study) had a Catholic concentration of only 17 percent. The percentages of Catholic population are too small to permit firm conclusions about how Catholics voted in the election.[13]

If Bean had pushed his study of "Catholic counties" a bit further, he would have made two interesting discoveries. First, the most Catholic county in the state—St. Mary's County, which boasted a Catholic population of 80 percent—actually gave Tydings a narrow victory over Butler. Second, in the three most Catholic counties and in the city of Baltimore, Tydings ran consistently ahead of the only other Democrat running on a statewide ticket—the incumbent governor, William P. Lane. (Lane lost badly to the challenger,

Theodore R. McKeldin, who took 61 percent of the vote.)[14] It may very well be, therefore, that Tydings did better with the Catholic vote than did either his fellow Democrat, Governor Lane, or his Republican opponent, John M. Butler.

The small scale of the Catholic population in Maryland should have discouraged hard and fast judgments about McCarthy's impact on the Catholic vote in the Tydings contest. It did not, however. The *New York Times* concluded (without supporting evidence) that the "combination of the Catholic vote and the labor vote" probably made up a "large bloc of the sentiment that unseated" Tydings.[15] Even less cautious was the McCarthyite Catholic weekly *Our Sunday Visitor*, which reported enthusiastically that Tydings had been "almost solidly opposed by Maryland Roman Catholics," who were the group chiefly responsible for his demise. Noting that McCarthy's enemies had fallen in other states, the *Visitor* concluded modestly that "the masses of Catholic electors have sensed . . . that they, and perhaps they alone, can save the world."[16]

The *Visitor* notwithstanding, the Maryland election had hinged on factors that went far beyond the Catholic vote. What were they? First, the Democratic vote in Maryland had long been in decline, a trend that had started in 1938 and had continued despite the state's heavy Democratic registration. Second, Tydings's deeply conservative record had cost him much of his support among union members and blacks as well. Third, the state's Democratic organization in 1950 had split badly into two contending factions, thus depriving Tydings of the help that he needed in an election promising to be hard fought and very close. Finally, Tydings may well have suffered from charges that his investigating committee had "whitewashed" McCarthy's indictments against the administration, though it is impossible to say precisely how much this might have hurt him.

The reality of the Maryland election was thus a complex set of voting patterns, party factions, and shifting structures of party loyalty. As often happens, however, the reality escaped the attention of observers, and a convenient myth took its place. In the case of

Millard Tydings and the election of 1950, the myth was the invincibility of Joe McCarthy, who had routed the enemy from office.[17] Franklin Roosevelt had tried in 1938 to "purge" Tydings from the Senate but had failed miserably; yet McCarthy succeeded where Roosevelt had not. What did this say about McCarthy's vote-getting power? McCarthy had vowed to "get" Tydings and had clearly marked him as public enemy number one. Not even Tydings's undeniably conservative record nor his long tenure in the Senate (he was trying for his fifth term) could stop the Wisconsin steamroller, or so it seemed to McCarthy's fearful colleagues in the Senate.

With the myth of McCarthy's invincibility went a companion myth: the Maryland Catholics had routed Tydings and had put the McCarthyite Butler in his place. In the fearful ten months that followed the 1950 elections, the Democratic strategists in the White House found themselves haunted by a nagging question—would the Republicans be able to use the Communist issue to capture the Catholic vote in 1952? One of the most concerned of all was a youthful civil libertarian named Stephen Spingarn, who served as administrative assistant to President Truman. A devoted Fair Dealer and opponent of McCarthy and McCarthyism, Spingarn tried repeatedly to place anti-McCarthy Catholics on the various security commissions that the administration tried to create as a foil against McCarthyism.[18] Though nothing ever came of the administration's proposals, the lengths that Spingarn and his associates went to in order to secure "liberal" Catholics for the commissions shows how sensitive some of the Truman aides were to Catholic feeling on questions concerning security.

At the same time that Spingarn was maneuvering behind the scenes to build Catholic opposition to the senator, a blunt challenge to McCarthy's Catholic entourage came from one of the leading Catholics in the administration, Secretary of Labor Maurice Tobin. A former mayor of Boston and governor of Massachusetts, Tobin had a reputation as a tough opponent of racism, an advocate of New Deal and Fair Deal social programs, and an outspoken defender of freedom of speech. Though known as a Catholic, he avoided making public displays of his religion and seldom mentioned it in public. Joe McCarthy made him modify his policy.

Tobin first denounced McCarthy in October 1950, when he said that McCarthyism, like communism itself, preaches that a mere accusation is sufficient proof of guilt.[19] Lest Catholics miss his point, a year later he denounced McCarthy in a speech before the Knights of Columbus in Rapid City, South Dakota. Tobin agreed with those who said that it was essential for Catholics to fight against communism, but it was equally important for them to avoid using the "weapons of slander and terror that have become popular in this country." Catholics could rightly rejoice that they were among the "most militant anti-Communists" in America, he said, but at the same time they should take every effort to disassociate themselves from a "campaign of terror against free thought in the United States."[20] Though he avoided mentioning McCarthy by name, it was clear enough whom he meant.

Tobin's views on McCarthy provided an excellent illustration of how Democratic Catholic leaders looked on McCarthy. If asked for the "root of their thought" on McCarthy, the Democratic Catholics would have been hard pressed to find a precise answer, but an examination of their statements makes their motivation clear. When one reflects on Chavez's speech on McCarthy—as well as the many statements of Eugene McCarthy, Maurice Tobin, Stephen Mitchell (the Democratic national chairman), and the other Catholic Democrats who denounced McCarthy—it seems most obvious that each of them spoke first as a Democrat and only secondly as a Catholic. Since they were liberal Democrats above all, McCarthy's conservative Republicanism violated everything they stood for: they detested his isolationistic and chauvinistic views on foreign policy, his adamant opposition to progressive social legislation, and his knife-edged incursions into civil liberties. Joe McCarthy, in other words, was a threat to the Democratic party that they loved—the party that they believed had brought the nation its greatest glories and that stood the best chance of delivering the nation from the threat of communism at home and overseas.

At the same time, McCarthy's visceral attacks on the Democrats' loyalty struck hard at their most cherished possession, their reputation as faithful and patriotic Americans. Though worried that their party was indeed vulnerable on the issue of security, they wanted to believe that they had done the best they could to cleanse both themselves and the government of Communist subversives. Thus they feared that in raising the Red specter, McCarthy had seized an issue that would cripple the party and wreck its political future. The Catholic Democrats worried especially about the effect that McCarthy's rabble-rousing tactics might have on the traditionally Democratic vote of the urban Catholics. Would the Eastern European Catholics—the ones from Poland, from Czechoslovakia, from Hungary—all flock blindly to his banner? Would the Irish fall for his mindless appeals to patriotism? As Catholics, the Mitchells and the Tobins were acutely aware of the threat that McCarthy posed to the Catholic wing of their party.

Though concerned about these problems, the Catholic Democrats agonized deeply when forced to confront McCarthy "as Catholics." Some of them, like Dennis Chavez of New Mexico, blustered and shouted. Still others, like John F. Kennedy of Massachusetts, reacted with acute embarrassment and tried to skirt the issue entirely. Like Stephen Mitchell, who roundly condemned McCarthy for disgracing the *Irish* Catholics, some of them felt more at home on ethnic grounds. For all of them, discussion of the Catholic dimensions in the McCarthy debate was a most distressing process, and more often than not they slipped back naturally (and no doubt with a sigh of relief) into the old, familiar political arguments. Even Catholic politicians who had received extensive training in Catholic theology and political theory—Eugene McCarthy among them—seldom used specifically "Catholic" theses against the senator; they preferred to debate McCarthyism on its political terms. The invocation of specifically "Catholic" arguments against McCarthy came more naturally to the professional publicists like John Cogley of the *Commonweal*. Yet when one reads deeply into Cogley's editorials, it quickly becomes clear that they too were more at home in the political arena than the religious one. Perhaps all of this was inevitable, since McCarthy was a political problem, and political answers came more easily to mind than the more subtle ones drawn from ancient Catholic tradition.

Not surprisingly, the Catholic Democrats found their patron saints in the pantheon of the Democratic party, numbering such Democratic stalwarts as Thomas Jefferson, Woodrow Wilson, Al Smith, Franklin D. Roosevelt, Harry S. Truman, and Adlai Stevenson. Their dogmas were the platforms of the Democratic national conventions, and their heresies were the right-wing tenets of the Robert A. Tafts, the William E. Jenners, and the Joseph Raymond McCarthys. The Catholic Democrats, in short, opposed McCarthy primarily because he posed a threat to their party and only secondarily because he menaced their status as Catholics.

The essentially political nature of their thought becomes even clearer when we look at the non-Catholic Democrats. Jewish Democrats such as Herbert Lehman, senator from New York, used the same arguments against McCarthy as did Mitchell and Tobin, and they reacted as violently as did the Catholic Democrats when told that an attack on McCarthy was an attack on the Catholic church. Protestant Democrats like Harry Truman shared the same views on McCarthy. All of this demonstrated that Catholics had become so thoroughly assimilated into the Democratic party that they hardly stood out as Catholics. It was still another example of how far the Catholic community had entered into the national fabric and had become "Americanized."

The more McCarthy attacked the Democrats for their supposed softness on communism, the more the Catholic liberals cried "smear" and "slander." Until he set upon Adlai Stevenson in late 1952, nothing so shocked them as his violent assault on Secretary of State George C. Marshall in June 1951. Marshall had long been a likely target for McCarthy, just as he had long been the bane of the Republican isolationists and the "China Lobby" as it was called. The conservatives believed that America had "lost" China in the postwar era because of the incompetence and even the "treason" of the nation's Democratic diplomats. They labelled the Acheson-Marshall-Truman foreign policy "appeasement" and called it a strategy designed to do the work of the Kremlin. The indecisive conclusion of the Korean War, followed by President Truman's firing of General Douglas MacArthur in April 1951, brought the anger of the conservative isolationists to the boiling point. Marshall stood the best chance of receiving these hostile sentiments, since he had served as special presidential emissary to China in 1946 and as secretary of state from 1947 to 1949. His argument in favor of limited war with the Communists ran directly counter to the liberationist thesis of General MacArthur and his followers.

Although McCarthy had attacked Marshall before, he waited until 14 June 1951 to deliver his considered judgment on him, by unburdening himself in a droning three-hour address that sent spectators moving toward the exits. (After three hours he had finished only one-third of the 60,000 words that made up the manuscript.) The notion of conspiracy—"a conspiracy of infamy so black that, when it is finally exposed, its principals shall be forever deserving of the maledictions of all honest men"—dominated the speech.[21] The Communist apparatus in America had cost the nation its allies in the Far East, long years of tension in Europe, and the weakening of our position across the world, he said. Implicated somehow in this tangled web of conspiracy was George Catlett Marshall.

McCarthy never claimed credit for the speech, which was indeed radically different from his usual slashing, vituperative, gut-level style. Heavily burdened with documentation and quotations, it reflected the "Georgetown school" of revisionist historiography, which held that American diplomacy from the 1930s through the cold war had failed because American foreign policy had not concentrated single-mindedly on the problem of Soviet power. Thus FDR had been wrong in recognizing Russia in 1933, in aiding the Russians in 1941, in bringing the Russians into the Pacific War, etc. The leading exponents of this interpretation were Charles Tansil and Stafan Possony of Georgetown University's Department of Government. Richard Rovere wrote that there was "little room for doubt" that McCarthy's speech was the work of a member of the university or of "someone heavily influenced by it."[22] On the face of it, Rovere's suggestion that a Georgetown faculty member had written it seemed reasonable enough, since everyone believed that Georgetown's Edmund Walsh had inspired McCarthy in the first place and Professor Charles Kraus of the same Department of Government was thought to be a "close friend" of McCarthy. As we have seen, however, Walsh had little to do with McCarthy, and Kraus ended his brief friendship with McCarthy long before the Marshall speech.

No evidence has appeared indicating that any Georgetown University faculty member (or a Jesuit) wrote McCarthy's rambling speech.[23] Nevertheless, it is important to note how closely the argument given in the address parallels that of the Georgetown "revisionists." Both came out of the "siege mentality" of the conservative isolationists, an embittered faction that believed that the best way to deal with the Russians was to avoid dealing with them at all, except in terms of confrontation and counteraggression. It is equally important to note that though the speech contained no obvious "Catholic" influences, it was nevertheless congruent with much of contemporary Catholic thought on communism. Catholics (as well as revisionists) saw communism as a deadly conspiracy; both groups looked on communism as an "enemy of mankind"; both viewed it as dehumanizing and degrading, and both believed that it stood defiantly opposed to the freedom of the individual. All of these motifs, however, were common to the larger conservative ideology of the 1950s, and undoubtedly this broad stream of political thought best accounts for McCarthy's speech on George Marshall. American conservatives of any stripe could (and already had) subscribed to McCarthy's thesis that Marshall was the conscious agent of world communism.

If the origin of the speech was obscure, its message was not. McCarthy said that at every point in his postwar career, Marshall had abetted the Communist cause, sometimes by appeasing the enemy and failing to act, at other times by deliberately following policies that led inevitably to Communist success. McCarthy's attack on Marshall united a disparate group of Catholics, all of whom took deep offense at the senator's remarks. In its first real criticism of McCarthy, the Jesuit weekly *America* found his speech "unfair and unjust" since it smeared a man with a long and brilliant record of loyalty to his country.[24] Even Congressman John McCormack, who avoided the McCarthy controversy as if it were malaria, remarked in a speech on the floor of the House that Marshall would be remembered favorably long after the names of his attackers were remembered "only with contempt."[25] The *Commonweal* also scored McCarthy, criticizing his "sheer intellectual dishonesty and recklessness."[26]

The McCarthyites could dismiss the *Commonweal* as hopelessly liberal and fuzzy minded, but they could not fairly say the same thing for *America* and the Catholic Speaker of the House, John McCormack. What had happened to prompt this about-face? Most likely, they saw the attack on Marshall as an assault on his *patriotism*, which no one had ever questioned before. Catholics had long shown a special sensitivity toward the issue of patriotism because they had suffered for so many years from charges that they were an "alien" people, hence unpatriotic. As one who had demonstrated his patriotism both in war and in peace, Marshall held a reputation for loyalty that Catholics had long revered. In the eyes of many Catholics, therefore, an attack on Marshall was tantamount to an attack on loyalty itself.

One man's patriotism was another man's perfidy, however. The senator's Catholic defenders noted that McCarthy had never actually called Marshall a "traitor" but had merely said that Marshall had minimized the nature of communism's threat to world peace.[27] (To Marshall's irate Catholic supporters this was a semantic nicety utterly devoid of meaning.) In the *Brooklyn Tablet's* view the speech was a "blazing indictment" of Marshall that no one had yet answered, if indeed an answer could be made at all. It was especially impressed by the documentation of the speech, pointing out that "probably 90 percent of the speech is made up of quotations."[28]

All during the summer of 1951, McCarthy hammered away relentlessly at Truman, Dean Acheson, and liberal Democrats everywhere. As he carried on his campaign of vilification, he succeeded not only in raising the political temperature of the nation but in driving Catholics further apart than ever. Keeping the political pot boiling became even easier after August 1951, when Senator William Benton of Connecticut introduced a resolution asking for the expulsion of McCarthy from the Senate. (Benton had received appointment to the Senate in late 1949, finishing the term of Senator Baldwin who had assumed another office. Connecticut law decreed a two-year term for United States senators, thus forcing Benton to run for reelection in November 1950, when he won by an exceedingly narrow margin.) A liberal Democrat and a self-made millionaire, Benton had long detested McCarthy's methods and had denounced him on several occasions. What prompted him to definitive action, however, was the congressional investigation into McCarthy's role in the notorious Tydings–Butler campaign of 1950. The report that the investigators issued following their inquiry hit vigorously at McCarthy, accusing him of running a gutter campaign against the incumbent Tydings. Deeply worried that the investigators' findings would be filed away and forgotten, Benton decided to force the issue by demanding McCarthy's removal. After some hesitation the Senate detailed a special committee under the chairmanship of Senator Guy Gillette to examine Benton's list of charges against McCarthy. Benton's bill of particulars covered McCarthy's entire Senate career. For the next year and one-half, while McCarthy and Benton exchanged taunts (McCarthy called Benton a "mental midget"),[29] the Gillette committee met intermittently to discuss its findings. Not until early January 1953 did the Gillette report finally come before the public. Although showing the effects of senatorial compromising and McCarthyite harassment, the report nevertheless revealed a McCarthy whose financial dealings were suspect in the extreme and whose treatment of the Gillette committee itself had been contemptible.[30]

As a senator from a state where the Catholic population was considerable, Benton quickly became aware of the Catholic-McCarthy problem. To his grief he found that many of the conservative Irish Catholics in Connecticut were convinced McCarthyites, but at the same time he discovered a number of Catholic liberals who fought McCarthy at every turn. The finest of the liberals, in his view, were the editors of the *Commonweal*, whose articles on McCarthy he vastly admired and used repeatedly in his campaign for reelection.[31]

McCarthy's long struggle with Benton helped move *America* from its consistently neutral position on the junior senator. Its early editorials on the Benton-McCarthy feud had been scrupulously factual and devoid of editorial comment, but they were becoming increasingly critical; finally the magazine wearily concluded that McCarthy's "boorish manners and strategy of 'the best defense is a good offense' are finally catching up with him."[32] Yet a feeling of weariness with the senator was not a rejection of him, and some six months passed before *America*'s editor, Father Robert Hartnett, decided that it was time to open fire on the senator.

Meanwhile a flood of letters, most of them favoring his campaign against McCarthy, was coming into Benton's office. A few of the letters, however, showed a curious anti-Catholic bias as well. Thus one writer congratulated Benton for "showing Pius XII McCarthy up for the rat he is." In a reference to McCarthy's education under the Jesuits at Marquette University, the author said that the "Jesuit bum" was a "cancer on the Senate which should be cut out."[33]

While Benton was running against McCarthy and the Catholic McCarthyites, he received some unexpected help from the American Catholic bishops. In November 1951 the bishops gathered once again in Washington for their annual meeting. In the public statement that they always issue at the end of their deliberations, the bishops addressed themselves to the subject of "public and private morality." After laying down general norms for moral action, they concluded by detailing specific rules for the conduct of education, economics, and politics. It was in this final section on politics that the bishops dropped their bombshell. After condemning the policy that "anything goes" in politics, they concluded, "Dishonesty, slander, detraction, and defamation of character are as truly transgressions of God's commandments when resorted to by men in political life as they are for all other men."[34] Did they mean Senator McCarthy?

Both McCarthy's Catholic and non-Catholic opponents concluded immediately that the prelates had McCarthy in mind. Overjoyed at the hierarchy's seeming endorsement of their stand, they proceeded to use the declaration to the fullest. William Benton was a case in point; he immediately asked his Catholic friends and supporters if the bishops were referring to McCarthy. Assured by them that the bishops certainly were pointing at McCarthy, Benton proceeded with great confidence to use the statement in his campaign.[35]

For Senator McCarthy's outspoken critics in the press, the document came as sweet news indeed. The *Madison Capital-Times*, carrying on the fiercest anti-McCarthy campaign of any publication, believed that there was "little doubt" that McCarthy was the object of the bishops' censure and wondered if McCarthy would continue to accuse his enemies of "playing the game of the Communists," since the hierarchy had spoken.[36] Drew Pearson praised the statement as a "scathing" indictment of the senator, one that the bishops had handed down because he had smeared innocent people, had entered the Communist hunt too late, and had approved quickie divorces while a judge in Wisconsin. Pearson reported that "word from inside the Catholic hierarchy" was that Bishop Emmet Walsh of Youngstown, Ohio, had engineered the condemnation.[37] (There is no evidence of any kind to support any of Pearson's claims.) Pearson's associates Jack Anderson and Ronald May wrote exultantly that the bishops had "struck" McCarthy with an "ecclesiastical bolt."[38] Pearson, Anderson, and May could well have taken a lesson from the *New York Times*, which showed a laudable sense of caution; the *Times*'s editorial and political writer John B. Oakes noted merely that the document "could well be construed as an attack on McCarthyism."[39]

Protestant liberals joined the anti-McCarthyites in praising the hierarchy's pronouncement. At a national meeting of Protestant ministers held in Washington shortly after the bishops' gathering, the ministers called the document a "direct slap" at McCarthy and lavishly complimented the Catholic bishops for their action.[40] Coming at a time when tensions between Catholics and Protestants were rising alarmingly, this was a significant move in the opposite direction.

Were the senator's opponents correct in concluding that the bishops had condemned McCarthy and none other? The first scholar to study the problem carefully, Professor Vincent DeSantis of the University of Notre Dame (and a renowned anti-McCarthyite at that), doubted that they meant the senator.[41] Is his conclusion still justified? Unfortunately, too little evidence is available to draw a firm judgment about the declaration. Since the bishops do not keep minutes of their annual discussions, the investigator has to rely on the testimony of the meeting's surviving delegates. The two bishops who are willing to discuss the meeting do not recall any discussions about McCarthy, though it is only fair to point out that both gentlemen are advanced in years and the gathering occurred twenty years ago.[42] Monsignor George Higgins, who was intimately associated with the bishops because of his work in the National Catholic Welfare Conference, is sure that the statement came from the pen of Cardinal Edward Mooney of Detroit, a social-justice liberal who dominated the meetings of the early fifties. He notes that the document gives a good reflection of the views of the cardinal, who was broadly leftist on social issues, sympathetic to political liberals and intellectuals as well, and partial to a moderate stand on domestic communism.[43] He was a poor candidate for McCarthyism, though he said nothing in public about it. Agreeing with Higgins is Father John Cronin, who was equally close to the bishops. He thinks that if Mooney wrote the document (as seems likely), then McCarthy was the politician in question, since "McCarthy just wouldn't be his [Mooney's] style."[44] It is doubtful that any two men in America knew more about the bishops, or knew them more intimately, than Higgins and Cronin. The language of the document may also be revealing: the political writers of the times often used the words "slander," "detraction," and "defamation of character" to describe what McCarthy was doing, and the bishops' use of these words may well have betrayed a veiled reference to him. It is possible, surely, that the bishops were in fact speaking about the junior senator from Wisconsin, though it is unlikely that we will ever know for sure.

If the prelates obscured the force of their declaration by failing to name names, it was equally true that they came far closer to condemning McCarthy than to approving of him. This point was not lost on either Catholic liberals, Protestant intellectuals hostile to McCarthy, or McCarthy's critics in the press and in academe, all of whom could rally around the 1951 statement. Above all, it came as welcome news to William Burnett Benton, who thought that he had found a silver lining in the dark clouds of Catholic McCarthyism.

The election of 1950 and its aftermath thus proved to be an exercise in confusion and indecision. Neither the Catholic McCarthyites nor the Catholic liberals could fairly claim that the Maryland and Wisconsin elections had vindicated their position, and even though the McCarthyites quickly claimed a victory in Maryland, they soon reverted to older and more familiar themes. So, too, did Senator McCarthy, who began rehashing his old charges, though he seemed to be looking for new victims and new revelations of subversion in high places. The Democrats in the Truman administration and the Catholic politicians who played a large role in the party also seemed uncertain, confused, and frustrated. The Catholic Democrats seemed particularly out-of-sorts when confronted with the "Catholic issue," though they dared not ignore it: the Catholic vote played a critical role in the party's plans for the 1952 campaign. As matters stood, however, few Catholics had yet taken a truly decisive stand on the matter of the junior senator. A Roper poll taken in May 1952 showed that the masses of Catholics (as well as the rest of the populace) had only vaguely defined ideas about McCarthy. When asked, "Who has done the best job of handling the Communists in America?" only 9 percent of the Catholics polled named McCarthy; 56 percent pointed to the FBI. (The figures for the non-Catholics were virtually the same.) The same poll also asked if the respondents disapproved of the way the Communist problem had been handled by the FBI, the State Department, the Congress, President Truman, and Senator McCarthy. The results must have come as a shock to the politicians and conservatives who had made anticommunism a way of life: a majority of the Catholics (52 percent) said that they had no opinion, and 14.6 percent said that they disapproved of McCarthy. (Again, the rest of the country showed virtually the same opinion.)[45] In short, it seemed that after a fast start McCarthy had lost ground as a political celebrity, and both Catholics and non-Catholics alike seemed to be taking their time deciding what they thought about him.

In a way, the halting and cautious declaration of the Catholic bishops was symbolic of the hesitancy felt by the larger Catholic community: perhaps the 1952 elections might bring a clarification of the Catholic attitude on McCarthy, for the senator's own campaign for reelection would surely be a crucial test of his Catholic following, and possibly Adlai Stevenson's expected attack on McCarthyism would help force the issue. The elections of 1950 proved nothing at all, except that any kind of defeat for McCarthy's opponents became an instant victory for McCarthy, no matter how ambiguous the reverse or complex the causes. The campaign of 1952 merited a careful watch, as did the vote that concluded it.

Chapter 5
The 1952 Elections

Seldom has a speech by a United States senator received as much advance publicity as Joe McCarthy's attack on Adlai Stevenson of 27 October 1952. For weeks before the speech, McCarthy toured the country (much to the embarrassment of Dwight Eisenhower and the other Republicans with deep reservations about him), promising that he would soon make a nationwide television address giving the whole story on Stevenson and his connections with the Communist party. On the night of the speech, a well-heeled crowd of 1,500 conservative Republicans, who had paid fifty dollars each for the privilege of seeing McCarthy in person, packed into the elegant grand ballroom of the Palmer House in Chicago. The "McCarthy Broadcast Dinner," as its sponsors called it, carried the senator's voice to a national audience estimated in the millions. His most widely heralded effort, the speech was addressed to the largest audience he would ever reach. With his wealthy Republican sponsors paying $78,000 for thirty minutes of air time, McCarthy meant to make the most of his opportunity.[1]

If the senator's words brought no surprises, they at least reassured his followers that he had not changed his message. "Tonight, I shall give you the history of the Democratic candidate for the Presidency who endorsed and would continue the suicidal Kremlin-directed policies of the nation," he said. He insisted that his was not a pleasant task, but nevertheless, "The American people are entitled to have the coldly-documented history of this man who says, 'I want to be your President.'" The "coldly-documented history" of Stevenson had by this time acquired a thoroughly familiar ring. In a rambling rehash of his previous charges, McCarthy alleged first of all that Stevenson had surrounded himself with leftist associates and speech writers who thought that Communists should be allowed to teach in the universities. One of the writers had even condemned the government's security program (oddly enough, so had McCarthy); another had attacked the FBI. And during World War II Stevenson himself had opposed the removal of Communist radio announcers from the United States Navy, McCarthy charged.

The climax of the speech came when McCarthy announced that his investigators had just discovered a barn in rural Massachusetts containing 200,000 documents belonging to a Communist-front organization, documents that the front had spirited away when government probers were about to expose them to the public. Most alarming of all, McCarthy found a connection between the documents, Adlai Stevenson, and the notorious Alger Hiss. Buried deep inside the documents was a letter that Hiss had written recommending that Stevenson be named American representative to an international conference on Asian policy. (McCarthy failed to note that Stevenson never attended the conference, nor was he even aware of Hiss's promotion of his name.) With the link between Hiss and Stevenson now somehow "established," McCarthy next reminded his listeners that Stevenson had submitted a deposition during the Hiss trials supporting Hiss's good character, his reputation for veracity, and his loyalty to the nation. Lest anyone fail to see the nefarious connection between Hiss and Stevenson, McCarthy noted that Stevenson had even gone so far as to invite Hiss to speak to the students at Northwestern University in 1946, when Stevenson was on the faculty of the university. The "hidden files" in the barn, the many "vouchers" that accompanied them, and the name of Alger Hiss (whom McCarthy resoundingly but inaccurately described as a "convicted traitor") all made up the "facts on the evidence in the case of Stevenson vs. Stevenson."[2]

McCarthy's deeply admiring audience in the Palmer House cheered, hooted, and whistled as the senator hammered away at Stevenson. Not even a pair of anti-McCarthy demonstrators in the rear of the ballroom could dampen the enthusiasm of the crowd, which had come to hear McCarthyism and relished every syllable of it. The consecrated phrase "I hold in my hand" brought an especially warm response, as the senator brandished the *New York Times*, the Communist *Daily Worker*, articles from the Americans for Democratic Action, photographs of the outside of the Massachusetts barn, and finally photographs of the inside of the same barn (the presence on the inside of a "beautifully paneled conference room with maps of the Soviet Union" seemed somehow sinister and conspiratorial when described by McCarthy). The speech was so predictably faithful to the McCarthy pattern that it might have attracted no more than the usual notice, had it not been for a calculated slip of the tongue that brought the Democrats and Stevensonites roaring to their feet. The phrase "Alger—I mean Adlai" occurred a third of the way through the speech, bringing a laugh and a shout of approval from the audience.[3] But the Democrats, like Queen Victoria, were not amused.

The Alger-Adlai remark, together with the violent response that it evoked from McCarthy's opponents, aptly symbolized the 1952 campaign, one of the bitterest and most vengeful in American history. It all began in Wisconsin, where McCarthy had to defeat his opponent in the Wisconsin Republican primary if he were to continue his crusade against subversion. At first glance Leonard F. Schmitt looked like a worthy candidate for the liberal GOP forces in Wisconsin to pit against McCarthy. A graduate of the University of Wisconsin, he had an impeccable record as a progressive Republican with close ties to such renowned Wisconsin progressives as Robert La Follette, Jr., Philip La Follette, and William T. Evjue, editor of the *Madison Capital-Times*. In a state that had long revered the La Follette name and where the label *Progressive* was still a good one to have, Schmitt seemed to have a fair chance against McCarthy. Liberal Republicans were especially happy with his stand on social issues, for they believed that his Fair Dealish tendencies would cut heavily into McCarthy's Republican following. And Schmitt made no secret of his detestation for McCarthy's methods, saying that he would hit the senator's record as hard as he could. His two-fisted approach to the senator earned him a reputation as a "fighter" who would "slug it out" with the Appleton mauler.[4] Finally, Schmitt was a practicing Roman Catholic and a member of the Knights of Columbus like McCarthy; his supporters thought that this would give him extra leverage with the Catholics, who formed a large bloc of the state's electorate. The *Milwaukee Journal*, long a vehement opponent of the senator, hoped that Schmitt's Catholicism would help remove religion as a factor in the race.[5]

Only the most naive of Schmitt's followers, however, could ignore their candidate's glaring weaknesses. First of all, he had come out on the losing side in the two most important elections preceding the 1952 campaign: he had labored mightily for Robert La Follette, Jr., in the 1946 Republican primary, only to see McCarthy edge out La Follette, and in 1950 he lost the Republican primary race for governor. Schmitt's unfortunate habit of losing Republican primaries did nothing to help his chances against McCarthy. Second, the national political tides seemed to be rolling toward the right wing and away from Progressivism, New Dealism, and Truman's Fair Deal social programs, all of which had somehow acquired the taint of corruption and communism. None of this did any good at all for Schmitt, whose liberalism and Progressivism might have looked suspiciously pinkish, especially when seen against the relentless conservatism of Joe McCarthy.

All during the primary campaign McCarthy's liberal critics worried repeatedly that Wisconsin's Catholics would turn in a massive vote for the senator. The *Christian Science Monitor* (in those years deeply fearful of the influence of "Catholic power" on the nation) reported that McCarthy's support had "come to a large extent from the considerable Roman Catholic voters."[6] Miles McMillin of the *Madison Capital-Times* wrote that many Wisconsin Republicans were afraid to oppose McCarthy because they feared he had enormous backing from his fellow Catholics. He told a story that illustrated their concern: when McCarthy came to one small Wisconsin town on a Catholic fast day, the local church authorities relaxed the fast and declared a "meat day" so that Catholics could attend the senator's talk.[7]

Nevertheless, the *Monitor* and McMillin were heading in the wrong direction. Wisconsin Catholics had already begun to divide along political, not religious, lines: McCarthy would receive little support that one could fairly label "religious" in its origin. McMillin was one of several Wisconsin observers who later recognized McCarthyism as a political phenomenon, not a religious or "Catholic" one. The *Monitor*, however, continued to believe that the masses of Catholics had some special affinity for Joe McCarthy. It was in good company, for it shared the viewpoint of Jack Anderson and Ronald May as well as that of Drew Pearson, Paul Blanshard, and the *Nation*, all of whom remained convinced to the end that Catholics were somehow "behind" McCarthy, scheming to use him against Protestants, liberals, and the American democratic system.

For Leonard F. Schmitt, regular attendant at St. Francis's Catholic Church in Merrill, Wisconsin, the battle with McCarthy was an uphill one from the start. Deeply frustrating to Schmitt was McCarthy's failure to wage a serious campaign (he was suffering from a hernia, so his staff reported). With McCarthy largely invisible, Schmitt had to attack a candidate who was more ghost than man. Adding to his woes was his fear that McCarthy was receiving massive support from Wisconsin Catholics: "They were completely taken in by Joe on the Communist issue," he recalls sadly.[8]

Schmitt waged a slashing campaign, charging McCarthy with pulling a "hoax" on the American public, with following ethical practices that were scandalous, and with favoring big business interests by his votes in the Senate.[9] He nevertheless faced tremendous handicaps: it was a conservative Republican year, he was politically unknown (compared to Joe McCarthy), and his platform smelled too much of the Trumanism and Rooseveltism that had fallen into disfavor. The handicaps foretold the outcome: McCarthy scored a landslide, gaining 500,000 votes to Schmitt's 200,000.[10]

A few observers tried to attribute McCarthy's overwhelming victory to the Catholic vote, but their explanations were strained and unconvincing.[11] McCarthy simply did well everywhere and with every Republican group, Catholics included. At the same time he polled his biggest pluralities in conservative strongholds such as his hometown of Appleton, where he won a smashing 79 percent of the count.[12]

For McCarthy's exultant Catholic followers across the nation, a landslide was a cause for unreserved rejoicing, no matter how it came about. The *Brooklyn Tablet* wrote that the "stooges" and "assorted pinks" who opposed McCarthy had been "stopped in their mud." The voters of Wisconsin had spoken in an "emphatic, democratic and convincing way," it believed.[13] To the McCarthyite *Catholic World* it was clear that the Wisconsin electorate had "talked back" to the "Parlor Pink," the radical, and the "pseudo-liberal" who had made a career of smearing McCarthy. They reported that the people of Wisconsin had turned out in record numbers to show how proud they were of the "fearless son" they had "sired."[14] But for Donald McDonald, liberal columnist for the *Catholic Messenger*, the election had been a sad day for America: fear—a fear of Russia and communism that McCarthy had "shrewdly exploited, for his own political advantage"—had gone to the polls, wrote McDonald. Using every trick "in the repertoire of the professional demagogue," McCarthy managed to establish himself as the "savior" of America.[15] Although only the nonbelievers agreed with McDonald that McCarthy was a demagogue, everyone agreed that his massive victory and the nationwide publicity that resulted from it had given him a momentum that would make him hard to beat. His opponent in the general election would be Judge Thomas Fairchild, whose thoughtfully liberal policies and mild appearance looked pale against McCarthy's virulent anticommunism.

Although McCarthy had swept the primary with much more than simply the "Catholic vote," his opponents still worried that Catholics would turn out overwhelmingly for him in the general election. Two of the most concerned were the manager of the Fair-child campaign, Patrick Lucey, and the chairman of the Wisconsin Democratic party, James E. Doyle, who worried most of all that McCarthy would sweep the vote of the Wisconsin Catholics from the Eastern European countries. The most important of these were the Polish Catholics located in Milwaukee's south side and in the Polish wards of Racine, Kenosha, and Madison. Lucey's informants told him that the Democrats would be "wiped out" on the south side, so strong was the bitterness of the Polish Catholics against communism. In addition to his reputation as the national anti-Communist *par excellence*, McCarthy was also a Catholic, a combination sure to cut deep into the traditionally Democratic strength of the Polish precincts. Recognizing the seriousness of the challenge, Lucey's forces worked strenuously on the south side, securing the support of organized labor and convincing the popular Congressman Clement Zablocki to support Fairchild. Lucey even ran advertisements in the Polish language newspaper with photos of Fairchild and Zablocki and a strong endorsement by Zablocki.[16] Zablocki put limits on his support, however, refusing to campaign outside of his district for the Democratic candidate. Ironically enough, McCarthy in turn went out of his way to speak well of Zablocki, telling the Poles in the fourth district, "You have a good man here, in my good friend Clem Zablocki." McCarthy even refused to endorse Zablocki's opponent, John Schafer.[17] McCarthy's support of Zablocki may seem curious at first glance, since Zablocki stood in the opposite camp from McCarthy on both domestic issues and foreign policy. At the same time, however, McCarthy could occasionally rise above both party and ideology when the reason was to support a "friend," to crush an enemy, or—as may be the case with Zablocki in 1952—to avoid losing votes by opposing a sure winner.

Yet at no time during the campaign did McCarthy raise a "religious" issue, or use his Catholicism to capture the Catholic vote. The veterans of 1952 are unanimous on this point, with the Democratic leaders the most emphatic of all. True, McCarthy did talk occasionally before Catholic groups such as the Holy Name Society (a fraternal organization given to pious and charitable exercises) or the Knights of Columbus, but usually the invitation came to him, not the other way around, and as any shrewd politician would, he accepted the bid. His confidant Charles Kersten is probably right when he says, "I don't think he went out deliberately to get the Catholic vote. He was not that kind of a designing guy."[18] Nor is it likely that he soft-pedaled the Catholic vote out of calculation (i.e., to avoid antagonizing right-wing Protestant fundamentalists). McCarthy was simply too unreflective, too little the strategist, too undesigning to have pursued so crafty and sinuous a course.

The 1952 campaign polarized around the conservative-McCarthy-GOP forces and the opposing liberal-Democratic phalanx. For the Republicans the campaign issues were domestic communism and the failure of American foreign policy; the Democrats, on the other hand, tried to divert the public's attention from McCarthy's emotional attack on subversives to what James E. Doyle called the "real issues"—such as housing, employment, and education.[19] Catholics lined up on both sides, as did Protestants and those without religious affiliation. The 1952 campaign, in sum, was almost entirely without religious overtones.

One reason McCarthy made no special attempt to snare the Catholic vote was that he spent so little time in Wisconsin during the campaign. "It was a great source of frustration to me, that Joe McCarthy ignored the fact that there was a contest going on," Patrick Lucey ruefully remembers.[20] As a self-proclaimed national political figure, McCarthy spent the campaign months touring the country, giving speeches against Adlai Stevenson, campaigning against William Benton in Connecticut, and assisting in the reelection efforts of McCarthy stalwarts like Barry Goldwater in Arizona. Most of the time he was out of the state, ignoring his opponent and seldom acknowledging that a contest was taking place.

The result was a close call for Joe McCarthy. Out of the eleven Republican candidates on the Wisconsin ticket, McCarthy ran last, winning by only 139,042 votes over Fairchild (McCarthy had dropped 112,616 votes from his 1946 total). Meanwhile, Eisenhower took the state by 357,569 votes, and Governor Walter Kohler, Jr., won reelection by 407,327. Most amazing of all was the vote for the Wisconsin secretary of state, Fred R. Zimmerman, a bitter opponent of McCarthy: he piled up a 505,300 vote margin, the largest of any candidate on the ballot.[21] It was in many ways a most unconvincing victory: McCarthy enjoyed heavy financing, he ran on a GOP ticket in a state that was swinging strongly into the Republican camp, and his reelection coincided with the first national GOP landslide in twenty years. Yet he trailed his ticket, he lost all the major cities in Wisconsin, and he did well only in the back-country areas where, as one scholar points out, "the voters had been dispassionately anti-Democratic since Roosevelt 'tricked' the country into war."[22] Clearly, the Eisenhower sweep carried McCarthy into the winning column, but his followers nevertheless proclaimed that he had won a "smashing victory."

If McCarthy's win was unconvincing, so was the thesis (advanced by a few) that he had taken the state's Catholics along with him. In the working-class Polish wards of Milwaukee, McCarthy polled only 28 percent of the vote; the other GOP candidates received at least 38 percent.[23] McCarthy also ran poorly in the Polish wards of Kenosha, Racine, and Madison, trailing far behind the rest of the Republican ticket and losing badly to his opponent.[24] The reason? One was that the Fairchild forces had concentrated their efforts in the cities, believing that if they could win the urban areas by a large enough margin, they could overcome McCarthy's expected bulge in the countryside. The Wisconsin labor unions adopted the same strategy, concentrating their efforts on the working-class wards in the cities, where the Poles made up one of the largest blocs of voters. In addition, the liberal newspapers of Milwaukee and Madison waged a furious campaign against McCarthy, hoping that they could reduce his chances for reelection. The result of all this concerted activity was that the Catholic laboring groups, made up largely of Eastern Europeans, voted heavily against the senator. The point is worth emphasizing, for the Wisconsin Poles made up the largest single group of Catholics in the state. When Louis Bean studied the Catholic vote in Wisconsin, he found that in the largest Catholic centers McCarthy ran poorly. In the counties with the largest concentrations of Catholics, McCarthy polled 6 to 7 percent less than in counties with only a few Catholics. He notes, however, that the factor of population was much more striking than Catholicism in its relation to the McCarthy vote: the greater the population density, the worse McCarthy's loss was. Although most of Wisconsin's rural counties were heavily Protestant, the few that were Catholic voted like the other rural areas for McCarthy.[25] All of this means, quite simply, that Catholics generally followed the pattern of the rest of the state, voting against McCarthy when they lived in cities and with him if they lived in farming, back-country areas. His support among Catholics, therefore, was not "Catholic" as much as geographical and political. Bean was correct, then, in concluding that McCarthy's vote-getting power among Catholics was "not as solid or as extensive as is generally assumed."[26]

And yet the myth survived that Catholics had overwhelmingly turned to McCarthy. Even Clement Zablocki, who should know better, still thinks that McCarthy carried his own fourth district. "The same people who voted for me voted for McCarthy," he says.[27] They did no such thing. McCarthy failed miserably in Zablocki's district, losing 76,408 to Fairchild's 135,852; yet Zablocki himself won still another smashing victory, piling up 131,098 votes to his opponent's 72,869.[28]

In the fifth district Charles Kersten ran on a conservative platform (though not an avowedly pro-McCarthy one) and narrowly defeated his liberal opponent, Andrew Biemiller, 112,048 to 105,013. McCarthy fared slightly better here, though he still lost badly, 128,660 to 91,719. The senator's strength lay solely in the wealthy and conservative Republican suburbs along Lake Michigan. In the rest of the city, he trailed his liberal rival as much as three and four to one.[29]

McCarthy's biggest margin (69 percent of the vote) was in the Fox River Valley, comprising his hometown of Appleton and the manufacturing areas around Green Bay.[30] Long a conservative Republican enclave, the Fox River Republicans turned out in force to vote for the local favorite. The state's Democratic leaders are correct when they say that Catholics in the area (who made up about one-half of the local residents) voted with Fox River conservatives of every type to put McCarthy back in office.[31]

Therefore, the efforts of some scholars to explain why Wisconsin Catholics voted for McCarthy seem to beg the question. An example is Michael Paul Rogin who, presuming what needs to be proven, suggests that "Catholics voted for McCarthy" because (1) he too was a Catholic (Rogin calls this the "favorite son effect") and (2) Catholics were generally voting Republican in the years 1950 to 1956 because it was a way of expressing their new and higher status.[32] Considerations of status may have moved some Catholics to vote for McCarthy, and some may even have voted for him because of his Catholicism, but Rogin provides no evidence for his conclusions. Indeed, the available evidence suggests that urban Catholic Democrats voted for Fairchild and conservative rural Republican Catholics voted for McCarthy.

If McCarthy gained another six years in the Senate, he also earned the undying enmity of a most formidable and stubborn opponent, the Jesuit editor of *America*, Father Robert Hartnett. Long an admirer of the Democratic party's social-reform programs, Hartnett had supported both the Truman administration's Fair Deal legislation and Stevenson's bid for the White House. Like many another convinced Democrat, he held his peace with McCarthy until he found himself able to do so no longer. McCarthy's televised speech of 27 October against Stevenson, in which he referred slyly to "Alger—I mean Adlai," moved Hartnett into action. An ardent Stevensonite with a high-minded view of political ethics, Hartnett bristled at McCarthy's abrasive slur. He became especially incensed when McCarthy waved a photostatic copy of the *Daily Worker* before his audience and said that the *Worker* had endorsed Stevenson's candidacy for the presidency. That was too much for Hartnett. After a delay of several weeks, during which he painstakingly gathered together the copies of the *Worker* that he needed, Hartnett published a broadside against McCarthy. With his copy of the *Worker* for 19 October lying before him, Hartnett wrote, "Now this writer holds in his hands, not a photostat but the actual complete copy of the *Daily Worker* for October 19. It says just the opposite of what McCarthy claimed it says. . . . Governor Stevenson is not even mentioned in this editorial." McCarthy's "cheap stunt" with the *Worker* was a good example of "what are euphemistically called McCarthy's 'methods,' " wrote Hartnett. Nothing could have been less convincing than McCarthy's photostats, because he made off with them immediately after the address, in spite of "ostentatiously promising" during the speech to let the reporters examine them as soon as he was through speaking.[33]

McCarthy quickly replied to Hartnett's attack on him. In a long letter to the editor, he accused Hartnett of carrying a "completely and viciously false" article about his Chicago speech. The *Worker* editorial did indeed urge its readers to vote for Stevenson, McCarthy said, and it was simply not true that he had vanished with the documents after completing his speech. The burden of McCarthy's letter was not his argument about the speech, however, but how he felt about the Jesuits at *America*. Wrote the senator:

I realize that your magazine has been extremely critical of my fight to expose Communists in government. Obviously that is your right. I am sure you will agree with me, however, that while you owe no duty to me to correct the vicious smear job which you attempted to do on me, you do owe a heavy duty to the vast number of good Catholic people who assume that at least in a Jesuit operated magazine they can read the truth.

Being an ardent Catholic myself, brought up with a great respect for the Priesthood, which I still hold, it is inconceivable to me that a Catholic Priest could indulge in such vicious falsehoods in order to discredit my fight to expose the greatest enemy of not only the Catholic Church, but our entire civilization.

If you do not see fit to correct the falsehoods in this article, then it would seem that common decency would demand that you publish not only the letter but also the Daily Worker editorial to which I referred at Chicago so that your readers may determine the truth.[34]

McCarthy's riposte failed to impress Hartnett. He immediately published McCarthy's long letter in toto, as well as the disputed article from the *Worker*. Once again he plowed through the pages of the *Worker*, attempting to see if McCarthy's interpretation of it had any validity at all. He found, first of all, that McCarthy had confused different editions of the *Worker* for 19 October and in doing so had mixed up an editorial on Stevenson with an article on the same man. Far more serious, however, was Hartnett's pained discovery that the *Worker* for that date had positively disavowed Stevenson's candidacy, saying that he was as unacceptable a nominee for president as was Dwight Eisenhower. Lest McCarthy fail to get the point, the *Worker* on 29 October attacked him for saying that it had ever approved of a "slick warmonger like Stevenson." Hartnett concluded that the McCarthy version of what the *Daily Worker* had said was a "badly garbled and distorted account" of what really appeared in the newspaper.[35]

In the weeks that followed, Hartnett continued to attack McCarthy, calling his Stevenson address a "tissue of innuendoes."[36] McCarthy responded by reasserting his earlier claim that he was "an ardent Catholic" whose "very religious mother" had implanted in him "a deep and abiding respect for the priesthood." What could he say, now that those very Jesuits whose "religious zeal, high intelligence and complete integrity" he had come to know at Marquette University were actually obstructing the fight against "atheistic communism"?[37]

Unhappy with Harnett's continued recalcitrance, McCarthy wrote directly to Hartnett's Jesuit superior in New York City, Father John McMahon. McMahon answered McCarthy politely, saying only that he had read the senator's letter "with interest."[38] The McCarthy-McMahon correspondence is important because it marked the first of a long list of attempts by people outside the order to force Jesuit superiors to bring pressure to bear on Hartnett.

Public reaction to *America*'s bout with McCarthy ran clearly in its favor, as the mail seemed to show. The *Washington Post* summed up the feelings of *America*'s supporters when it denounced McCarthy's handling of the dispute as a "case history of McCarthyism."[39] In its second and more decisive encounter with McCarthy, the journal would enjoy the support of the liberal press once again, but the mail would tell a different story.

For Hartnett, the first debate was strictly a political affair. He paid no attention at all to McCarthy's repeated and insistent attempts to bring Catholicism into the argument, nor did he invoke the traditional arguments drawn from Catholic ethics and doctrine, arguments that he knew very well and had previously used quite effectively. Looking at the senator in exclusively political terms, he used the standard Democratic (and liberal) arguments against McCarthy: he misused his evidence, he imputed statements to the opposition that it had never made, he hinted at insidious connections between liberals and Communists that had no basis in fact, and he defamed the reputations of honorable men. At the same time, however, Hartnett's personality and background gave a peculiar cast to the liberal thesis he was developing. He had researched the documents of the case with a dogged thoroughness that few would have attempted. He pursued McCarthy's misstatements and innuendoes with immense rigor, checking even the minutest details. The Catholic Democrats who opposed McCarthy had acquired a stubborn and resourceful leader in Robert Hartnett, whose entrance into the realm of the anti-McCarthyites was all the more important because of his reputation among Catholics as a cautious and responsible journalist, one whose opinions had always seemed "safe," sober, and reliable.

Yet 1952 was not a good year for the anti-McCarthyites, Catholic or otherwise, because they had few such victories as the dramatic change in policy at *America* to cheer them. Good as it was to have *America* on their side, the liberals took no comfort in the reelection of

McCarthy. Nor were they happy with events in such places as Connecticut, where his leading opponent in the Senate went down to defeat.

McCarthy vowed that he would "get" William Benton the way he had unseated Millard Tydings in 1950. Benton, it will be recalled, had been reelected to the Senate in 1950, but thanks to the vagaries of Connecticut law, he had to run for reelection in 1952. McCarthy had entered the Connecticut election campaign in 1950, hoping to defeat both Benton and Senator Brien McMahon, who had announced some mild reservations about McCarthy. His junket failed miserably, however, probably because he was not then the potent national figure that he was to become later on.

Much stronger by 1952, he wasted little time getting into Connecticut. He made three trips into the state, speaking to large and vociferous crowds; denouncing Acheson, Benton, and Truman as "Commiecrats"; and insisting that only a Republican sweep in November could end Communist influence on the government.[40] As usual, he avoided making a special appeal to Catholic voters, though Benton remained convinced that McCarthy had a great following among Connecticut's conservative Irish Catholics.[41] Yet both Benton and his advisers seem to have confused the Irish leadership of the Democratic party in Connecticut with the Catholic voters of the state. Connecticut was rightly known as "one of the most Catholic states," but the statement was misleading, if true. It was in fact the third most Catholic state, but its proportion of Catholics stood at 37.3 percent, considerably less than the "overwhelming number of Catholics" that one often heard mentioned in discussions of Connecticut politics.[42]

Whatever the mood of the Catholic electorate, Benton had to discern it without the advice and assistance of the politician with the greatest influence over the Connecticut Catholics, Senator Brien McMahon. The latter had died suddenly in July 1952, leading many Democrats to wonder whether Benton would be able to take the Catholic vote in 1952, especially since he had won election in 1950 by only 1,000 votes. They theorized that if McMahon were alive he might be able to hold the Catholics in line for Benton, just as he had apparently held them in 1950 when both returned to Congress.[43] With Benton running against William Purtell, a candidate who was both Irish and Catholic, the experts feared that McMahon's loss would be ominous indeed.

In the November election Benton did well enough with the Connecticut Catholics, though he lost his seat in the Eisenhower landslide. A careful statistical study of the election showed that Benton did as well in the most Catholic counties of the state as in the least Catholic counties. The study concluded that if there were any religious influence at all on the election, it was "so small as to be quite indiscernible."[44] Still another analysis revealed that McCarthy's campaigning against Benton actually gave him 5 percent more votes than he would have received if McCarthy had not campaigned at all.[45] The conclusion seems to be that if McCarthy helped Benton gain votes, then he probably enjoyed little success in getting Catholics to vote against Benton.

Benton's strong position with the Connecticut Catholics becomes even clearer when we examine one of the most Catholic centers in Connecticut, the manufacturing community of Waterbury. The third largest city in the state, Waterbury boasted a Catholic population of approximately 80 percent. In the 1950 election it voted for Benton by the narrow margin of 26,003 to 25,794. Though Benton's victory in Waterbury was razor thin, he seems to have fared quite well with the Irish Catholics: our study of the ten predominantly Irish wards revealed that eight out of ten such wards voted for Benton; the cumulative tally showed 7,362 votes in the Irish wards for Benton and 5,660 for Purtell.[46] Apparently Purtell's position as an Irish Catholic did little to enhance his chances against Benton. As a result, the traditionally Democratic Catholics of Waterbury stayed in the fold, choosing the Democratic candidate for the Senate. In view of the returns from Waterbury, one wonders if Benton might have taken Connecticut, had the proportion of Catholics in the state been even higher than it was.

The Eisenhower landslide of 1952 defeated William Benton, just as it swamped Ernest McFarland in Arizona. McCarthy's victory in Wisconsin, however, coupled with the losses of his opponents in Connecticut and Arizona, added to the legend of McCarthy's omnipotence. And since Connecticut was rightly known as one of the "most Catholic states," the fable that McCarthy had the Catholic vote in his pocket also gained currency.

When the smoke of battle had cleared, Benton received a letter of encouragement from another Democratic candidate for the Senate who knew what it was like to run for office with the McCarthy question hanging over one's head like Damocles' sword. Senator-elect John Fitzgerald Kennedy of Massachusetts wrote him saying that he regretted that Benton would not be in the Senate and added, "I have greatly admired your courageous service." Benton was certain that Kennedy was referring to his own problem with the McCarthy issue.[47] Courage, however, was precisely what many liberals found lacking in Kennedy when it came time for him to wage his own contest with the junior senator.

When young Congressman John F. Kennedy of Boston declared his candidacy for the Senate in April of 1952, he not only had to run against a strong and experienced incumbent in the person of Henry Cabot Lodge, but he had to deal with the McCarthy matter as well. In no part of the Union, so it seemed, did Joe McCarthy have a more enthusiastic following than in Kennedy's own Massachusetts. The 750,000 Irish in the state were among McCarthy's most ardent admirers (though an embattled minority opposed him), and no one was more acutely aware of this than John Kennedy and his campaign staff. No matter what position Kennedy might take on any other issue, he had to deal with the McCarthy question: either supporting him (and earning the ire of Massachusetts's academics and liberals) or opposing him (and facing the anger of the state's McCarthyites). Failing either of these two alternatives, he could simply pretend that McCarthy did not exist—a policy that would of course succeed in alienating everyone. Every position was fraught with peril, for neither the McCarthyites nor the anti-McCarthyites had any patience with the politician who tried to take a neutral position on the senator.

McCarthy and Kennedy had known each other for a long time. If Roy Cohn is correct, McCarthy and Kennedy first met in the Solomon Islands during World War II.[48] The meeting, if it took place, seems to have made little impression on either man, since neither one ever mentioned it in later years. In 1946 Kennedy was elected as a freshman congressman representing Boston's "North End" (Italian section) as well as the suburbs of Charlestown, Cambridge, and East Boston. In the same election Joe McCarthy won a seat in the Senate, following his triumph in the Republican primary over Robert F. La Follette, Jr.

The relationship between the two men seems to have been casual and perhaps a bit distant, but certainly not unfriendly. Kennedy made it a point to "get along" with everyone, even bizarre types like Vito Marcantonio and John Rankin.[49] He "got along" well enough with Joe McCarthy, though a difference of opinion on public-housing legislation led them into a debate on nationwide radio.[50] It attracted little attention.

Although Congressman Kennedy maintained a moderately Fair Dealish stand on domestic issues and a firmly anti-Communist one on foreign policy, Joe McCarthy quickly developed his own reputation for controversy and conservatism. As time passed, the two men came to know each other a bit more, though they moved in different social and political circles. Always exceedingly careful about what he said in public, Kennedy studiously avoided expressing his personal thoughts about McCarthy, except when alone with friends. What he told them, however, was plainly contradictory: to James MacGregor Burns and Leonard Bernstein, for instance, he indicated his acute displeasure with McCarthy, but he told Supreme Court Justice William O. Douglas and Senator George Smathers that he actually liked McCarthy.[51] Wily politician that he was, John Kennedy clearly said different things to different people about Joe McCarthy. What emerges from all of the testimony of Kennedy's confidants, nevertheless, is clear evidence that Kennedy felt a keen repugnance for what McCarthy was doing, for his excesses and his extremism. "Style" was what most sharply differentiated the two men, and McCarthy's boorish, gashouse style may well have been what most repelled Kennedy. John Kennedy may have retained a kind of sympathy for McCarthy as a person, and at times he may even have relished his Irish garrulousness, but the McCarthy style was quite beyond endurance.

Vastly complicating Kennedy's relationship with McCarthy was the tight web of personal contacts that bound McCarthy to the Kennedy clan. Chief among these was the fondness of the Kennedy patriarch, Joseph P. Kennedy, Sr., for the senator. Joe Kennedy genuinely liked McCarthy, and he invited him on occasion to the family manse on Cape Cod for a drink and dinner. The senior Kennedy also admired the senator's tough fight against communism and may even have thought that his highly controversial methods were as valuable as his goals.[52] An even warmer friendship developed between McCarthy and Robert Kennedy, who served on McCarthy's Permanent Senate Subcommittee on Investigations for six months in 1953 before leaving because of a personal feud with McCarthy's chief counsel, Roy M. Cohn. Bobby never disavowed McCarthy, remaining loyal to the end.[53] In sum, when John Kennedy dealt with the McCarthy problem, he had to consider not only the senator and his unswerving adherents in Massachusetts but the Kennedy family in addition.

However ambiguous Kennedy's posture toward McCarthy may have seemed, he showed no equivocation at all in his stand on communism. As a young and ambitious congressman, Kennedy accurately mirrored the fervent anticommunism of his constituents in his heavily Catholic district.[54] The Irish, Italians, and Eastern Europeans whom he represented wanted "something done," as they put it, about the Communists, and they showed their hearty approval of what Kennedy was doing by reelecting him in 1948 and

1950. Kennedy took a back seat to none in the determined efforts he took to thwart communism: in 1949 he startled the House of Representatives by telling the members that "the responsibility for the failure of our foreign policy in the Far East rests squarely with the White House and the Department of State." Since the Speaker of the House had given him permission to speak for only one minute, he quickly made the most of his brief opportunity by adding, "This House must now assume the responsibility of preventing the on-rushing tide of communism from engulfing all of Asia." That was quite enough for House Speaker Sam Rayburn, who promptly gavelled the young upstart into silence.[55] A few days later, however, in Salem, Massachusetts, Kennedy repeated the same motif, saying that the "Lattimores and the Fairbanks" had "frittered away" our chances in China by undermining the Nationalist government, thereby clearing the way for a Communist takeover in that country.[56]

In later years Kennedy expressed his regret over these two speeches. Arthur Schlesinger, Jr., loyally defends him by saying that they were "out of character" with him.[57] Kennedy may well have had qualms of conscience in subsequent years, but the remarks that he had made were by no means "out of character" with his earlier, hammer-fisted style of anticommunism. In defense of Kennedy, however, we ought to note that on one occasion he condemned those who preached only anticommunism and nothing else, saying that America's "great weakness" had been its relentless negativism on communism: "We have been anti-Communist," he said. "We have been 'Pro' nothing."[58] By the standards of his time, however, Kennedy was a vigorous Communist hunter, earning praise from one Catholic publication as an "effective anti-Communist liberal."[59] The reputation stemmed largely from his exposure of Harold Christoffel, a former union organizer in Massachusetts, whom Kennedy successfully accused of pro-Communist leanings.[60] John Kennedy, in sum, was a stalwart anti-Communist, but at no time did he partake in the hysterical rabble-rousing that marked the worst days of the Red-hunt era.

The leading rabble-rouser, in the view of most of the civil libertarians of the times, was of course Joseph Raymond McCarthy. What did Congressman John F. Kennedy think of the flamboyant performance of his fellow Catholic in the Senate? In his aloof and detached way Kennedy seemed to stand apart from the rancorous issue of McCarthyism, quizzically surveying those aspects of the argument that interested him, and occasionally commenting on it in an offhand and disarming way. The best example of his attitude was his much-discussed appearance before a gathering of Harvard professors and students in November 1950. Asked what he thought about Senator McCarthy, he said that he rather respected McCarthy and thought that he "knew Joe pretty well and he may have something." If he had intended to shock his Harvard audience, he could hardly have chosen a better way to do it, for Harvard was a hotbed of anti-McCarthy sentiment. As if his pro-McCarthy remarks were not enough, he told his auditors that he approved of the Internal Security Act and was also happy that Richard Nixon had defeated Helen Gahagan Douglas in the California senatorial race.[61] Kennedy won no votes that day at Harvard.

The Harvard professors and students need not have concluded that Kennedy was unequivocally on McCarthy's side, however, for a year later he said on the "Meet the Press" television program that he thought the issue of communism in the executive branch had "more or less died out." Furthermore, he believed that the determined efforts of the past few years to rid the government of Communists had succeeded "on the whole."[62] In both the Harvard incident and the appearance on "Meet the Press," Kennedy seemed to be toying with ideas and speaking off the top of his head. The truth is, as Arthur Schlesinger points out, that Kennedy had not yet taken McCarthy seriously.[63]

The time soon came, however, when Kennedy was forced to take McCarthy very seriously indeed. With his announcement in April 1952 of his candidacy for the Senate, he immediately ran into the McCarthyism question, and it haunted him for the rest of the decade. The Kennedy staffers (and Kennedy himself) did everything they could to avoid the McCarthy issue, realizing that it could destroy the Kennedy campaign completely. For that matter, the forces of Henry Cabot Lodge did the same, and the McCarthy question was kept almost entirely out of the battle.[64]

By way of placating the vehement anti-Communist feeling in Massachusetts, Kennedy's staff carefully devised a strategy designed to show off their candidate as a bona fide anti-Communist. The Kennedy literature emphasized the following points: (1) Kennedy's efforts in the Christoffel case; (2) his long-standing opposition to "atheistic communism," a phrase certain to appeal to his Catholic constituents; (3) his efforts to prevent a Communist takeover in China; (4) his support of the Marshall and Truman Plans; and (5) his opposition to the selling of American goods to Red China.[65] Lest his opponent appear to have the stronger anti-Communist credentials, the Kennedy forces asserted that Lodge had missed his chance to do something about communism when he had received an assignment to the Tydings committee but had failed to attend most of the hearings.[66] This was a risky gambit to take because it meant skirting the edge of the McCarthy issue, but it seemed to work well enough.

Acutely aware of the ethnic groups making up his constituency, Kennedy elicited letters of support from the Massachusetts Italians, Poles, Germans, Russians, Lithuanians, Hungarians, Czechs, and Greeks, each of which took careful notice of his stand against communism.[67] Finally, Kennedy took steps to appease the civil libertarians in Massachusetts's many colleges by enjoining Gardner "Pat" Jackson and his cohorts from the academic world to send a letter to the Massachusetts professors assuring them that though he would be "unremitting in his fight against communism," he would not let the methods used to fight communism undermine "the very civil liberties our nation is taking leadership to preserve."[68] Kennedy's main problem, however, clearly was not the professors. It lay with the McCarthy following in Massachusetts's cities, a constituency heavily Irish and Catholic, which did not lightly suffer attacks on the honor of the senator. All observers looked carefully at McCarthy, therefore, to see what he would do. Kennedy's friend Patrick Mulkern remembers that Kennedy worried for a while that McCarthy might come into Massachusetts. Dave Powers, another intimate, recalls that the whole Kennedy staff was relieved that McCarthy stayed out of the state.[69]

Of course, much depended on Senator Lodge. As a Republican running for reelection, would he call on help from Senator McCarthy, a fellow Republican also seeking another term? As logical as this tactic might have seemed at the time, Lodge avoided it completely, probably because he disliked McCarthy. The Wisconsin senator, for his part, entertained little enthusiasm for Lodge. But in spite of the obvious factors militating against a McCarthy visit, both candidates continued to worry about McCarthy. What if he defied all prognostications and came anyway? No one knew what the "wild man from Wisconsin would do," as Burns writes. "Both candidates pretended he did not exist."[70] Kennedy remained tight lipped about McCarthy right to the end of the campaign, even refusing the request of the Democratic national leadership to give a radio speech against McCarthy a week before the election.[71]

To the vast relief of both the Kennedy and Lodge forces, McCarthy stayed away from Massachusetts. Although we may never know with certitude why he did this, it seems probable that he refrained from coming to Massachusetts out of respect for his old friend Joseph P. Kennedy, Sr. Money may have cemented an already firm friendship: the story is still current that the elder Kennedy gave McCarthy $50,000 in the fall of 1952, ostensibly to help McCarthy with his own campaign in Wisconsin, but in reality designed to make sure that McCarthy stayed out of Massachusetts.[72] Although the incident is not impossible, there is no firm documentary evidence to support it.

Much better founded is the famous "Beacon Hill" affair, in which Joe Kennedy exploded in wrath at an attempt to get his son to renounce McCarthy and McCarthyism. The story goes that the liberals among Kennedy's advisers had long been pushing him to make a bold anti-McCarthy statement, one that would appeal to the anti-McCarthy feelings of the liberals in Massachusetts's electorate. After some hesitation Kennedy agreed to sign such a declaration, provided that Congressman John McCormack, always a power in Massachusetts, agree to sign it with him. When McCormack announced that he was ready to go along with the arrangement, Gardner Jackson prepared the statement and brought it to Kennedy's apartment on Beacon Hill in Boston to obtain the candidate's signature.

As Jackson entered the room, he was surprised to see that a large crowd had gathered there—with Joe Kennedy, in a rare visit to the apartment, seated on the sofa. When Jackson began reading the statement, the senior Kennedy violently interrupted him, shouting that Gardner and his liberal friends were trying to wreck his son's career. He praised McCarthy, saying that he supported him enthusiastically, and vowed that the anti-McCarthy advertisement would never reach the newspapers (as indeed it did not). Young Kennedy heard his father's performance from the nearby bedroom but said nothing. Asked about it later, he replied laconically that it was just his father's "pride of family."[73] Several years afterward the elder Kennedy tried lamely to deny the whole story, but the evidence supporting the incident is too strong to discount.[74] If nothing else, the affair demonstrated beyond dispute the sensitivity of all the Kennedys to McCarthy's political power in the Bay State.

Thanks to excellent organization and a furious campaign that saw him visiting every one of the 351 cities and towns in Massachusetts, Kennedy was able to defeat Senator Lodge and the Eisenhower landslide by the narrow margin of 70,737 votes.[75] Without question a McCarthy intervention in Massachusetts would have had momentous consequences for the campaign, so strong did his following among Catholics in that state seem to be. Most political commentators have concluded that if Kennedy had made a false move on the McCarthy issue, he would have gone down to certain defeat. Eric

Sevareid, for instance, wrote in 1960 that if Kennedy had taken a bold stand against McCarthy, "he would have been overwhelmingly defeated."[76]

Since McCarthy did not enter the Massachusetts race, we will never know for sure whether the pundits were right in their dark assessment of the McCarthy problem. One suspects, however, that Schlesinger is right when he says that Kennedy would have gained support as well as lost it, had he come out foursquare against McCarthy. True, some of the Irish in his state would have grumbled, Schlesinger explains, but they would not have left the Democratic fold. Furthermore, Kennedy would have gained support from other groups as well. Schlesinger points to the example of Brien McMahon in Connecticut. Though representing a state with a sizable contingent of Catholics, McMahon nevertheless took a strong stand against McCarthy in the campaign of 1950 and won reelection.[77] If Kennedy had shown more profile than courage in his first bout with McCarthyism, he nevertheless had another chance in 1954, when the Senate debated the resolution to censure McCarthy.

One might well ask why Catholic McCarthyism seemed so much more virulent in Massachusetts than in McCarthy's own Wisconsin or even in heavily Catholic Rhode Island or Connecticut. Some possible reasons come immediately to mind: first, the Irish dominated Massachusetts Catholicism (as well as the state's politics). This gave an activist and politicizing character to the state's Catholic community that was not true in Wisconsin, where the Poles and Germans tended to play a more passive role in political affairs. Second, the Massachusetts Catholics had a long history of feuding with the area's liberals, Brahmins, academics, and Protestants, and this tradition carried over into the McCarthy question. With liberals and Protestants solidly and publicly arrayed against McCarthy, it may have seemed to many Catholics in the state that the only logical course was to opt for McCarthy. After all, some of the Boston Irish may have thought, a man whom the *Christian Science Monitor* and Harvard disliked so much could not be all bad. Third, Boston's

Catholics had lived from 1906 to 1944 under the rule of one of the most conservative prelates in American Catholic history, Cardinal William O'Connell. Following his largely reactionary leadership, the Boston Catholics developed the habit of suspecting liberals, Protestants, and intellectuals (though the cardinal himself, ironically enough, was highly intelligent and enormously well read). Some of this negative feeling may have added to McCarthy's reservoir of support, even though O'Connell's successor, Archbishop Richard Cushing, took a more benign attitude toward non-Catholics and the academic community. Finally, McCarthy himself was not unlike the perennial hero of the Boston Irish, Mayor James Michael Curley. Like the mayor (who supported McCarthy) the senator was seen as one who was going after the "big guys" (as the Catholic Bostonians put it), the "higher-ups" in Washington who collected fat salaries and made big names for themselves but were too good for the "little people." McCarthy, like Curley, slyly broke the rules and winked roguishly while doing it—but all for a good cause.

All of this added up to a situation that was nearly unique in America. The most identifiably "Catholic" sector of the country, Massachusetts posed a problem for John F. Kennedy that other politicians faced only in a much lesser degree. When the Kennedy forces took a nationwide sampling of public opinion on McCarthy in 1954, they learned with certainty what they had suspected all along: Massachusetts had the highest proportion of McCarthyites in the land.[78] Kennedy was right to assess the situation shrewdly and to weigh his moves with great care: the Catholic McCarthyites in his home state were ready to stand up and fight if he decided to duel with the junior senator from Wisconsin.

If McCarthy seemed reluctant to enter the Massachusetts contest, he showed no hesitancy at all about the senatorial race in West Virginia, where his antagonist, Harley Kilgore, was running for reelection on the Democratic ticket. Tackling the West Virginia race with his usual enthusiasm, McCarthy apparently supported the circulation of a scurrilous book called *Kilgore's Red Record*, which tried to make Kilgore appear a Communist sympathizer. Worried about the impact of the book on the state's 100,000 Catholics, as well as the effect of McCarthy's campaigning in Catholic areas, Senator Kilgore and one of his aides went to see the Catholic bishop of West Virginia shortly before the election. The prelate told them not to worry about the book and also gave them his private assurances that the church would not interfere with the election.[79]

Kilgore was one of the McCarthy enemies who managed to survive the Eisenhower sweep of 1952 and went on to vote for McCarthy's censure in 1954. The Catholic vote in West Virginia, as in Wisconsin and Connecticut, failed to go McCarthy's way. A statistical examination of the Catholic balloting in that state revealed that McCarthy's campaigning in Catholic areas had not hurt Kilgore in any way. The evidence showed, in fact, that Kilgore did better in the counties with a greater Catholic concentration than in those with a smaller percentage of the same.[80] When Kilgore's staff made its own analysis of the Catholic vote in West Virginia, it arrived at much the same conclusion: McCarthy exercised only slight impact on the Catholic vote.[81]

In spite of their intensive campaigning in Wisconsin, Connecticut, and West Virginia, the McCarthy forces clearly failed to capture the allegiance of Catholic voters. Instead, Catholics voted much the same as the rest of the electorate, sometimes tending to follow the Eisenhower landslide or sometimes joining in a local move to retain a popular incumbent, such as Kilgore in West Virginia. Nevertheless the myth of "McCarthy invincibility" survived, and along with it came its corollary, the fear of the Catholic vote. So concerned was the Democratic National Committee about McCarthy's impact on Catholics that it gave two of its staffers, Kenneth Birkhead and Henry L. Rofinot (a Catholic liberal and anti-McCarthyite), the task of monitoring Catholic opinion on McCarthy.[82] The Democrats worried especially about McCarthy's impact on the Catholic vote in the presidential campaign, fearing that his emotional anticommunism would have a devastating impact on Catholics worried about persecution of the church abroad and subversion at home.

Two years later Drew Pearson confidently proclaimed that McCarthy had delivered the Catholic vote for the GOP, and a later study concluded that "the agitation of the McCarthyites" helped cause the exodus of the Catholics from the Democratic to the Republican party in 1952.[83] Although the Eisenhower landslide cut deep into the Catholic vote, it nevertheless seems certain that Stevenson managed to do better with the Catholics than did Eisenhower: two careful studies of the 1952 presidential vote have revealed that 43.5 percent of the Catholics opted for Stevenson and that Eisenhower captured only 41 percent of the same vote.[84] True, the Democratic share of the Catholic vote slipped badly in 1952, but there is no evidence at all that McCarthy was responsible for this change. In fact the crucial Irish vote seems to have gone by a lopsided margin to Stevenson, with Adlai taking 55 percent to Eisenhower's 38 percent.[85] Furthermore, one can rather easily attribute the Catholic defection from the Democrats to a number of other causes: Catholics, like everyone else, were sick of Korea and suspected the Democrats of corruption. With their rising position in status and income, Catholics may also have seen a vote for Eisenhower as a way of expressing their newfound affluence. Finally, Catholics may have joined the millions of other Americans who believed that twenty years of Democratic rule was quite enough. With all of these motives in operation, it hardly seems necessary to attribute the Republican gain in the Catholic vote to McCarthyism.

Only by stretching one's imagination beyond all endurance can one possibly interpret the election of 1952 as a McCarthy triumph with the nation's Catholics. They had once again gone their own way, largely oblivious to the special pressures that so many politicians believed would push them into the McCarthy camp. The shrill and hysterical appeals of the McCarthyites seem to have little appeal for them, just as they seemed to sway so few of the non-

Catholic voters in 1952. Nor does one find much evidence that some Catholics voted for McCarthy because he was a "good Catholic man" or a "devout Catholic" or even "the only one in Washington who is doing something about the Communists." For the most part, they did what other Americans did: they voted Democratic if they were liberally inclined, if they were habitual Democratic voters, or if they disliked McCarthy and McCarthyism to begin with. The remainder voted Republican if they were conservative or isolationistic or "fed up with Truman."

The Catholic division over McCarthy represented far more than simply a difference of opinion over politics. Seen at the deepest level, it symbolized the status that American Catholics had attained in the postwar decade. After years of feeling estranged from the rest of American society, Catholics were at last well on the way toward attaining full status as Americans: they were no longer Catholics who happened to be Americans but rather American Catholics who had become fully American and fully Catholic. In the matter of Senator Joe McCarthy, Catholics failed to vote their religion because they were ready to vote their conscience, their party, their region, or their status. The Catholics of the 1950s felt less threatened than they had felt in the past: the overt religious warfare of the 1920s was gone, as were the years of privation that marked the decade of the thirties. With the World War giving further proof of their patriotism, they could enter the mainstream of American life confident that for most Americans their Catholicism was no barrier to full acceptance as American citizens. To be sure, the more thoughtful Catholics worried that the rest of the nation was taking less interest in their Catholicism because it was taking religion itself less seriously than in the past: America had gained a civic religion based fully as much on the red, white, and blue as on Protestantism, Catholicism, and Judaism.

Still, the signs persisted that Catholic distinctiveness was disappearing. What did *not* happen in the 1952 election was fully as instructive as what actually transpired: the bishops gave no instructions to Catholics on how to vote, McCarthy was scrupulously careful to avoid using his own Catholicism to gain Catholic votes, the editors of the Catholic newspapers and magazines blithely went their own way without direction from the hierarchy or from Rome, and all parties decried the injection of the religious issue into the McCarthy debate (even though some of the same parties occasionally violated their own principles by injecting the very same issue).

But what is obvious now was not so apparent in 1952. If many observers failed to see how far Catholics had assimilated themselves into the national fabric, one of the reasons was that they still thought that Catholics formed a monolithic army of McCarthyites. This failure in perception should come as no surprise. McCarthy had won reelection and stood a good chance for "promotion" because once again the Republicans controlled the Congress. The powerful Joe McCarthy was also a Catholic, and it was common knowledge that Catholics had a special problem with communism. The argument concluded, with seeming plausibility, that Catholics favored McCarthy by an overwhelming margin. The myth, which had become a permanent feature of the American political landscape, persisted in the years to come. McCarthy and the Catholic church had become inseparably linked in the minds of many observers, even though the next two years brought intensified strife among Catholics over the matter of the junior senator from Wisconsin.

Chapter 6

Protestant–Catholic Tensions and the McCarthy Issue

As Dwight Eisenhower began the first of his eight low-key years in the White House, political observers still disagreed over whether McCarthy had been the beneficiary of a landslide or a true winner in his own right. Everyone admitted, however, that his power was greater than it had ever been before. Without question he had turned a corner in his career, achieving a notoriety that few people thought he would ever reach. The new Congress, in Republican hands once again after four years of Democratic control, promptly granted him the chairmanship of the Permanent Subcommittee on Investigations, an arm of the Government Operations Committee. Though the Senate hoped to restrict McCarthy's maverick behavior by denying him the exclusive right to investigate Communists, he soon began using his committee to fire at will against alleged Communists in the federal government. For the next year and one-half he possessed his own bully pulpit from which to proclaim his accusations and to publicize an unending stream of documents purporting to prove the existence of Communist subversives in key government positions.

What did the Eisenhower administration do about McCarthy? Eisenhower himself preferred to say little and do less, thinking perhaps that the McCarthy problem would go away if ignored. Nor does he seem to have paid any attention at all to the impact that McCarthy might have had on the country's Catholics, possibly because he looked upon such issues as the unseemly "political" questions above which he had promised to rise. His aides in the White House had little more to say about the problem. Emmet John

Hughes, Eisenhower's speech writer and personal assistant who came into the administration with an extensive background in social-justice Catholicism, paid almost no heed at all to McCarthy's effect on Catholics, nor does he remember that the Eisenhower staff ever discussed it.[1] They seem to have presumed that the question of Catholic reaction to McCarthy was one for the Democrats to worry about, since Catholics traditionally tended to vote Democratic, a habit that the 1952 election had modified but had not entirely reversed.

A poll of national opinion on McCarthy taken in March 1953 showed that few Americans, Catholics included, had made up their minds about the junior senator. A clear majority of the Catholics interviewed (56.6 percent) said that they had no opinion at all about him. Catholics who said that they had a favorable opinion numbered a scant 16.6 percent; virtually the same number (17.4 percent) entertained an unfavorable view of him. (Protestants were slightly more critical of McCarthy, as was the nation as a whole.)[2] The lesson seemed clear enough: if McCarthyism was an issue in the early months of the Eisenhower administration, it was a question for politicians and pundits, not for the masses of voters. Catholics formed no exception to the rule.

To the surprise of no one familiar with his past, McCarthy charged into a fresh packet of investigations as soon as the new administration had taken up its duties. In the weeks that followed, he accused the State Department of allowing subversive literature into its overseas libraries (established by Congress for the purpose of informing citizens of other lands about life in the United States). He also found time to denounce the "Voice of America" program, to make an unsuccessful try at blocking the nomination of Charles E. Bohlen as ambassador to Russia (Bohlen had been present at the Yalta Conference and had refused to repudiate it), and even to negotiate a private "deal" with some Greek shipowners to keep them from trading with Communist China and North Korea.[3] Catholic reaction to these and all of McCarthy's adventures followed generally predictable lines.[4] In the same period young Robert F. Kennedy went to work for McCarthy, but his Catholicism seems to have had little to do with either his decision to work for McCarthy or his subsequent determination to leave him. Suffice it to say that he was anxious to be near the center of political action, his father wanted him to be on McCarthy's staff, and he thought that McCarthy was "doing something" about the security problem.[5]

On two occasions, however, Catholic response to McCarthy departed from the usual course. The first came in March 1953, when a nationally known Catholic intellectual gave McCarthy a vigorous verbal drubbing. Dr. George N. Shuster, the president of Hunter College in New York City, attracted national headlines when he announced that the time had come for the colleges of the nation to do some investigating of their own. The object of their inquiries? The junior senator himself. "No doubt the time has come to ask on what meat this our Caesar has fed," he said in a Washington speech that virtually every anti-McCarthy journal reported at length. Shuster added that the colleges ought to review McCarthy's activities "with the utmost objectivity, calm and chilly resolution," for he fancied that "the day on which the senator is summoned before the bar of American history and social science will not be the least revealing of his career."[6] The newspapers gave Shuster star billing because he was the first college president in the land to denounce McCarthy, but they took due notice of Shuster's Catholicism as well. The *Madison Capital-Times*, the *New York Post*, the *Nation*, and many other liberal publications all described Shuster's religious connections in detail, noting especially his earlier career as editor of the *Commonweal* and his national reputation as a Catholic intellectual and author.[7] Shuster's mail from his fellow Catholics, meanwhile, reflected the usual split between McCarthyites and their opposite numbers.[8]

The *Commonweal*'s bitter argument with McCarthy reached a decisive point in June 1953, when the senator insinuated that the magazine had once harbored a writer who was a security risk and a Communist sympathizer.[9] When McCarthy pushed his innuendoes a step further and implied that the *Commonweal* had deliberately given refuge to a Communist, the magazine challenged him to make a "public correction." McCarthy replied to the *Commonweal* but ignored its challenge, concentrating instead on the *Commonweal* itself. The journal was undeserving of the description "Catholic magazine," McCarthy averred. "So that there will be no doubt in your mind as to how I feel about your magazine, I feel that you have done and are doing a tremendous disservice to the Catholic church and a great service to the Communist Party." He believed that papers like the *Daily Worker* could be of little benefit to the Communists, but a magazine that "falsely and dishonestly masquerades under the title of being a mouthpiece for the Catholic Church can perform unlimited service to the Communist movement."[10] Since the *Commonweal* had long believed that McCarthy himself was hurting the church and helping the Communists, it did not deign to make a lengthy reply to the senator. Concluded the editors: "We are indebted to Senator McCarthy for one thing: He has again demonstrated, more effectively than we could ever hope to do, the level of his 'crusade.' "[11]

McCarthy's attack followed the same lines as his assault on *America*: first a charge loaded with innuendo, then a repetition of the charge and a refusal to answer questions about it, and finally an assault on the religious fidelity of the magazine. McCarthy's letters to the *Commonweal*, however, were somewhat more restrained and less angry than the ones he had written to *America*. McCarthy seemed to be saying that he could not take the *Commonweal* very seriously since it was flagrantly leftist, but because *America* was supposed to represent the standard of reasonable Catholicism, its criticism of his policies posed a real threat both to his crusade and to the church itself.

If the first six months of the Eisenhower administration brought few unique developments in the story of Catholic reaction to McCarthy, they nevertheless saw a deepening of the long-standing hostility between Catholics and Protestants. Though the McCarthy question did not bring Catholics and Protestants into open conflict until 1953, the struggle had been building ever since McCarthy first entered the scene in February 1950. Furthermore, the foundations had been laid for such a battle long before McCarthy came on the scene, thus making an outburst all but inevitable.

Though tensions between Protestants and Catholics had declined slightly during the war years (even Catholics were better than Nazis, and even Protestants stood a cut above the Japanese) the postwar years witnessed a renewal of religious conflict. The two most important issues (in the view of the closest student of the topic) were the question of an American ambassador to the Vatican and the problem of federal aid to parochial schools.[12] Other issues—among them the attempts of Catholics to make their church's positions on moral issues (such as abortion and birth control) the law of the land, the repeated efforts of Catholics to censor or condemn "dirty movies," and their campaigns to strip public libraries of books that they deemed "anti-Catholic"—added fuel to the fire. On top of all this, Catholics were enjoying a population boom that made them by far the largest single denomination in the land. This remarkable growth in numbers, plus their success at winning converts from Protestantism, did little to endear Catholics to Protestants, especially since they seemed to delight in bragging about their unparalleled success. To the Protestant community all of this reeked of "Catholic power," which many Protestants believed was the age-old attempt of Catholics to turn America into a bastion of the pope.

Underlying all of these conflicting currents was the problem of communism. Though the religious conflicts raised by communism seldom took as many headlines as did the Vatican problem in the late forties or aid to parochial schools in the fifties, it was the most consistently divisive issue, the one that never seemed to go away. Catholics and Protestants fought over communism even after the school debate had quieted down and even after Mark Clark had decided in 1951 not to seek the post of envoy to the Vatican.

The McCarthy question greatly intensified the hostilities already existing between Catholics and Protestants. One can find a number of causes for this. First, many Catholics believed that Protestants opposed McCarthy simply because he was a Catholic. The specter of Al Smith's failure to win the White House in 1928 because he was a Catholic once again loomed ahead; a number of Catholics (mostly conservative Republicans) believed that should a Catholic rise to prominence in American public life, the Protestants would always push him down. But more important than this, many Catholics had come to see the war against communism as "their" issue: their church had opposed Marxism since the *Communist Manifesto* first appeared in 1848. Their popes had repeatedly and solemnly declared their opposition to communism and all its works and pomps, and their denomination had repeatedly suffered persecution at the hands of the Communists, beginning in Russia in the 1920s and continuing unabated in most of the countries locked behind the iron curtain. What could Protestants possibly understand about world communism (and Communist spies at home) since they had come to the issue so late, so uninformed, and so completely unscathed by it?[13]

Many Protestants, on the other hand, believed that McCarthy enjoyed vast Catholic support and that Catholics approved of him simply because he was a Catholic. (The assumption, of course, was dead wrong—Catholic liberals opposed McCarthy just as much as did non-Catholic liberals.) At the same time many Protestants began to see in Joe McCarthy the lurid image of everything they had come to fear in American Catholicism: like many Catholics he showed a certain disinterest in civil liberties, he demanded conformity to his own set of opinions, he was intolerant of all opposition, he dogmatized mindlessly, and he made a shambles of the democratic process by abusing the witnesses who came before his congressional committee. In sum, Joe McCarthy had come to represent what the Roman Catholic church had always seemed to be.[14]

Not surprisingly, the first Protestant spokesman to link the Catholic church with Joe McCarthy was the leading American critic of Catholicism, the redoubtable Paul Blanshard. Blanshard raised the Protestant alarm against McCarthy in 1951, saying that the senator's "campaign of disgraceful villification" against his enemies had received "wide acclaim" in the Catholic press. McCarthy's activities had probably done more "to discredit American democracy in Europe than any event in American politics in recent years," he believed. [15]

The Protestant liberals who opposed McCarthy felt a deep chill two years later when the senator aggressively questioned the religious programming director of the Voice of America, Mr. Roger Lyons. (By that time McCarthy had received the chairmanship of his own congressional investigating committee.) McCarthy asked Lyons whether he believed in God (he did), if he attended a church (he had not done so in the past month), if he was a member of a church (he was not), and whether he contributed to the support of a church (he did). What was the reason for McCarthy's testy grilling of Lyons? The sole cause for McCarthy's antics was Lyons's one-time description of the American Legion's "Back to God" program on the Voice of America as "drivel." The *Christian Century* (a weekly representing a liberal Protestant viewpoint) took angry exception to McCarthy's rigorous questioning of Lyons, saying that the senator was attempting to apply a "strictly unconstitutional religious test" to a public official. The incident gave vivid proof of what happened to religious liberty when someone "acting in behalf of the state" tried to "impose an official religion." [16] The magazine was plainly worried that Joe McCarthy, the Catholic, was trying to impose his religion on the nation's Protestants.

As the McCarthy years went by, both Protestants and Catholics wrote letters to their political representatives, venting their feelings about McCarthy. In doing so, they vividly illustrated the growing religious argument over the senator. Thus one Protestant minister in Ohio wrote President Truman that both Catholics and Communists were trying to get control of the whole world; both believed that the end justified the means, and both were utterly godless, he asserted. [17]

The nation's Catholics, of course, had their own views on the matter. One Irish Catholic gentleman from New Jersey wrote hysterically to the president saying, "Communism is the cradled baby of Protestant Bible interpreters . . . and they have grown into a God-less [sic] race of pleasure seeking, flesh adoring illiterates. . . . May God have mercy on them."[18] Writing in a less passionate vein, a New York priest chided Senator Herbert Lehman (D., New York) for his criticism of McCarthy and asked why he had failed to protest against the "anti-Catholic" attacks currently directed at the senator. Lehman replied vehemently, insisting that he had always opposed religious bigotry in every form. He would accept criticism from no one on that score.[19]

The conservatives who formed the vanguard of McCarthy's Roman Catholic following had a skilled leader in Richard Ginder, popular columnist for *Our Sunday Visitor*. "The Senator would not have nearly so many enemies if he were a high-ranking Protestant and a Mason," Ginder complained in 1953. Though many Catholics agreed with Ginder, a few took the opposite view. The Reverend Francis Lally, liberal editorialist for the *Boston Pilot*, said that in the minds of many people "Protestantism seems to take on a kind of pink hue." A number of Americans seemed to think that "if the Reds are not in the pews they are at least in the pulpits." Lally objected strongly to the Ginder line of thought, saying that "the body of Protestants" had indeed recognized the menace of communism and that many of them had even "suffered bravely side by side with the rest of us" in the lands where communism ruled. He said that Protestants had fought communism "bravely and boldly" and that "reasonable men everywhere" had been "grateful" for what they had done.[20]

One of the questions that worried Protestants most of all was whether McCarthy would run for president. From early 1950 until 1954, rumors flew about repeatedly that the senator would seek the Republican nomination in 1952 or 1956. If the Republicans gave him the nod, would he capitalize on his Catholicism to win the Catholic vote?[21] McCarthy himself seemed to have written off the possibility of his being the "first Catholic President" when he told an interviewer for the *Madison State Journal* that he would not run for the presidency because of his religion.[22] McCarthy's interview stirred up an angry altercation between Protestant liberals and conservative Catholics. The *Christian Century*, fearing that McCarthy's declaration was merely the first move in a projected campaign for the White House, called upon the Catholic hierarchy to repudiate his candidacy.[23] The conservative Catholic weekly *Ave Maria* bitterly denounced the *Century*'s editorial, saying that if the Catholic bishops ever took such an action they would be committing "an unpardonable interference by the Church in matters of State." Taunted *Ave Maria*, "Haven't you been telling us how keen you are for complete separation of Church and State? Well, just what are you for?"[24]

The religious dispute over McCarthy deepened perceptibly after the beginning of his second term in early 1953. In charge of his own investigating committee, he proceeded to hire a former leftist (and Stalinist) turned Methodist minister as his right-hand man and the head of his investigating staff. The Reverend J. B. Matthews, long known for his extreme right-wing political views, enjoyed close contacts not only with the conservative Hearst newspaper chain but with many of the businessmen and politicians who made up the Republican party's conservative elite. Though the members of the Democratic minority on McCarthy's committee resented Matthews's presence, he worked freely until he published an article entitled "Reds and Our Churches" in the July 1953 issue of the *American Mercury*. The first line of the essay roused a storm of debate, caused his ouster from the committee, and deepened the chasm between Protestants and Catholics over McCarthy. Matthews wrote, "The largest single group supporting the Communist apparatus in the United States today is composed of Protestant clergymen."[25]

Public reaction was instantaneous and furious. At the White House a group of Eisenhower's assistants opposed to McCarthy decided that the time had come to maneuver the president into making a public protest against McCarthy. While this was happening, the National Conference of Christians and Jews, an ecumenical body located in New York City, decided to make its own denunciation of McCarthy, though it wanted the support of the White House in its efforts. Since the White House staffers knew that it would be much easier to get a statement out of Eisenhower if he could appear to be responding to a respectable group like the NCCJ, they made strenuous efforts to coordinate the two actions.

After preliminary consultation the NCCJ decided that it would send President Eisenhower a telegram protesting Matthews's attack on the Protestant clergy; signing the telegram would be a Catholic priest, a Protestant minister, and a Jewish rabbi. President Eisenhower, in turn, was to send a telegram of congratulations to the three clergymen, taking the occasion to condemn McCarthyistic attacks on the ministry. Catholics figured prominently in the maneuvering at both the NCCJ and the White House. The priest whom the NCCJ selected to sign the telegram was the Reverend John O'Brien of Notre Dame University, a Catholic columnist known for his theological scholarship, his moderate political liberalism, and his keen interest in ecumenical affairs. Prime mover in the behind-the-scenes activity at the NCCJ was Dr. James Eagan, a scholarly and liberal Catholic layman whom the NCCJ employed to promote its many interfaith functions. To men like O'Brien and Eagan, devoted to the breaking down of denominational barriers and the building of social justice programs that all three major religions could support, McCarthyism and Matthews seemed destructive in the extreme.[26]

Working at breakneck speed, the NCCJ delivered its telegram to the White House, where it went into the waiting hands of Emmet John Hughes. A Catholic liberal with ecumenical sympathies, Hughes had long been looking for a chance to strike a blow against McCarthy, whom he viewed as a menace to American politics and an embarrassment to the Catholic church.[27] Hughes and his anti-McCarthy cohorts in the White House worked frantically to get a telegram of response from Eisenhower: they knew that McCarthy was preparing to dismiss Matthews anyway, and they wanted to beat him in reaching the wire services. They narrowly won the race with McCarthy, delivering a copy of both telegrams to the press less than an hour before McCarthy broke his own story. The clergymen's message denounced Matthews's attack as "unjustified and deplorable." They said that destroying trust in the leaders of Protestantism, Catholicism, or Judaism "by wholesale condemnation" had the result of weakening "the greatest American bulwark against atheistic materialism and communism." The president's reply, drafted by Hughes, assured the clergymen that he shared their convictions. It was from the nation's churches, he believed, that the American people would get the "spiritual strength" they needed to do battle "against the forces of godless tyranny and oppression."[28]

The president received about 150 letters reacting to his message, virtually all of them congratulating him on his stand. A majority of the letters, however, were from Protestant clergymen; he received no letters at all from Catholic priests or from others whom one could identify with certainty as Catholics.[29] The Catholics, it seems, were writing to Father O'Brien, denouncing him bitterly and accusing him of sympathy toward communism. Some even proclaimed that he was not a very good Catholic, much less a model Catholic priest. Although most of the mail was negative and extremely abusive, a few Catholics saluted him for putting the senator and Matthews in their place. O'Brien remembers especially a favorable letter from Professor Jerome Kerwin of the University of Chicago. A noted Catholic philosopher and intellectual with strong ecumenical sympathies, Kerwin wrote that he was gratified and happy that a Catholic priest had finally spoken out against the senator. For John A. O'Brien the incident was neither upsetting nor anything new; as a longtime journalist who had fallen into controversy before, he had learned to expect a virulent reaction from his fellow Catholics whenever he made a statement they were likely to oppose. He had learned also that the Catholics who wrote letters usually were those who had something negative to say.[30]

Protestant-Catholic Tensions

By all accounts the Matthews affair ought to have lessened the strains between Protestants and Catholics, since Protestant and Catholic liberal leaders had joined together in rejecting both Matthews and McCarthy. In reality, however, it actually widened the chasm between Protestantism and Catholicism. What was the reason? It appears that many Protestants saw the Matthews attack as a Catholic assault on their loyalty. How did they come to this curious conclusion? First, they remembered that McCarthy, who never repudiated Matthews's article and released him only after coming under great pressure, was a practicing Catholic. They seemed to believe that what McCarthy the Catholic had done, the Catholic church had done. Second, Catholic conservatives openly rejoiced in Matthews's indictment of the Protestant clergy, saying that it proved what they had known all along: the vaunted liberalism of the American Protestant ministry was nothing but a mask over their leftist (and even Communistic) sympathies. Third, liberal Protestants still believed that Catholics were a reactionary group, ready to support a Matthews-style attack on their patriotism. True, Catholic liberals leaped at the chance to attack Matthews and McCarthy, but their attempts to defend the Protestant clergy against Matthews were less than convincing, at least to the Protestant clergymen whom Matthews had offended. Protestant liberals, as a result, felt little inclination to try to heal the old wounds.[31]

Protestants were especially angered that some Catholic McCarthyites gloated openly over the Matthews article. For instance, the *Los Angeles Tidings* (the Catholic paper for that city) said that Matthews had attacked the Protestant clergy because a "disconcerting number" of such clergymen "have brought dishonor on the regiment. . . . Honor will return only with the purge or the penance."[32] The Catholic news service's dispatch on the Matthews story hinted darkly that Matthews's charge of Communist infiltration into the Protestant clergy was "still a public question."[33] Protestants also took umbrage at an editorial appearing in the *Brooklyn Tablet*. Long known for its policy of relentless anti-Protestantism, the *Tablet* stopped attacking the Protestants long enough to praise Matthews as an "outstanding Protestant" and a distinguished national authority on communism. Nevertheless, it believed that Matthews's indictment of the Protestant clergy was both reasonable and moderate. Did Matthews say that seven thousand Protestant clergymen in America were pro-Red? If so, the article asserted, he had really been quite kind to the nation's Protestants, because if there were 250,000 Protestant ministers in the United States, then he had singled out only 3 percent of them![34] When McCarthy finally dropped Matthews from the committee, Richard Ginder joined the *Tablet* in honoring Matthews by describing him as "something of a martyr to the faith."[35] Other prominent Catholic conservatives, such as Louis F. Budenz, agreed with the *Tablet* that the people who had slandered Matthews were the same people who had smeared McCarthy in the past.[36]

Protestants were quick both to deny Matthews's accusations and to react against Catholic support for him. One of the Protestant ministers whom Matthews had singled out for special criticism, Dr. John A. MacKay, moderator of the Presbyterian Church USA, issued a statement denouncing Matthews and asserting that Protestants had to confront "the Twentieth Century American version of the Sixteenth Century Spanish Inquisition." In an obvious reference to McCarthy, Dr. Mackay said that the "new inquisition" even had its "Grand Inquisitor" who like his famous prototype "thinks in patterns which have been made familiar to the world by totalitarian regimes."[37] Mackay's reference to the "inquisition" was an unmistakable slap at the Catholic Joe McCarthy and Catholics in general, since Protestant liberals of the 1940s and 1950s often used phrases like "the Spanish Inquisition" and "inquisitor" to describe the modern Catholic church, which they believed was as authoritarian and illiberal as its medieval predecessor. Drew Pearson was only too accurate when he said that the "chief tragedy" of the Matthews dispute was the deepening of hostility between Protestants and Catholics; Matthews's known association with reactionary groups had aroused deep bitterness among Protestants because they feared that McCarthyism was "developing into a Catholic attack" on Protestantism.[38]

Catholic liberals did, of course, condemn Matthews. James E. Doyle, national cochairman of the Americans for Democratic Action, complained that McCarthy's hiring of Matthews had been an "attempt to intimidate and silence opposition from the Protestant clergy," and the liberal Catholic columnist Donald McDonald said that he was "extremely proud" of Father O'Brien's role in the public repudiation of Matthews.[39] Yet others were more guarded in their assessment of the Matthews issue. The *Commonweal* reacted strongly against Protestant demands that the Catholic church make an official condemnation of McCarthy. As much as it opposed the senator, it strenuously disapproved of abandoning "the tradition of non-intervention into politics by Church leaders just for the sake of another stick with which to beat McCarthy."[40] Furthermore, the critics of the Matthews article had "gone much too far out on a limb" when they gave the impression that no Protestant minister had ever followed the Communist party line or had belonged to any of its numerous fronts. If McCarthy or Matthews should produce a few real Communistic ministers, "the public is likely to end up thinking McCarthy was right all the time."[41] The Reverend Francis Lally of the *Boston Pilot* saw Matthews's criticisms of the clergy as "friendly" and "a kind of family criticism," though he regretted deeply the opprobrium the press had heaped upon the Protestant clergy.[42] From no sector of the Catholic church, therefore, did Protestant ministers and spokesmen hear the kind of ringing denunciation of Matthews that they believed they had a right to hear. The Matthews episode had done nothing to draw Protestant and Catholic liberals closer together. More ironically, it does not appear that very many of the Protestant ministers ever succumbed to communism. A detailed study of the problem has found that little more than 1 percent of the Protestant ministers in America ever affiliated themselves with the Communists: the number of clergymen who actually joined the party may have been as small as fifty; it was certainly no more than two hundred.[43]

Besides intensifying the tensions already present between Protestants and Catholics, the Matthews affair also strengthened the subtle role that religion was beginning to play in the McCarthy question. The southern Democratic senators, all of them Protestants, who previously had gone along with McCarthy or had said nothing about him, were incensed by the attack of his right-hand man on their fellow Protestants.[44] Furthermore, it is worth emphasizing that it took a *religious* issue to force President Eisenhower to abandon his neutralist stance on McCarthy. The telegram to the three clergymen marked the toughest position he had yet taken against the senator, and he did not move as vigorously again until the Army-McCarthy hearings of early 1954. Finally, it seems clear that the press had long been looking for a religious dimension to the McCarthy controversy; having finally found one, it did all that it could to magnify the issue and keep it alive. This is not to deny, of course, that a religious issue truly existed. It is only to say that the press capitalized on the problem and probably gave it more publicity than it deserved. The almost obsessive coverage that the media gave to the Matthews incident did nothing to further the cause of interfaith relations.

Hardly had the furor over J. B. Matthews died down than the McCarthy debate exploded again because a prominent Catholic cardinal made a series of McCarthyite statements. Francis Joseph Cardinal Spellman, the Catholic archbishop of the see of New York, epitomized all that American Protestants feared and disliked in American Catholics. A stubborn if inarticulate polemicist, he carried on New York City Catholicism's grand tradition of warfare with the local Protestants, a tradition that went as far back as Archbishop John Hughes of the 1840s and 1850s. Again and again he fought bitterly with leading Protestant clergymen in New York City and Washington, most especially with G. Bromley Oxnam, James Pike, and Francis Sayre. Although the issues of government assistance to Catholic schools and appointment of an American envoy to the Vatican formed the cutting edge of the Spellman-Protestant debates, Protestant clergymen also disliked his strident patriotism, seeing in it the witless waving of the American flag that they believed characterized the worst of American Catholicism. His repeated statements praising American Catholics for their outstanding patriotism had also become a source of anger; was he saying that American Protestants, especially American Protestants with politically liberal sympathies, were somehow unpatriotic, somehow soft on communism? The cardinal's anticommunism seemed to many Protestants utterly without nuance, without intelligent qualification, and altogether compulsive. In his haste to exorcise American life of Marxism, Spellman seemed all too ready to reject social reform, socialistic forms of Christianity, and even liberalism itself. To convinced liberals like Blake, Pike, and Oxnam, Spellman's mindless and obsessive anticommunism was quite beyond endurance.

Finally, Spellman refused to cooperate with the efforts that many Protestants and Jewish leaders were making in the direction of ecumenism. Interfaith associations like the National Conference of Christians and Jews had to operate entirely without his cooperation, and sometimes even against his active opposition. Father George Ford, the one priest in New York City who had truly distinguished himself in ecumenical affairs, was constantly at odds with Spellman and eventually found himself living as *persona non grata* in the New York City archdiocese. Ford's positions as Catholic chaplain at Columbia University and later as pastor of the innovative Corpus Christi parish in New York City gave him excellent pulpits from which to preach the heady gospel of religious union, but he received constant reminders that his message did not please his superiors at the chancery office on Madison Avenue. Eventually, as he recalls, "They just gave up on me!"[45]

Both Catholic and Protestant liberals began giving up on Spellman when he decided to come out publicly for McCarthy. His first statement came in August 1953, when newspaper reporters asked him what he thought about the senator. "He is against communism and he has done and is doing something about it," Spellman replied. "He is making America aware of the dangers of communism."[46] Two months later the cardinal defended McCarthy against his liberal critics. Responding to the charge that McCarthy had abused the civil rights of those he accused of being Communists, the cardinal asserted firmly that neither the McCarthy investigating committee nor any other congressional committee had violated such liberties. "Anguished cries and protests against 'McCarthyism'" will not deter America from trying to root Communists out of the government, he promised.[47] Spellman paid no attention at all when his opponents accused him of advocating McCarthyism.[48]

Although McCarthyite publications like the *Chicago Tribune*, the *New York Daily News*, and the *Brooklyn Tablet* rejoiced in Spellman's comments on McCarthy, a prominent American divine expressed precisely the opposite viewpoint. Dr. Reuben Nelson, general secretary of the American Baptist Convention, said at an interfaith meeting in Cleveland that he was "deeply concerned" that Spellman should "advocate McCarthyism." The worst thing about McCarthyism, he believed, was its obvious similarity to past movements that had attempted to impose "formulas of thinking" over religious groups.[49] It seems clear, in retrospect, that Nelson voiced a fear that many other Protestants also shared.

It may well be, however, that Nelson and his colleagues were overreacting to Spellman. The cardinal's two statements, taken together, did not make him a wildly enthusiastic McCarthyite, even though his many liberal and Protestant critics believed that he was such. Rather he was expressing his support for McCarthy precisely as an *anti-Communist*. He had long championed anticommunism and anti-Communists and simply looked upon McCarthy as another, and perhaps more effective, foe of communism. He liked McCarthy because he thought that the senator was "doing something," as he said, about communism instead of "just talking" about it.[50]

These precisions were lost, however, on the cardinal's Prot-

estant opponents, who demanded nothing less than an outright
Catholic condemnation of McCarthy or, failing that, at least a clear
declaration that Spellman and the church were not in league with him.
The cardinal's pronouncements simply confirmed their worst sus-
picions: Spellman, the Catholic church, and Joe McCarthy all shared
a common disinterest in civil liberties and a common willingness to
use strong-arm tactics to achieve uniformity of opinion. Romanism,
with an Irish demagogue at its head and a prominent Catholic
cardinal as its official sponsor, was once again abroad in the land.

The Presbyterians, too, worried about Catholic participation in
the congressional investigations into communism. Their General
Assembly, meeting in October 1953, issued a "Letter to Presbyterians" deploring the fact that some of the investigations had
become "Inquisitions" that trampled on personal freedoms, smeared
the reputations of "citizens of integrity," and threatened "our democratic traditions." A "painful illustration" of the damage these committees caused was the way in which they "publicly condemned"
innocent people "upon the uncorroborated word of former Communists," many of whom had merely transferred "their allegiance
from one authoritarian system to another."[51] (The "former Communists" to whom the Presbyterians referred undoubtedly included
Louis F. Budenz.) No one could reasonably doubt that the "Letter"
pointed in a special way at Catholics, since its author was the Reverend John A. Mackay, chairman of the General Assembly and lifelong
opponent of Roman Catholicism. Furthermore, the references to the
"inquisition" and the destruction of the "democratic tradition," in
addition to the remarks about the ex-Communist witnesses, all
clearly moved in a direction hostile to American Catholicism.

Long convinced that Roman Catholicism was a deadly foe of
American democracy, Mackay seldom passed up a chance to expound
upon the evils of the Roman church.[52] Especially certain that Catholics were using the congressional investigations to club Protestants
into submission, he shared this belief with his friend the Reverend
Eugene Carson Blake, the Stated Clerk of the Presbyterian Church

USA. Asked to comment on the Presbyterian letter, Blake said that the "Roman Church has been and still is, industriously spreading the false propaganda that the only safe church, fully anti-communistic, is the Roman Church." The letter aimed to counter this nonsense, he said, because even Protestants had come to believe it. Blake concluded that "where the Roman Church is dominant you regularly find communism stronger than where the free churches are dominant."[53] A few Presbyterians disagreed with Blake and Mackay, however. John Foster Dulles, the secretary of state (and a staunch Presbyterian), said in a letter to a friend that Mackay "is so violently anti-Catholic that he tends to feel a bond of sympathy with the Communists."[54] Mackay, of course, would have denied this strenuously and with every good reason, since he had never associated himself with Communists in any way.

As Joe McCarthy launched into the fifth and final year of his crusade against domestic subversion, Protestant liberals continued to blame American Catholics for McCarthyism and for all inquisitions everywhere. Early in 1954 three of the leading Protestant clergymen in Washington and New York joined in accusing the Catholic church not only of failing to repudiate McCarthy but of giving him massive support as well. The Reverend Robert McCracken, pastor of the fashionable Riverside Church in New York City, warned his congregation in February that McCarthy was a member of a church that "has never disavowed the Inquisition, that makes a policy of censorship, that insists on conformity."[55] Although the Catholic conservatives predictably condemned McCracken's position, Catholic liberals showed a curious tendency to blame Catholics themselves for his statement. The liberal Catholic newspaper columnist, Donald McDonald, told the University of Iowa Newman Club that many Protestants equated McCarthyism and Catholicism because of the large number of Catholics who had either remained silent about him or had "already canonized the man."[56] Vincent DeSantis, professor of history at the University of Notre Dame, agreed emphatically with McDonald, noting that only a few priests had joined Father

George Ford in condemning McCarthy; yet McCarthyite publications like the *Brooklyn Tablet* continued to give the impression that Catholics were lined up en masse behind the senator.[57]

To America's Catholics it must have seemed especially galling that the Protestant bishop who most often blamed the church for McCarthy was himself an ex-Catholic. The offending prelate, Bishop James Pike (Dean of the Church of Saint John the Divine in New York City), had received his college education from the Jesuits at the University of Santa Clara in northern California. He had renounced Catholicism, however, and had entered the Episcopal church, rising eventually to the top of that denomination's hierarchy. On 21 March 1954 Pike exchanged pulpits with Francis B. Sayre, Jr., Dean of the Washington Cathedral in the nation's capital, and both men used the occasion to ask why the Catholic church had not formally condemned McCarthy. By implication, at least, the two clerics were blaming Catholicism for McCarthy by hinting that the Catholic hierarchy's silence on the senator was somehow sinister and malign. Inspired perhaps by the solemnity of the occasion, both prelates condemned McCarthyism as spiritually destructive and viciously undemocratic.[58]

If Sayre and Pike thought that they would receive unanimous support from the nation's liberal press, they were destined for a painful surprise. The *Washington Post* condemned the Pike-Sayre declarations almost immediately.[59] (Oddly enough, many conservative Catholics looked upon the *Post* as an "anti-Catholic" newspaper because it occasionally opposed Catholic positions on morality and law.) Joining the *Post* were a number of anti-McCarthy Catholic liberals who found the statements reckless and anti-Catholic in the extreme. Typical was the judgment of a liberal Catholic priest from Michigan, who noted that the Catholic church had already disavowed McCarthy (in the form of *Commonweal* editorials, for instance) and maintained that the entrance of the bishops into the quarrel would bring "an even bigger brawl than the present one."[60] Many liberals agreed with him.

No one was surprised when the *Brooklyn Tablet*, *Ave Maria*, and *Columbia* (the conservative organ of the Knights of Columbus) also joined in repudiating the remarks of Pike and Sayre. For once they all expressed the same opinion as the Catholic liberals whom they had so often condemned in the past. That was truly newsworthy, for the postwar years witnessed fully as much conflict between conservative and liberal Catholics as between Protestants and Catholics. Both the liberals and the conservatives in American Catholicism joined in accusing Pike and Sayre of waving the red flag of religious prejudice with no justification whatever. In doing so, they had added a religious dimension to the McCarthy question that was both unnecessary and destructive. There was only one difference between liberal and conservative Catholic comment: the *Tablet* thought that Sayre and Pike were pursuing a line that was in thorough accord with the avowed policies of the Kremlin.[61]

Bishop James Pike, be it noted, was a man of his convictions. No sooner had the chorus of protest died down than he repeated the same thesis again, this time attacking no less formidable a McCarthyite than His Eminence the Catholic Archbishop of New York, Cardinal Spellman. Never an admirer of the cardinal, Pike exploded at a comment Spellman made on 25 March 1954 when present in Ogdensburg, New York, for the installation of a new Catholic bishop. Asked after the ceremony to comment on McCarthy, Spellman replied mysteriously, "We don't preach sermons about politics. We have other things to talk about." And what were the other things he wanted to discuss? Americanism, for one: "True Americanism is the best answer to communism in this country. Anyone who is a real American knows what America means, what communism does, and, as George Washington once said, 'the strongest support of true Americanism is religion.'"[62]

If Spellman's unique combination of piety and patriotism was enough for others, it was decidedly not enough for Bishop Pike. He wondered why Spellman had suddenly stopped preaching sermons about politics, since he had been doing it consistently "up to last week." He had no quarrel at all with Spellman's preaching about politics when "moral issues were involved," but he wondered why silence had suddenly descended on the scene when the McCarthy issue came up. It was a sad but true fact of American political life, he believed, that people raised the cry of "the church in politics" only when they disagreed with the position the preacher had taken.[63] Spellman ignored Pike's riposte, and for a while the two men stopped quarreling with each other.

In spite of so much religious bickering, the last year of McCarthy's crusade witnessed two attempts by Catholic and Protestant liberals to close ranks against the common enemy. The first came in March 1954, just before the Senate began its famous televised hearings into McCarthy's charges of Communist infiltration into the Army. The move originated at Freedom House, a New York–based organization whose purpose was the destruction of all forms of totalitarianism, both at home and abroad. Though not founded expressly for ecumenical purposes, its activities necessarily cut across denominational lines and repeatedly brought Protestant, Catholic, and Jewish leaders together. Indeed, the very foundation of the association had itself been something of an ecumenical endeavor: two of its leading architects were Father George Ford and an equally well-known clergyman from New York, Rabbi Nathan Perilman. The two clerics were not only deeply involved in ecumenical affairs for many years but were close friends as well. A mutual antipathy for Joe McCarthy deepened their friendship and their common devotion to liberal causes.[64]

The McCarthy forces brought deep anxiety to Ford and his cohorts at Freedom House, not only because McCarthyism ran counter to their civil liberties ethic, but because McCarthy's Catholic supporters repeatedly said that criticism of McCarthy meant criticism of Catholicism. This was too much for the men at Freedom House, who smelled totalitarianism lurking under a religious guise. Working at a hectic pace, they produced a forty-five minute film condemning McCarthy for his demagoguery. Although the film avoided an open discussion of the religious dimensions of the Mc-Carthy debate, it took several steps designed to counter the thesis that the Catholic church somehow favored McCarthy.[65] The president of Freedom House, Dr. Harry Gideonse, took pains to introduce Father Ford (the film's first speaker) as "a Paulist priest of the Roman Catholic Church." The principal speaker on the film, Bishop Bernard J. Sheil of Chicago (auxiliary bishop for Chicago's Catholic archdiocese), vigorously hammered away at the film's central message—forms of anticommunism like McCarthyism, themselves totalitarian, were no better than the totalitarianism they claimed to oppose.[66] (The choice of Sheil turned out to be a most fortunate one, for by the time the twenty prints of the film were available for distribution Sheil had become one of the nation's most celebrated anti-McCarthyites; on 9 April 1954 he delivered a slashing assault against McCarthy and McCarthyism that attracted headlines across the nation.) With Catholic clerics appearing at the beginning and the end of the film, Freedom House believed that it had taken a major step toward dispelling the myth that all of McCarthy's critics were anti-Catholic.[67]

The wide distribution that the film enjoyed in the next seven months not only added momentum to the anti-McCarthy movement but demonstrated a newfound solidarity among Catholics and non-Catholics as well. In short, McCarthyism succeeded in uniting a small but dedicated coterie of liberals drawn from the ranks of New York City's Protestants, Catholics, and Jews.

A similar ecumenical move against the senator came in the waning days of the McCarthy controversy, as the Senate entered into a protracted debate over what to do about its most controversial and obstreperous member. In November and December of 1954, as the argument raged in the Senate chamber and across the nation, a coalition of Catholics and non-Catholics called the Citizens for the Censure of McCarthy came into existence in Boston. A prominent Catholic labor leader and a Protestant layman who was a professor of government at Harvard University headed the group. The Catholic, John C. Cort, had joined forces several years earlier with Professor Samuel Beer (a Presbyterian who was active in his church's affairs) to form a Boston College–Harvard University discussion group whose purpose was to bridge the gap between the city's Catholics and non-Catholics.[68] Encouraged by the enthusiastic support they had received up until then from liberals of both Catholic and non-Catholic origin, Cort and Beer decided that the time was right for an ecumenical assault on the walls of McCarthyism. The group organized a citywide drive to collect signatures of prominent citizens for an anti-McCarthy petition. Their goal (an ambitious one) was to strengthen the anti-McCarthy drive by soliciting support from every segment of Boston society, but especially its religious leaders. Though the Catholic clergy refused to get involved ("There was a good deal of timidity" among them, Cort recalls), prominent Catholic laymen did support the movement, as did well-known Protestant ministers and leaders from the Jewish community.[69]

Though the efforts of Freedom House and the Boston Citizens group failed to attract national headlines, they added a measure of force to the McCarthy censure campaign. More important still, they demonstrated a willingness of liberal Protestants, Catholics, and Jews to support interfaith activities when outside forces seemed to threaten the liberal beliefs common to all of them. In their own small way they anticipated the more important ecumenical efforts that marked John Kennedy's campaign for the presidency in 1960. Just as liberal and intellectually oriented Protestants, Catholics, and Jews joined in condemning the injection of the religious issue into the McCarthy debate, so they closed ranks in rejecting the use of the same issue when a Catholic once again ran for the White House.

To be sure, the divisive forces were stronger and far more apparent than the ecumenical ones. Just as detente between communism and American capitalism awaited another era, so the full exploration of ecumenism was still five years or more away. It could hardly have been otherwise with the rhetoric of the times reaching such a shrill and hysterical level.

One has to look beyond all of the rhetoric, however, to find the underlying causes of the antagonisms of the period. If one looks past the charges of "treason" and "Communist sympathizer" that Catholics hurled at Protestants and beyond the charges of "Inquisition" and "undemocratic" that Protestants in turn flung at Catholics, one finds such a cause: Catholics and Protestants were arguing over the question of patriotism. In the loyalty-obsessed atmosphere of the cold-war years, they mercilessly attacked what every American regarded as his most precious possession: his credentials as a patriotic citizen.

With patriotism the name of the game, some strange things happened on the religious scene. Witness, for instance, the utter lack of conflict between such religiously contradictory figures as Francis Cardinal Spellman and the fundamentalist minister Carl McIntyre; though each represented a theological tradition that viewed the other side as heretical, each shared a common political viewpoint, and in the supercharged environment of the fifties, the political position seemed to matter the most.

As a consequence, most of the fighting over the issue of loyalty raged not between Catholics and fundamentalist Protestants (as one might have expected) but rather between Catholics and liberal Protestants. To Protestant liberals such as Pike and Oxnam, the Catholic church's support for McCarthy (which they always assumed but never demonstrated) gave just another proof that Catholicism was undemocratic, conformist, intolerant, authoritarian, politically reactionary, hyperpatriotic, and antiintellectual to boot. To say all of this was to say that Catholicism was, in sum, a menace to the Republic (hence "disloyal" in the largest sense). For many Catholics, on the other hand, the attitude of liberal Protestants toward McCarthy helped confirm their own set of presuppositions. Catholic conservatives were certain that Protestants were soft on communism (they thought that this was especially true of such avowedly liberal Protestants as Pike and McCracken). The McCarthy debate, they believed, had finally ripped off the liberal mask that Protestants loved to wear so ostentatiously and had shown what lay beneath— the face of the Communist sympathizer. The Catholic right-wingers were above all convinced that Protestants opposed McCarthy because he was a Catholic. After all, Protestant intellectuals and liberals were leveling the same criticisms against McCarthy that they had long been aiming at Catholics in general.

Perhaps most unfortunate of all, the McCarthy debate also strained relations between liberal Protestants and liberal Catholics. Catholic liberals thought that their Protestant counterparts were all too ready to dismiss the whole of American Catholicism simply on the basis of their church's right-wing fringe. They were deeply incensed at the unseemly haste with which Protestants rejected the whole American Catholic church as undemocratic and neofascist. It is ironic to read the pages of the *Commonweal* and the *Nation* for the McCarthy period, noticing that their views on McCarthy are virtually indistinguishable and yet seeing the two publications constantly at war with each other. The reason for this painful state of affairs was that their views on religion, and on political questions touching on religion, were simply too far apart. Though liberals all, they continued to debate the church-state issues as if they had nothing in common.

Yet the period was not entirely without hope for ecumenism. Though not apparent at the time, it is obvious now that beneath all the bombast a series of forces were at work that were laying the basis for a renewed effort at interfaith cooperation in the decades to follow. First of all, Catholics clearly overestimated the extent of popular anti-Catholic feeling in America. What was true of the editorial board of the *Christian Century* and the *Nation*, for instance, was not necessarily true of the ranks of Protestant churchgoers, or even of America as a whole. Opinion polls taken during the days of

McCarthy showed that few people entertained deeply hostile feelings against Catholics. One of the most revealing surveys asked the respondents if they thought that any religious, racial, or ethnic group posed a threat to the country. When the question was asked in 1953, only .7 percent thought that Catholics formed such a menace; when the pollsters asked the same question in November 1954, only .4 percent identified the Catholics.[70] Furthermore, few Americans seemed to think that anti-Catholicism was much of a problem for the nation. A poll taken in November 1954, shortly before the McCarthy censure, asked the respondents if they had heard any criticism or talk against Catholics in the past six months. Eighty percent said that they had not; only 20 percent answered that they had heard such talk.[71] The conclusion seems to be that the anti-Catholicism of the period was narrowly restricted to a small coterie of dedicated anti-Catholics.

Not only did most Americans entertain good feelings about Catholics, they remained unconvinced that Catholics stood as a group behind Senator McCarthy. When asked in November 1954 what kind of people would be for McCarthy, a slight 6 percent of those polled identified Catholics. The same poll asked the respondents if they had heard Catholics criticized because they favored McCarthy, and only 2 percent answered that they had.[72] Once again, the battle over McCarthy seemed to be taking place on an elite level. The masses of Americans did not seem to think that Catholics had jumped on the McCarthy bandwagon—only a small band of Protestant ministers, editors, political writers, and politicians seemed to be of that persuasion. In other words, the Protestants and Others United for Separation of Church and State and Paul Blanshard represented an anti-Catholic elite that spoke far more for itself than it did for rank-and-file Protestants.

Furthermore, both Protestants and Catholics shared a set of common beliefs that could eventually bring the two sides into closer harmony. Though each article of faith sounded like a cliché, each represented nevertheless a deposit of belief common to both Protestants and Catholics. Both sides stood opposed, at least in principle, to the injection of the religious issue into the McCarthy debate. (The fact that both sides proceeded to inject it repeatedly only proved that the principle was difficult to put into practice; it did not prove that either side had abandoned it in theory.) Both Protestants and Catholics condemned the religious issue because both sides clung with a blind tenacity to the principle of separation of church and state. Again, if both Protestants and Catholics sometimes violated their own principles, it did not prove that they had stopped believing in them but rather that such high-sounding goals were hard to achieve in practice. Contradictions abounded, and a little hypocrisy touched both sides, but the principles remained intact. If ever the two sides could sit down to discuss their common assumptions in a calm manner, they might find grounds for agreement and for interfaith cooperation.

In short, it was possible that the debate over communism, loyalty, and McCarthy could lead to greater understanding in the future. Both sides agreed that communism was evil (though perhaps Catholics were more vehement than Protestants in their denunciations of what they called its "atheistic" and "materialistic" qualities). Clearly, the Marxists were no real friends of the Christians; by the 1950s most American Christians had come to recognize this. Both sides protested their undying loyalty to the nation, their undiluted fidelity to true Americanism, in short, their mutual affection for the flag. If patriotism was the last refuge of scoundrels, it was also the common resting place of both Catholics and Protestants. In a later age this too might offer a basis for ecumenism.

The ecumenical effort had to wait, however, until the matter of McCarthy had passed from the scene. If Pike, McCracken, and their allies in the liberal Protestant fold spoke passionately in early 1954 against Catholic McCarthyism, it was because the McCarthy contest had at last reached its climactic and final stages. Late in 1953

McCarthy began his investigations into the United States Army, an inquiry that soon turned into the celebrated Army-McCarthy hearings. It thus came to the ultimate choosing of sides, the last and sometimes hysterical summation of arguments. During the hearings Cardinal Spellman dropped all pretense of neutrality on the McCarthy issue and gave the senator the biggest boost he ever received from the Catholic church. But another Catholic bishop gave him one of the worst drubbings he received from any quarter, religious or secular. In the fierce atmosphere of the Army-McCarthy hearings, the religious conflict continued unabated.

Chapter 7

The Army-McCarthy Hearings: The Opening Clash

His voice hot with anger, Senator McCarthy stabbed a finger at the man sitting at the witness table. "General, you are a disgrace to the uniform. You're shielding Communist conspirators. You are going to be put on public display next Tuesday. You're not fit to be an officer."[1] It mattered little that in the days following his outburst, McCarthy denied that he had ever insulted Brigadier General Ralph Zwicker. (Since the committee had met in secret, McCarthy could plausibly deny that he had ever said anything of the sort.) What mattered enormously was that in February 1954 the senator was riding the crest of his popularity and that in his own private pursuit of the political millennium he had seen fit to challenge that most formidably established of all government establishments, the United States Army.

For over a year he had been hurling his challenges at the generals in the Pentagon, accusing them of "coddling Communists," of failing to remove security risks from the military, and (most important of all) of harassing a recent and famous army draftee, one G. David Schine. Private Schine, as everyone knew, was an intimate friend of McCarthy's assistant, Roy Marcus Cohn.

When McCarthy discovered in November 1953 that the army had honorably discharged an army dentist with a questionable security record (the famous Dr. Irving Peress), he summoned Peress's commanding officer, General Zwicker, and attempted to locate the source of the army's lax security procedures. It became a matter of subsequent dispute whether McCarthy really had told Zwicker that he was "not fit to be an officer" and that the general did not have the "brains of a five-year-old."[2] The dispute became academic, however, when McCarthy publicly bullied, browbeat, and sledge-hammered the starchy General Zwicker. Said McCarthy, at the end of a long and pulverizing cross-examination of Zwicker: "General, you should be removed from command. Any man who has been given the honor of being promoted to general and who says, 'I will protect another general who protected Communists,' is not fit to wear that uniform, General. . . . I intend to repeat to the press exactly what you said. So you know that. You will be back here, General."[3] When Zwicker asked for protection from the secretary of the army, Robert Stevens, the secretary ordered him to refuse to appear before the committee. McCarthy exploded once again, telling Stevens over the telephone, "Just go ahead and try it, Robert. I am going to kick the brains out of anyone who protects Communists! Just go ahead. I will guarantee that you will live to regret it."[4]

And so it went, day after day, as McCarthy lunged into new discoveries of spies in the army and as the men of the Pentagon wrestled in deep frustration with their newest antagonist. What did Catholics think about all this? If the Gallup polls were any indication, Catholics thought very highly indeed of McCarthy; his squabbles with the army raised his stock with Catholics and with Protestants as well. A survey taken in December 1953 showed his popularity with Catholics reaching a new high of 51 percent; only half that number (24 percent) said they disapproved of his work. As before, Protestants were slightly more critical of McCarthy, with 43.8 percent approving and 29.9 percent disapproving of him. Still, it was clear that Protestants and Catholics were not very far apart in their estimate of the senator.[5]

The poll for the next month showed an even more dramatic gain for McCarthy, as he registered strong improvement with both Protestants and Catholics. The sample for January brought McCarthy the highest rating he ever received with Catholics: an impressive 58 percent said they approved of him, and only 23 percent disapproved. This, the smallest negative vote he had ever received from his fellow Catholics, stood until November 1954, when Catholics rallied to his banner at the eleventh hour. Protestants, too, seemed to think that McCarthy was "on to something," as his supporters liked to say. His popularity with them, standing at 49 percent, had risen six points since December. (Just as in all the polls ever taken on McCarthy, the national opinion of McCarthy was virtually the same as Protestant opinion; at the same time, the Jewish respondents continued to reject him overwhelmingly.)[6] For Joe McCarthy it was the top of the mountain, the gala victory parade, and the realization of a long and elusive dream. But it did not last. After January his popularity declined steadily; by April he had lost his great national following, including his Catholic constituency.[7]

One does not have to look very far to find the reasons for his sudden jump in popularity and his immediate decline thereafter. The mass of publicity that the Army-McCarthy controversy brought him in November, December, and January may have convinced the public that he was accomplishing something—after all, he was in the headlines every day. Many people were beginning to think that he must be uncovering some vast network of espionage. After four months of table-thumping histrionics, however, he seemed to tire the public, especially since his "discoveries" of spies in the army appeared to be more form than substance. By the time the famous TV hearings began in mid-April, he had fallen sharply from his excellent position of early January. And the televised proceedings simply accelerated the process. Perhaps the public had reached the same conclusions as *Commonweal* and *America*: McCarthy was not only unreliable, he was not even interesting.

Though one can speculate on the reasons for McCarthy's demise and fall, one fact is not open to speculation: Catholic opinion and national opinion ran in parallel courses. As McCarthy's popularity rose with Catholics, it rose with the nation as well; as Catholics began to lose patience (or perhaps interest) with McCarthy, so did the rest of the country. The only important difference was the size of McCarthy's Catholic support: from December 1953 until September 1954, Catholic approval for McCarthy ran seven to nine points higher than his support among Protestants and with the nation as a whole. It would be wrong to place too much stress on McCarthy's Catholic advantage, however, since a seven-to-nine-point bulge is hardly a major statistical difference. Important here is the unmistakable fact that Catholic opinion was obviously following the course of national sentiment in its risings and fallings.

Nevertheless, the Catholic McCarthyites for a time enjoyed the immense favor that the nation seemed to be lavishing on McCarthy. His Catholic following seemed especially intense around New York City, where the Catholic War Veterans gave him their "Americanism" award on 30 January 1954 and where the *Brooklyn Tablet* hailed the Gallup poll for that month as showing that he was "more popular than ever before."[8] Even in his finest hour, however, McCarthy's Catholic enemies made themselves heard. For example, the student newspaper at McCarthy's own alma mater, Marquette University, protested his threat to investigate the nation's colleges. The student journalists feared that his reckless charges against higher education would "make education disreputable in the eyes of the entire country."[9]

None of this had any effect on McCarthy's loyal Catholic following. Especially concerned about the senator was the *Wanderer*, which saw anti-Catholicism lurking in the wings: the enemies of the church were out to destroy "not only McCarthy, but also the Church of which he happens to be a member."[10] As usual, the Reverend James Gillis landed the sharpest punch. When Agnes Meyer, wife of the publisher of the *Washington Post* and a prominent liberal spokeswoman, said that McCarthy's abusive treatment of Zwicker was "merely the newest manifestation of a plague that has engulfed the country like a prairie fire," Gillis remarked that "the poor lady is so mad that she mixes her metaphors. She seems to have a nightmare in which a tidal wave, a conflagration and an epidemic are one and the same thing and the one same thing is McCarthy."[11]

Gillis and the *Wanderer*, however, were beginning to wage a losing battle. Three months of hand-to-hand combat over McCarthy had done the senator's cause no good at all. The Gallup poll for March 1954 showed that McCarthy's stock with Catholics had fallen slightly from 58 percent in January to 56 percent in early March; at the same time his Catholic opposition had increased from 23 percent in January to 29 percent. (His popularity with Protestants had declined correspondingly.)[12] Nevertheless, in the most heavily Catholic sector of the country, New England, his favor remained as strong as ever. A special poll showed that McCarthy's support in that area was greater than anywhere else in the country. (Nevertheless, it would be dangerous to overestimate the extent of his Catholic following there, since the pollsters made no attempt to isolate Catholic sentiment from the rest of public opinion.)[13]

Symptomatic of American Catholicism's growing hostility to McCarthy was the defiant stand taken in February and March by the Democratic National Chairman, Stephen Mitchell. Both Catholic and Irish in his background, he had long worried about McCarthy's impact on the traditionally Democratic vote of the nation's Catholics: he was especially concerned about the effect of the conservative Catholic leadership and press on Catholic political opinion.[14] As a Democratic politician passionately dedicated to the advancement of his own party, Mitchell had long disliked McCarthy; he particularly detested the way in which the Republicans had used him to club the opposition party on the issue of security. When the opportunity finally arrived to denounce him, Mitchell leaped at the chance. In February 1954 the Irish Fellowship Club of Chicago invited both Mitchell and McCarthy to speak at its annual St. Patrick's Day dinner. Mitchell indignantly refused the invitation, saying that he would not "break bread" with a man who had accused the Democrats of treason. (He was referring to McCarthy's 1954 Lincoln Day speech in which the senator had said that the Democratic party was the party of "treason.")[15] Mitchell might have said nothing further, had an official spokesman for the club not accused him of failing to oppose communism. "The longer I looked at that letter, the madder I got," Mitchell said later.[16]

The man around whom the controversy swirled, Senator Joseph R. McCarthy, seemed bemused by the whole fracas. When told of Mitchell's angry refusal to attend the banquet, McCarthy said, "It won't hurt my dinner not to have him here."[17] Nor did it hurt the dinner's ticket sales, which "boomed" (as the club reported) after Mitchell had spoken his mind against McCarthy.[18] Chicago's Irish Catholic politicians made the witty, quotable remarks for which Irish politicians are supposed to be famous; when asked if he would "break bread" with McCarthy, Mayor Martin Kennelly said that he would not be breaking bread with the senator "because they're going to have corned beef and cabbage." Richard E. Daley, chairman of the Cook County Democratic party and future mayor of the city, said diplomatically that he would be at the speaker's table "to honor a great people, a great saint, and a great day." He added cautiously, however, that he would not have picked McCarthy as speaker for the occasion.[19]

As St. Patrick's Day approached, interest in McCarthy's appearance at the Chicago affair continued to grow: by the time he arrived at the Palmer House to give his speech, a "sellout audience of 1200" was waiting to hear him.[20] The banquet's chairman, John J. Kelly, introduced McCarthy as a man known all over the world as the greatest enemy of Soviet Russia. Responding to the lavish introduction, McCarthy noted that "St. Patrick drove the snakes out of Ireland, and the snakes didn't like his methods, either."[21] The audience loved it, hooting and stamping in appreciation. Noting that Chicago's Democratic mayor was sitting near him, he said, "I like to share the stand with my good Democratic friends. I like to get out of Washington once in a while and get back to the United States."[22] His Irish Catholic audience liked that, too.

Launching into the substance of his remarks, he described at length his investigations into the army. The Communists had been trying to set the Eisenhower administration against him, he said, but in spite of their obstructionist tactics, his work had succeeded in forcing at least twenty people to leave the government. This was an accomplishment that no one could lightly dismiss. True, Secretary of the Army Robert Stevens had proved troublesome and uncooperative, but "I don't blame Stevens," McCarthy said, adding that he was just too naive to "cope with the politicians in the Pentagon." Did his liberal critics still cavil at his methods? He had an answer for that, too: "Traitors are not gentlemen," and the investigator has to use rough methods to deal with such people. The struggle of the free world with the Communists was a "struggle of brutalitarian [sic] power to enslave the world." If America wanted to win this conflict, he concluded, then the two great political parties had to learn how to work together.[23] McCarthy could hardly have put together an effort more calculated to please his roisterous Irish audience. He gave them the kind of hard-hitting anti-Communist message they wanted to hear and spiced it up with a little Irish "malarkey" as well. He was a roaring success.

Stephen Mitchell meanwhile reported that public reaction to his attack on McCarthy was running strongly in his favor. Following his refusal to speak to the Chicago Irish, he accepted an invitation from the Friends of Saint Patrick in Troy, New York. His speech to the Troy group was as determined a criticism of the Catholic Joe McCarthy as anyone ever made. Mitchell said that besides all the other evils McCarthy brought in his wake, he had also caused a "revival of religious prejudice against the Catholic Church." He noted that a prominent New York clergyman (Robert J. McCracken) had recently described McCarthy as a member of a church that had never renounced the Inquisition and that insisted on conformity to its own beliefs. It was clear that McCarthy was giving the church a bad name, and Mitchell declared that he personally resented "the transfer of his reputation to that of my Church." Even though Protestants were wrong in thinking that Catholics were conformists and undemocratic, he continued, nevertheless it was imperative that Catholics (and the Irish as well) oppose McCarthy so vehemently that everyone would see how divided Catholics were over McCarthy. Fortunately, magazines like *America* and *Commonweal* had been showing the way, but they could not carry on the battle alone, he said. He concluded with an oratorical flourish worthy of his Irish forebears: "Let those of Irish ancestry stand up and be counted as defenders of the American traditions of decent methods and fair play. Our ancestors came here for love of liberty—to escape tyrannies. And the Irish who stayed behind fought and died for liberty." He hoped that the present-day Irish Catholics in the United States would do the same.[24]

Though Mitchell's audience was much smaller than McCarthy's, it responded warmly to his impassioned rejection of McCarthyism. Of course, Senator McCarthy disagreed. After reading about it in the Chicago newspapers, he professed that he could "hardly believe it and I sincerely hope he will retract it. It is evil and viciously un-American for the head of any political party to willfully and maliciously attempt to arouse religious bigotry."[25] The *Wanderer* and the Catholic newspaper of the Albany, New York, Catholic diocese agreed with McCarthy's sentiments, but the *Commonweal* predictably took Mitchell's side.[26] Meanwhile Stephen Mitchell reported that public reaction to his speech, like the response to his earlier statement about the invitation to McCarthy, had been favorable.[27]

The Mitchell-McCarthy episode spoke volumes, not only about the two protagonists, but about Chicago Catholicism and the Irish Catholic community as well. Though Mitchell had couched his assault on McCarthy in terms of Catholicism and ethnic pride, the burden of his remarks was on patriotism, loyalty to one's country, and the best way to deal with the problem of subversion. In other words, he had spoken as would any Democrat in the same circumstances, addressing himself to McCarthy's conservative Republicanism and his threat both to the Catholic vote and to the vitality of the Democratic party. In his remarks on McCarthy in the months that followed, Mitchell dropped the Catholic and Irish arguments and returned to the more familiar political ones.

At the St. Patrick's dinner McCarthy showed that he had little to say about the Irish and less about the church, though his witticism about the "snakes" shrewdly catered to the Irish jingoism of his audience. He followed true to his own form, insisting that his battle was less one of party (he welcomed the Democrats present at the dinner) than of region (he liked getting out of Washington and back into America) and of style (he scorned the "gentlemen" traitors in the government). The deeper he drew into his battles with the army and the administration in the months that followed, the more it became *his* battle—a war against his enemies in the government and a search for the spies that he alone seemed able to discover.

And what of McCarthy's Catholic following in Chicago? Though the city's Irish Catholic leaders were conspicuously present at the banquet, none of them had either national or local reputations as enthusiastic McCarthyites. As Democrats, Irish-Americans, and Chicago Catholics they had a solemn duty to be present at the St. Patrick's Day gathering, and they honored that obligation with the expected fidelity.

It was no accident that so few of Chicago's Catholics (most of whom were Democrats) failed to enlist in McCarthy's ranks. The archdiocese had long been the most liberal in the nation and the envy of liberal Catholics living in other, less progressive dioceses and archdioceses. Two of its previous prelates, Cardinals George Mundelein and Samuel Stritch, had pressed the Chicago Catholics into a variety of social reform programs. As a result, the Chicago archdiocese received national attention in the 1940s and 1950s for its programs of racial relations, welfare, ecumenism, and labor affairs. Bishop Bernard J. Sheil founded the Sheil School for Social Studies that taught the city's Catholics the principles of the social encyclicals, trained Catholic leaders in union work, and exhorted the faithful to involve themselves in such varied problems as housing, integration, health, education, and local politics. Other groups, such as the Young Christian Students and Christian Family Movement, inculcated the same progressive ideals in young Catholics and Catholic adults. No

Catholic city in America was more innovative, more experimental, more open to change. The liberal clergymen and lay people who dominated the archdiocese truly monopolized the pulpits and press, thus giving Catholic McCarthyites little chance to develop a strong following for the senator.

What then of the cheering Irish Catholics who seemed to take such delight in McCarthy's St. Patrick's Day address? It appears that they represented a small but vociferous minority of Chicago's Irish Catholics. Had they spoken for a Catholic-McCarthyite majority, their strength would have manifested itself in many other ways. For instance, they would have put the kind of pressure on Senator Paul Douglas (a critic of McCarthy) that Boston's Catholics placed on John Kennedy, or they would have joined in petition drives and attended public meetings for McCarthy, as did their fellow Catholics in New York City. Yet no such organized Catholic McCarthyism ever developed in Chicago; in November 1954 Chicago voted overwhelmingly for Douglas, and petition drives and public demonstrations failed to materialize. Like the Irish conservatives in Connecticut whom William Benton knew so well, the Irish McCarthyites in Chicago probably made a noise out of all proportion to their small numbers. Chicago was no bastion of open and militant McCarthyism, least of all *Catholic* Chicago, which had learned its liberal lessons well.

Finally, the incident demonstrated with compelling clarity the split that existed in the Irish Catholic community over Joe McCarthy. It simply was not true as some observers said then (and a few still say) that the Irish in America had taken Joe McCarthy's cause to heart. To be sure some had, but some had not. Not even in Boston or New York could McCarthy count on undisputed affirmation from the Irish-American citizenry. In sum, the nation's Irish divided on McCarthy about as much as the rest of the Catholic populace.

As McCarthy continued to flail away at the army, growing evidence emerged that Catholics were becoming more evenly divided than ever before. In March at Georgetown University, a debate over McCarthy between the national chairmen of the two major political parties, Stephen Mitchell and Leonard Hall, produced an equal number of cheers for Mitchell (who angrily attacked McCarthy) and Hall (who reluctantly defended him).[28] Even more convincing was the Gallup poll for April which showed a continued deterioration in McCarthy's popularity with all groups, but with the greatest drop coming among Catholics. McCarthy's Catholic following, which had declined ten points since March, stood at 46 percent. For the first time since March 1950, when the pollsters took their first sampling of opinion on McCarthy, the senator's Catholic support stood at less than a majority. Meanwhile, 41 percent of the Catholics said in April 1954 that they disapproved of him; this marked an increase of 12 percent over the previous month. (Among Protestants his decline continued as before, with 37 percent favoring him and 46 percent disapproving.)[29] Clearly, McCarthy was losing whatever advantage he had enjoyed with his fellow Catholics.

It seemed clear that Catholics were shifting sides against the senator. Four straight months of intensive McCarthyite investigations into the army had turned up nothing more than "one pink dentist," as one wag put it. Catholics, like other Americans, had seen charges and countercharges come and go, but nothing tangible or convincing seemed to emerge. If the army had not proven its case that McCarthy and Cohn had tried to secure special privileges for Private G. David Schine, neither had McCarthy proven his case that the army was soft on communism. Though the American public, Catholics included, seemed inclined at times to wish a plague on both houses, Senator McCarthy was clearly the principal casualty of the nation's growing disgust with the proceedings.

By early spring of 1954, a national movement against McCarthy was beginning to develop. Spearheading the offensive was the attempt of his opponents in Wisconsin to recall him from the Senate. The Joe Must Go movement, as it was called, attracted national attention during the spring and summer months of 1954, whipping up a furious statewide campaign to oust McCarthy from the upper chamber. Although Catholics did not stand out from the ranks of those making up the movement, they helped with the tedious work of collecting signatures, distributing anti-McCarthy literature, and sponsoring advertisements for use in Wisconsin publications.[30] More important, the editors of the Joe Must Go campaign literature made it a point to feature statements from Catholics opposed to McCarthy, especially the anti-McCarthy editorials in the *Commonweal*.[31] Since the sponsors of Joe Must Go wanted to explode the myth that Catholics all favored McCarthy, declarations from prominent Catholics opposing him seemed to serve this purpose nicely.[32]

April 1954 was the cruelest month, both for the McCarthyites and the anti-McCarthyites in American Catholicism. During that month two prominent Catholic bishops spoke out definitively on McCarthy, one for him and the other against. If ever the American church made plain its divided feelings on the senator, it was when Francis Cardinal Spellman of New York fully endorsed McCarthy only five days before Bishop Bernard J. Shiel of Chicago roundly rejected him. Both men were prompted into action by the increasing vehemence of the struggle between McCarthy and the Pentagon, a conflict in which the army first stood up defiantly against McCarthy, then capitulated abjectly, then reversed itself again and tried to halt his incursions into military authority.

Only a few days after his altercation with Bishop Pike, Spellman made his most dramatic endorsement of McCarthy. It was a high point, not only in his own career, but in that of the junior senator from Wisconsin as well. The setting was New York City, where the police force's chapter of the Holy Name Society (a social and devotional organization for Catholics) had invited McCarthy to attend a communion breakfast in his honor. Seeing fit to accept the invitation, McCarthy on 4 April interrupted his hearings in Washington in order to attend early Mass and communion at St. Patrick's Cathedral. When the services were finished, an informal parade led the senator and his entourage to the Hotel Astor, where the Holy Name Society had arranged a postcommunion breakfast. McCarthy had agreed to deliver remarks suitable to the occasion. The chaplain of the force, Monsignor Joseph McCaffrey, had the honor of introducing the senator to the 6,000 policemen present. The patrolmen shouted lustily when McCaffrey first mentioned McCarthy's name and cheered "for fifty seconds" (the *New York Times* carefully noted) when McCaffrey said that the senator had devoted his entire life to the "exposure and uprooting of Communists." When he said that McCarthy's mistakes "have been few," cries of "No! No!" rejected the implication of error. McCaffrey was still introducing the honored guest when Cardinal Spellman strode dramatically into the room, shook the senator's hand, and sat down near him on the dais, all to thunderous applause.[33]

Cheered by the enthusiastic reception the Catholic police had given him, McCarthy delivered a slamming, two-fisted speech on the sins of the Pentagon. Interrupted twelve times by loud applause, the senator talked about the failure of the army to sweep Communist sympathizers out of its ranks and excoriated the "bleeding hearts" who were trying to keep him from conducting the tough, thorough investigation he wanted to direct. "We are at war," he declared, a struggle that Karl Marx had declared on behalf of all the Communists.[34]

When he had finished with his remarks on the Pentagon, he proposed to end the speech, but cries of "More, more" and "Go ahead, give it to them, Joe," and "You're only warming up" encouraged him to talk further. This time "the professors" felt the senator's wrath. A college professor who follows Communist discipline is "ten times as dangerous" as a traitor in an atomic plant, he warned, because he has a "captive audience." He issued a caution, however, which undoubtedly escaped his uproarious audience: he urged that the American people refrain from going off "half-cocked" simply because some professor had "screwy ideas." The nation had little to fear, he believed, provided that the teacher was a "free agent" and not under Communist discipline.[35]

Riotous applause broke out at the end of the address. When the ovation finally subsided, Cardinal Spellman rose to speak briefly. It was unnecessary to say anything about Senator McCarthy's remarks, he said. "However, I do wish to say one word, if I may. Senator McCarthy has told us about the Communists and the Communist methods. I want to say I'm not only against communism—but I'm against the methods of the Communists." Loud cheering followed the cardinal's words, and shortly afterward he left the breakfast. He was not available later to clarify what he had said. [36]

Few commentators paid much attention to the themes that McCarthy had discussed, so familiar were they and so expected. Rather, they focused on the tumultuous reception that he had received and Cardinal Spellman's participation in the event. These had "sent his listeners away chattering," as the *Times* put it. McCarthy himself said afterward that the police force's ovation was one of the most enthusiastic he had ever received, if not the greatest of all. [37] In short, the policemen's cheering reception of McCarthy, together with Spellman's warm words of encouragement, made the police communion breakfast a *cause célèbre* in the story of the church and McCarthyism.

One might well ask why the New York police jumped on the McCarthy bandwagon with such enthusiasm. Some observers tried to explain their applause for him by saying that the police liked his two-fisted, anti-intellectual approach. Indeed they did, but such an explanation begs the question, because we have to ask *why* they liked his style so much. The reasons are not hard to find: few of the officers had the educational background that would have encouraged them to read the "highbrow" Catholic publications, like the *Commonweal*, that opposed McCarthy. One suspects also that the Irishness of McCarthy endeared him to the Irish policemen who made up an overwhelming majority of the audience. Furthermore, Catholic lay groups in New York City such as the Holy Name Society and the Catholic War Veterans had long espoused McCarthy's cause with unrestrained fervor: it was only natural that some of this devotion would rub off on their members in the police force. Finally, the Catholic policemen undoubtedly noticed that the city's Catholic leadership was overwhelmingly in favor of the senator, and this may have encouraged them to take a strong stand for McCarthy, especially since the cardinal and the clergy were saying what they already believed to be true. Hardly anyone in New York City's official Catholic circles had spoken out against McCarthy: the tiny number of dissidents who opposed him usually found themselves quickly dismissed as "eggheads" or as "fuzzy-minded liberals" who were "soft on communism."

And yet the police did *not* begin a citywide Catholic stampede for McCarthy. Impressive as the force's ovations and Spellman's endorsements were, in retrospect the event looked like a one-day affair. What did not follow it was fully as significant as what actually happened. McCarthy went on to other adventures, the police returned to their beats, and even the cardinal himself refrained from saying more about the event. If Spellman had meant to inspire a New York Catholic crusade for McCarthy (as seems unlikely), he could not have failed more spectacularly. An examination of his correspondence reveals that few Catholics even bothered to write him about the breakfast and its attendant political dimensions.[38] One suspects that the city's Catholics took a more casual attitude toward the affair than did the press, which viewed with alarm and pointed with pride as never before. For most Catholics the Holy Name Society's communion breakfast was a brief sensation; after that they returned to business as usual.

The anti-McCarthy press, however, took instant offense at the cardinal's actions. Most concerned of all was the *New York Post*, which feared that the "handshake and applause he bestowed on Joe will be widely exploited by McCarthy's fans." It worried that "his participation in the rally will be remembered" long after his "enigmatic remark" about opposing the methods of communism no less than the Communists themselves. It concluded sadly that McCarthy had used the occasion "to strengthen the impression that he is the beleaguered spokesman of Catholicism in America."[39] The *Post*'s political columnist, Murray Kempton, noted that Monsignor McCaffrey had failed to quote the New Testament in McCarthy's favor. Nevertheless, Kempton thought that he knew of an appropriate verse: "The relevant passage, if Father McCaffrey will forgive me, is a very short and simple one. It is: 'Jesus wept.'"[40] (One suspects that Kempton's partisan use of the Scriptures gave offense to his Catholic readers, even the anti-McCarthyite ones.) The *Christian Century* saw an evil design not only in the Cardinal's remarks (he "fixed the impression that he was in the front row on the McCarthy bandstand") but in the Holy Name Society itself (it was one of the groups that the church used to "serve the ends of Catholic power").[41]

The Catholic liberals said nothing publicly about the incident, though their discomfiture was at once profound and painful. Monsignor George Higgins remembers feeling "most distressed" at the cardinal's action. He realized full well that New York was not the entire country and that a communion breakfast was not the whole church, but he was disturbed nonetheless.[42] The nationwide coverage given to the event, Cardinal Spellman's position as virtual spokesman for the American church, and his previous comments favoring McCarthy all added up to an episcopal blessing that left the Catholic liberals shocked and angry.[43]

In Spellman's view, however, the affair was simply a repeat performance of his earlier comments on the senator. Just as before, his purpose was to show his support for someone who was "doing something," as he said, about communism. His friendship with McCarthy and the senator's Irish background, on the other hand, may have impelled him on this occasion to act with a bit more zeal than usual. What vastly complicated the affair was an old habit that Spellman had developed over the years: he enjoyed posing in public with important political figures, but he had a disconcerting way of pretending to ignore the political implications of what he was doing. On one such occasion, for instance, he had appeared in public with Dwight Eisenhower when the general was campaigning for president in 1952; on another he had publicly embraced General Douglas MacArthur when the latter made a triumphant parade down Fifth Avenue following his dismissal by President Truman.[44] In both cases an uproar followed his seeming "benediction" upon each man, but he chose to say little and explain nothing ("Let the public draw its own conclusions," he said mysteriously). This time was different, however; although his critics had tended to overlook his earlier statements on McCarthy's behalf, they could not ignore what he had said and done at the policemen's breakfast. They remembered the handshake, the words of appreciation, and his enthusiastic joining in the applause for McCarthy. The war of rhetoric escalated again.

If Cardinal Spellman had brought gloom to the ranks of the country's anti-McCarthyites, they did not have long to wait before another Catholic bishop brought them the opposite message. Just five days after the Spellman incident, the auxiliary bishop of Chicago, Bernard J. Sheil, gave a vehement condemnation of McCarthy that showed once again how deeply divided the church (and probably also the episcopate) was on McCarthy.

To those who knew Sheil at all well, his ringing critique of McCarthyism came as no surprise at all. His attack on McCarthy's anticommunism for its "emptiness" and "negativism" sprang naturally enough from his profound liberal convictions. Long known as a staunch defender of the popes' social encyclicals, Sheil had a nationwide reputation as an advocate of racial equality, of fair-housing laws, of unions, and even of civil liberties (which made him something of an anomaly among the American Catholic bishops).

Though passionately anti-Communist, Sheil had no patience with what he called the "witch-hunting" brand of anticommunism. Rather, he favored the more "positive" anticommunism expounded by the Catholic liberals and intellectuals who ran the *Commonweal*. Sheil subscribed enthusiastically to the *Commonweal*'s theses on communism: witch hunts destroyed American rights and freedom, thereby accomplishing what communism failed to do; the church ought to help lead the attack on communism, but in doing so it ought to defend democratic values as well. He not only read his *Commonweal* regularly, but he frequently called on its editors for their services, especially for speech writing.[45] Although no intellectual himself, Sheil profoundly admired the intellectuals on the magazine, seeing that their liberalism fitted in so well with his own viewpoint on most issues, especially communism.

One day in March 1954 John Cogley, the executive editor of the *Commonweal*, received a telephone call from Sheil in Chicago. Sheil said, "I've had it with this guy McCarty [sic]." He wanted Cogley to write a speech against "McCarty," and he wanted it "tough." Cogley naturally agreed, but since he knew that Sheil would say "McCarty" instead of "McCarthy," with mass confusion resulting, he left the senator's name out of the speech and simply referred instead to "the junior senator from Wisconsin." Since Sheil read it that way, no one missed the point.[46]

The forum for Sheil's speech on 9 April was a gathering of 2,500 members of the United Auto Workers–CIO in downtown Chicago's Civic Opera House. Thanks to Saul Alinsky's meticulous advance preparations, banks of bright lights welcomed the large crowd of reporters and photographers from across the country that was on hand to see what the bishop had to say. And he had plenty to say. He told his labor union audience that he had come to talk about anticommunism; but he did not support just any kind of anticommunism, however. Far from it. He was in favor of a brand of anticommunism that was "moral," that was in line with the American values of democracy and freedom, and that was effective.[47] He said that it was high time to cry out in protest against the kind of anticommunism that "mocks our way of life, flouts our traditions and democratic procedures . . . feeds on the meat of suspicion and grows great on the dissension among Americans which it cynically creates and keeps alive by a mad pursuit of headlines." If America ever gave a free rein to that kind of anticommunism, it would have nothing left to lose to the communists, "not even the shining image of its victorious junior senator from Wisconsin," he said. By that time the crowd was roaring its approval, shouting and whistling and stamping with great delight. The "city slicker from Appleton" has been taking us in "like country rubes," he said, treating the nation to a game of false and misleading charges, a game of headlines, a game of playing with people's reputations. "Anticommunism is a serious business," he believed, and not "a game to be played so publicity-mad politicos can build fame for themselves."[48]

Though he violently disapproved of what McCarthy was doing, Sheil nevertheless wanted it made unmistakably clear that he was speaking not for the church but for himself. Any Catholic could disagree with him, and he freely admitted that many did. The Catholic church does not take positions on such matters "of public controversy," he said; yet the church does speak out against "lies, calumny, the absence of charity and calculated deceit." These practices were wrong, they were "morally evil and to call them good or to act as if they were permissible under certain circumstances is itself a monstrous perversion of morality," he declared. "They are not justified by any cause—least of all by the cause of anticommunism, which should unite rather than divide all of us in these difficult times."[49] A standing ovation greeted the bishop when he finished. Clearly he had said not only what Catholic liberals wanted to hear but what his union audience already believed. Walter Reuther rose to thank him and cracked, "Let's restore the good old name of McCarthy to Charlie—where it really belongs."[50]

The anti-McCarthy press exulted in Sheil's blast at the senator. The *New York Post* gave it the expected rave review, saying that it was one of those "rare" speeches that "decisively affects the course of events." The *Post* took special comfort in the fact that his talk had so closely followed Spellman's announcement of support for McCarthy, and it believed that Sheil's remarks had "blasted the notion that criticism of Joe McCarthy is tantamount to an attack" on Catholics.[51] Like many other newspapers and magazines, the *Post* reprinted long sections of the speech.[52] The *Madison Capital-Times* lauded the address as an "answer to those who charged that the hard core of . . . Mc-

Carthy's support in this country comes from the Catholic Church." It hoped furthermore that Sheil's statement would ease the religious tensions that had arisen over the McCarthy issue. Many other major newspapers and magazines shared the *Capital-Times*'s enthusiasm for Sheil's effort.[53]

The bishop's address drew not only the expected comment from the press but thousands of letters of approval from Catholics. Saul Alinsky, who handled the mail and divided it painstakingly into categories of "favorable" and "unfavorable," reported that out of the 21,763 letters and telegrams that Sheil received, 21,351 approved of his stand, and some 15,574 of these were from Catholics.[54] (The overall response was nine to one for Sheil, his assistants reported.)[55] Many of the Catholics who wrote Sheil said that they had long hoped that someone like him would denounce the senator.[56]

Did the favorable letters that Sheil received from Catholics reflect the thinking of most of his coreligionists? Since no one took a poll of Catholic opinion on Sheil, it is impossible to answer the question with the degree of certainty one would like. It seems clear, however, that the anti-McCarthyites represented a growing sector of Catholic thought, as the monthly Gallup polls unmistakably revealed. Without doubt, the thousands who wrote to Sheil had demonstrated the existence of a wellspring of support for Sheil and for others like him who wanted no more from the junior senator.

Of course the bishop had his Catholic critics as well. The Reverend Edward Lodge Curran of Brooklyn, one of that city's numerous spokesmen for conservative Catholicism, attacked Sheil's "glittering or rather frittering generalities," noting (perhaps with relief) that Sheil was the only member of the hierarchy who had attacked McCarthy.[57] Agreeing with Curran were the two most conservative journals in the Catholic diocesan press, the *Brooklyn Tablet* and the *Wanderer*. The *Tablet* reported that the *Daily Worker* was in "high glee" over the address, and the *Wanderer* sharply condemned Sheil for his "rabble-rousing" tactics.[58]

Some of the letters that Catholics wrote to their diocesan newspapers and to the Catholic periodicals showed an undisguised hatred for Sheil. One letter to the *Commonweal* said, "May Bishop Sheil, the editors of *America*, and the editors of the *Commonweal* go straight to hell and burn for all eternity. Sincerely yours."[59] Letters from Catholic readers to the *Boston Pilot* followed the same line, one of them saying that the "biggest burlesque" in the world next to the Kremlin was "the prattle of the good bishop."[60] A few letters praised McCarthy for his Catholicism or linked him by prayer to the Almighty. A Catholic from Wisconsin, for instance, told Sheil to "stick to your own profession and say a few prayers for our 'Beloved Savior,' our Joe McCarthy. God and Joe will save us from having the hammer and sickle flying over us."[61]

Although they tried to deflate the speech, the McCarthyites had suffered a major blow. The theory that Catholics stood as a bloc behind the senator looked more than ever like the myth that it had always been. Following Cardinal Spellman's benediction of McCarthy as closely as it did, it not only refuted the myth of monolithic Catholic McCarthyism, but it showed that even the bishops could disagree with each other about the senator. Most important of all, the Sheil affair demonstrated that McCarthyism was absolutely incompatible with the church's tradition of social justice. The persistent opposition of McCarthy and his Catholic followers to programs of social betterment was becoming ever more obvious to American Catholic social reformers. They were hardening their stand against the anticommunism of Joe McCarthy, not because it was anticommunism, but because they believed that it was sterile, unproductive, and supremely un-Catholic.

The story of Bishop Sheil and Senator McCarthy might have ended there, were it not for a sudden and most remarkable event: on 2 September 1954 Sheil dramatically "resigned" from his position as director general of the Catholic Youth Organization in Chicago, giving no reason for his action. The CYO was Sheil's favorite project (though he had many others); it was the one in which he had achieved his greatest fame and into which he had poured immense amounts of energy and money. The anti-McCarthyites feared that his resignation could only have one meaning: church authorities had fired him because of the speech he had given against McCarthy. Although newspaper photographs showed Cardinal Stritch (his superior) standing with his arm around Sheil, saying that he accepted the resignation "reluctantly,"[62] it was not enough to dispel the gloom that overwhelmed the ranks of McCarthy's Catholic critics. Sheil himself did nothing to lessen those fears when the reporters asked if his resignation had any connection with the McCarthy speech. He replied enigmatically, "I've already had my say about McCarthy and I have nothing to add."[63] The *Commonweal* fretted that his resignation, coming so soon after the speech, would cause "a great deal of sour speculation and suspicion." It hoped that the "proper authorities will soon quiet the suspicion of those who think Bishop Sheil may have paid the price McCarthyism demands of all who venture to speak against it."[64]

Meanwhile, the rumor that the church had fired Sheil because of the McCarthy speech became part of the "accepted truth," gaining credibility simply because everyone believed it. *Time*, for instance, wrote darkly that "big financial contributors" had forced the resignation, angered as they were over the UAW speech. The *New York Times* headline read, "No reasons are given for his resignation—Speech scoring McCarthy is recalled."[65] The accepted truth thus became a dogma of sorts, and few have ever questioned its veracity. The matter needs to be reopened, however, since all of Sheil's closest associates have insisted that he was not fired at all but simply quit on his own. They claim that he resigned because of financial reasons that had nothing to do with Joe McCarthy. Bishop Sheil, they insist, overextended the activities of the Chicago CYO, committing the organization to projects for which he had raised insufficient amounts of money. Though unquestionably a gifted fundraiser, he handled his resources poorly, sometimes spending far more than he had in the bank. Seeing himself caught in a deteriorating situation, he finally resigned when the finances began to look hopeless.[66] In characteristically flamboyant fashion, he acted without warning and in the presence of the entire Chicago press corps. One of Sheil's most trusted advisers was in Cardinal Stritch's office when word came that he had called a press conference to announce his retirement from the CYO. He reports that Stritch was thunderstruck at the news, since he had received no warning from Sheil about what he was going to do.[67]

Unfortunately, we do not have enough firm evidence to be able to solve definitively the problem of Sheil's resignation. Sheil's papers were either lost or burned, and the archdiocesan archives, which might have materials bearing on the question, are closed to scholars. The weight of available evidence, however, suggests that no one dismissed Sheil but that he quit of his own volition. It seems more likely that the CYO's undeniably bad financial and administrative position was the reason for his resignation, rather than the McCarthy speech that he had given almost five months before. If Cardinal Stritch had seen fit to fire Sheil, then why did he wait so long after the speech against McCarthy? Moreover, such a crude public demonstration of power was entirely out of the cardinal's style, since he preferred to work in private and avoided public controversies whenever possible. Finally, it is important to emphasize that no evidence of any kind has yet appeared to show that the McCarthyites (Catholic or non-Catholic) forced Sheil out of the CYO directorship.

These qualifications notwithstanding, the cause of anti-McCarthyism suffered a reverse when Sheil resigned. The church never gave an explanation for his withdrawal, and its failure to do so brought undoubted worry and uncertainty to the anti-McCarthyites and to all of Sheil's supporters. The memory of the speech, however, loomed larger than the bishop's resignation. More significant still, McCarthy's popularity had declined sharply by the time Sheil resigned in September. The senator's opponents could console themselves with the thought that the speech had already effected whatever good it might accomplish, since it had come during the critical days of the Army-McCarthy controversy.

The conflict between Spellman and Sheil threw a glaring light on the painful division that had long existed in the ranks of American Catholicism, the split between liberal Catholics and conservative Catholics. Sheil and his cohorts were part of the larger liberal tradition in American politics, the one identified most often with the New and Fair Deals. Thus they favored the achievement of social justice (full employment, equal rights, just working conditions, and government intervention to secure what they called "justice and decency" for all). At the same time they tried to play down those church teachings that puzzled or exasperated non-Catholics (for example, censorship of forbidden books or laws against birth control). Spellman and his forces, on the other hand, represented the conservative political tradition, identified with the conservative wing of the Republican party. They tended to feel little urgency about the realization of a just social order, and as religious conservatives they made little attempt to soften the church's harsher practices. With the coming of the cold war and the spy hunts of that era, the gulf between the two factions became wider than ever. Though both sides repeatedly announced their opposition to domestic communism, both favored policies that were diametrically opposed. Liberal Catholics believed that all was lost if the spy hunts destroyed the civil-liberties tradition, but the conservatives held that civil liberties could take a temporary backseat to the more important business of finding out who the spies were. Each group, in short, wanted a church that was fully anti-Communist (as well as fully American and fully Catholic), but neither could agree on what it meant to be truly American, authentically Catholic, or effectively anti-Communist. Thus the central question was how to achieve the age-old goal of full Americanization for the church. For the Spellmans, the Catholic police, and the members of the Catholic War Veterans, the answer was disarmingly simple: attack the Truman-Stevenson-Acheson phalanx that had "brought on" the cold war by its wartime alliance with Russia, by its failure to save China from the Communists, and by its persistent "coddling" (to use their favorite word) of Communists in Washington. For the legions of Catholic conservatives, it was so important to prove one's patriotism that no demonstration of it could ever bring embarrassment. Nor did the conservatives shrink from questioning the patriotism of others, especially those who sought sanctuary behind the Fifth Amendment when summoned before congressional committees.

For the Sheils, the Eugene McCarthys, and the editors of the *Commonweal* and *America*, the answer was not quite as simple but equally clear. If it was vital to ferret out subversives hiding in the government, it was equally important to preserve the constitutional rights of those subversives (and of those merely accused of subversion). If the United States were to keep the free nations of the world from going the way of China, then it ought to repudiate the brinkmanship of Eisenhower and Dulles, supporting instead the democratic movements struggling to survive in those threatened countries. Finally, public displays of patriotism were little to the taste of the Catholic liberals, especially when such demonstrations seemed "excessive" or "mindless," as they liked to call them.

Both factions drew more deeply on American politics than they did on church teachings or the Scriptures. The Catholic liberals, to be sure, cited the social encyclicals of the popes, but more often they drew their inspiration from the American labor-union movement, the legislative programs of the Roosevelt and Truman administrations, and the editorial pages of the liberal press. In sum, the beliefs of Harry S. Truman had a larger influence on their thought than the doctrines that Pope Leo XIII expressed in his *Rerum Novarum* (1891) or that Pope Pius XI enunciated in his *Quadragesimo Anno* (1931). The Catholic conservatives, by the same token, sometimes cited the passages in papal documents that rejected communism and socialism. More typically, they drew sustenance from the conservative political convictions of Robert A. Taft, William F. Knowland, or Dwight Eisenhower. ← *The*

What did all of this say about the position of Catholics in American society? It seemed to show that in the area of ideology, at least, Catholics were rather more assimilated into American life than unassimilated. Probably they were more fully integrated into American society than was commonly supposed at the time. Most important of all, it demonstrated that the religious and political convictions of American Catholics had become inextricably entwined. Religious practice had become politicized, and political beliefs had been elevated to the status of religious creed. Religious and political values were thus tending to merge and to reinforce each other. To be sure, this was nothing new in Catholicism: in the long history of the church, many theological positions had come into being because political forces had advanced them as their "platforms." Nor was this anything new in American religion; the Prohibition movement, for instance, represented both a theological position characteristic of a cluster of American churches and a political posture as well.

Yet all American churches, Catholics included, subscribed to the venerable American doctrine of the separation of church and state (even atheists and Catholics could subscribe to that). If the doctrine meant anything at all, it ought to have said that the churches should be scrupulous about separating their political and their religious creeds from each other. Instead, the opposite happened: anticommunism became fully as much a political tenet as a religious one; fervent patriotism was fully as much a religious belief as a political one. In short, the political destinies of the nation became identified with the spiritual destinies of the churches. What Will Herberg described as the "American Way of Life" became a dogma common to both Republic and religion. The "civil religion," compounded of equal parts of Fourth of July oratory and Holy Writ, seemed to have replaced the biblical tradition of prophetic (or critical) utterance. To a few Catholic dissenters such as Dorothy Day of the Catholic Worker movement, it seemed that in gaining respectability the church was in danger of losing its soul.

In the story of Joe McCarthy and the Catholic bishops, ironies abounded. Most observers agreed that the church was an authoritarian institution, yet in the McCarthy controversy the Catholic laity openly denounced a member of the hierarchy. All Catholics agreed that the church was somehow one (that is to say, a sign of its "truth" was that the church was manifestly an indissoluble union); yet in this instance the bishops openly disagreed with each other. All Americans agreed on the sanctity of separation of church and state, yet Catholics pressed their argument to move for (or against) their fellow Catholic, Joe McCarthy. All Catholics would agree that the church ought to speak out on imperative moral issues, yet the bishops not only disagreed about whether McCarthyism was such an issue but whether they ought to discuss it at all. Finally, most non-Catholics still assumed that Rome was the dominating force behind American Catholicism, yet the American church was blithely choosing its own course without any apparent sign of direction from the pope. American Catholicism, in short, was fully Americanized (Gibbons, Ireland, and the other Americanizers of the 1890s would have liked that), but how Catholic was it?

As the decade advanced, Americanization proceeded apace, and so did the national dispute over McCarthy. The argument between the Sheil faction and the Spellman contingent helped focus public attention on McCarthy's duel with the Defense Department. After five months that bitter controversy entered its climactic and most critical stage. The hearings soon became a staple part of daytime television, thus bringing the debate into the American home. It seemed that the American family would have the last word on McCarthy. And the American Catholic family played a key role in that decision, not only because it made up over a fifth of the population, but because the Catholic hierarchy had succeeded so well in calling attention to the junior senator from Wisconsin.

Chapter 8

The Army–McCarthy Hearings: Conclusion and Aftermath

Exasperated by six months of fruitless warfare with McCarthy, the army finally mustered enough anti-McCarthy feeling in the Senate to force the issue against the senator. For the first time in the history of that body, a committee of the Senate voted to investigate both a list of charges proposed by a committee chairman and a set of accusations made against the same person. Thus on 16 March 1954 McCarthy's own Permanent Investigations Subcommittee (an arm of the Committee on Government Operations) began hearing the McCarthy–Cohn indictments against the army as well as the army's own bill of particulars against McCarthy and Cohn. From 22 April until 17 June 1954, the hearings appeared on nationwide television, reaching the largest audience in the history of the medium up to that time.

McCarthy's television image could hardly have been worse: he looked every inch the blustering, shouting bully that the *Commonweal* had always said he was. An audience estimated at twenty million watched in silent fascination as he made his endless "points of order," interrupted the testimony of witnesses, and shouted that the army was deliberately trying to evade his charges of misconduct and softness on communism.

The show that McCarthy and the Pentagon put on was lively (if unenlightening), and nowhere did viewers seem to enjoy it more than in Irish Catholic Boston, where a Trendex survey showed that Boston had the highest percentage of viewers in the country. A study by George Gallup showed something even more revealing about the Boston audience: Boston was the only city in the country where

Like a leaking balloon, nothing could plug the leak

viewers sided with Senator McCarthy against the army.[1] The senator's apparently heavy support among Catholics in Boston was all the more surprising in view of his continued decline across the nation. The Gallup poll for May 1954 showed that his popularity among Catholics had fallen from 46 percent in April to 43 percent. (The Protestant McCarthyites had dwindled to an all-time low of 30 percent.)[2] At the same time, however, it seemed that fewer and fewer Catholics entertained truly strong feelings about the senator; both Catholics and Protestants seemed to be pulling back from the controversy—except of course in Boston, where the citizenry seemed to be taking an unwonted interest in the senator. In the following months the sectors of both Catholicism and Protestantism with no opinion about McCarthy grew markedly, until by the time of McCarthy's censure in December, they constituted nearly one-third of both groups.

Meanwhile, the "hard core" of McCarthy's conservative Catholic following remained firmly convinced of the truth of his cause. The *Brooklyn Tablet*, for instance, wrote that the "higher-ups" in the government had decided to direct charges against McCarthy and Cohn in order to take attention away from the army. It also took aim at the Democratic members of the investigating committee—Senators McClellan, Symington, and Jackson—who had fought bitterly with McCarthy from the first days of his dispute with the military. It accused them of trying to smear McCarthy instead of attempting to find out the truth of his charges against the army.[3] Anxious as always to practice what they preached, the *Tablet*'s devoted readers sent copies of one especially strident article to President Eisenhower, but his aides filed them away without making a reply.[4] Sharing the *Tablet*'s viewpoint was Senator Patrick McCarran, conservative Catholic Democrat from Nevada. McCarran gave a rousing McCarthyite speech on 1 May 1954 before the Catholic War Veterans of Manchester, New Hampshire, warning that the Communists and their sympathizers were anxious to destroy McCarthy because he had become the very "symbol of anticommunism in America."

Concluding on the militant note he knew the veterans would like, he cried dramatically, "Catholic War Veterans, you who wear the uniform and beared [sic] your breasts against our foes, [you] face an even greater struggle today. You must don the shield and sword so that America may stand against the foe of communism."[5] In a few weeks the CWV in Manchester and New York City did precisely that: they donned the sword of justice and the breastplate of righteousness in a frantic eleventh-hour attempt to save McCarthy from the censure of the Senate.

Among the truly fervent McCarthyites, the notion persisted that McCarthy had become a kind of crucified Christ figure. An Irish Catholic gentleman in Iowa, for instance, wrote that as he looked at the Army-McCarthy hearings during "Holy Week and the Holy Season of Lent," the similarity between Jesus Christ and Joe McCarthy "seemed very striking." In the cases of both Jesus and Joe McCarthy, he noticed that the persecutors practiced the "same sly propaganda and mass hysteria." The "average person who condemns Senator McCarthy has no more reason" to condemn him "than those who cried 'Crucify Him' two thousand years ago."[6] *Ave Maria* took a more worldly view, saying that the hearings had distracted the nation and the Congress from the urgent business of getting at "the enemy" who is "boring from without and from within." It hoped that the hearings would end soon "because somebody is setting the house on fire while we are trying to fix a leak in the sink."[7]

McCarthy's embattled enemies within Catholicism had not changed their minds, either. The *Commonweal* thought that the televised hearings might actually do some good, because they would show the American public precisely what McCarthy's style was: "The doctored photo, the constant interruptions, the speeches under the guise of points of order," all of which had long been part of the "McCarthy operation," would be exposed to full view. The editors hoped that the nation would finally begin to move against McCarthy; more important still, they hoped that the country could finally start to take "effective action to deal with the Communist threat."[8]

The staff of the *Catholic Worker* (the weekly organ of the Catholic labor movement bearing the same name) found the spectacle both awesome and appalling. Dorothy Day (founder of the movement) described it as a "grim game being played for rank and reputation," with both McCarthy and his military opponents "trying to ruin each other." True to its belief that charity always came first, the *Worker's* staff lamented the manner in which "hatred" had begun to rule America: "Satan, the father of lies . . . is taking us for that proverbial ride to an historical junkyard."[9]

While the liberal Catholic press criticized McCarthy's role in the television proceedings, evidence appeared in other quarters of growing discontent with the senator. Catholic labor groups, which had vigorously opposed McCarthy from the start, began waging a public campaign against him. The labor publication *Work*, the organ of the Association of Catholic Trade Unionists in Chicago, said that McCarthy's brand of anticommunism was "half-baked, if not phony." What the world needed was a truly Christian social order, it said. "What good . . . have I done for my neighbor where I live and where I work?" it wanted Catholics to ask themselves.[10] Inspiring the editorial in *Work* was a speech that Bishop John F. Hackett of Hartford, Connecticut, had given to a labor group in that state. The bishop had denied that it was enough to be "merely against Communists. We must be for the necessities of a decent living. . . . This is the type of anticommunism which will keep America strong."[11] Like the other Catholic bishops, Hackett scrupulously avoided any direct reference to McCarthy.

Although Catholics divided angrily over the many bitter "incidents" that characterized the Army-McCarthy proceedings, they disagreed with especial vehemence over McCarthy's repeated attempts to persuade government employees to hand him classified government documents. Since the president had issued orders expressly forbidding federal workers from doing this, a sharp split was developing between the senator and the White House. The issue

The leaders and McCarthy's willingness to use it.

reached a climax in May 1954 when an unnamed army officer snatched a "secret" document from government files and delivered it to the senator. The liberals chorused their astonishment at McCarthy's breach of security as well as his assault on the authority of the chief executive. The *Commonweal* branded the officer's action "a kind of patriotic anarchy" designed to destroy the principle of authority in government. The magazine feared that if every clerk in Washington did what McCarthy's man had done, then anarchy would rule the nation. The *Commonweal* worried that McCarthy had set himself "above all law" in order to reduce the rest of the government to "impotence." "Here lies the seed of that anarchy which has so often been the prelude to dictatorship," it warned.[12]

The Reverend James Gillis strenuously demurred and reached into traditional Catholic theology to fashion an argument in defense of McCarthy's actions. The "young army officer" who handed over the document had acted according to his conscience, Gillis wrote, and he reminded his readers that the Catholic church had unfailingly insisted that one must always act according to the dictates of conscience. The "significant fact" in this case, Gillis observed, was that "McCarthy's view is equivalently that of Christian ethics." He gave the young officer great credit for following his conscience but noted unhappily that other Catholic publications had failed to do the same.[13] Father Gillis, however, overlooked a complicating factor in this argument based on conscience: what satisfied the young army officer's conscience clearly violated the moral scruples of McCarthy's opponents. In other words, what was one man's virtue was another man's vice. *Vice and virtue.*

At the same time that the televised hearings were bringing the Army-McCarthy show to millions of Catholic households across the country, they were causing a major crisis at the offices of *America* (the national Jesuit weekly) in downtown Manhattan. Since October 1952 the editor of the magazine, Father Robert Hartnett, and his Jesuit associates had been fighting the constitutional case against McCarthy, rebuking him for his encroachments on executive privilege and his cavalier attitude toward civil liberties. From the beginning of their anti-McCarthy phase, they had been under growing pressure from both their readers and their fellow Jesuits to recant, but the whirlwind of abuse and repression that they reaped in May and June of 1954 far exceeded anything that they had seen in the earlier days.

After a series of editorials rebuking McCarthy for his disruptive tactics in the hearings, *America* softened its line somewhat. It went out of its way in late March and April to praise the "wholly admirable" instincts of McCarthy's Catholic adherents, insisting only that the "particular good" of rooting Communists out of the government ought not to interfere with the more important "common good," or the welfare of the whole nation.[14] What *America* said was not soft enough, however, to mollify its Catholic critics, who sent it an avalanche of protest mail. "The situation here is undoubtedly becoming awkward," Hartnett worried, noting especially the "emotionalism" of the Catholic McCarthyites.[15]

In mid-April *America* published most of the mail it had received on McCarthy, and nothing gave a better illustration of the verbal mayhem that had crept into the Catholic dispute over the senator. A priest in upstate New York, for instance, wrote that he would not be canceling his subscription to the magazine since he had been wise enough not to have one in the first place. Nevertheless, he believed that if enough subscribers did so, "it might bring you to your senses. Please accept my prayers for your conversion." A reader in Toledo, Ohio, wrote curiously, "Senator McCarthy is a good Catholic. . . . Look at his enemies: the Daily Worker, Tito, and Stevenson—a divorced man and member of the ADA."[16] (The writer erred grievously on the last two points. Stevenson's wife had sued him for divorce, and not the other way around; many Catholics made this same mistake, however, and with Catholics so firmly convinced of the "evils of divorce," it was no small matter with them. Nor had he ever been a member of the ADA, though many conservative Catholics unaccountably thought that he was.)

Notwithstanding its Catholic critics, *America* still had its supporters in the church. A man in Connecticut wrote that he dreaded the "slowly developing but perceptible undercurrent of public opinion that whispers that the Church approves of Senator McCarthy because he is a Catholic." Others shared his viewpoint and took *America*'s side in the dispute.[17]

America might well have been able to ride out the stormy seas of McCarthyism had it not been for a blistering attack that Hartnett administered to McCarthy in the issue for 22 May 1954. No Catholic essay on McCarthy, either for him or against him, ever attracted as much attention as Hartnett's vigorous editorial, "'Peaceful Overthrow' of the U.S. Presidency." (The occasion of the piece was McCarthy's acceptance of the classified documents from the "young army officer.") Hartnett's editorial warned of the "grave constitutional issue posed by Senator McCarthy's 'methods.'" His actions seriously threatened the "rule of law," which was the "hallmark of free government," Hartnett wrote. The president was the choice of all the people and was responsible to all of them, he continued. Therefore it was the obligation of the whole country to decide whether the president was properly discharging his duties; McCarthy had no business arrogating the nation's duty to himself. Hartnett feared that McCarthy was bringing about a "peaceful" but nevertheless "piecemeal" overthrow of the presidency, an act of rebellion that might well do immense harm to the American system of government.[18]

Liberal newspapers across the country took note of Hartnett's editorial, some of them printing long passages from it.[19] All of this was too much for the *Brooklyn Tablet*, which immediately attacked *America*. It quoted "a number of prominent Jesuits" who said that the publication represented the thinking of only a "small number" within the order. One Jesuit even wrote the *Tablet*, "From the logic of the article it sounds as though Eleanor Roosevelt wrote it." (The former first lady, be it noted, was no favorite of the Catholic conservatives, who not only disliked her liberal views but had come to the bizarre and unfounded conclusion that she was anti-Catholic.) The *Tablet* argued that McCarthy was seeking, "not to destroy the Presidency, but to save it from its enemies within the Government itself."[20] The national press also picked up the *Tablet*'s rejoinder to *America*, thus making a national event out of a debate between two Catholic weeklies.[21] Never one to ignore an unfounded attack, Hartnett wrote an immediate reply to the *Tablet*, saying that there simply was no "official Jesuit position" on McCarthy and that the Jesuit editors of the periodical were completely free to say whatever they believed was just and reasonable. Becoming a little defensive, he concluded that the superiors of the order had chosen the editors because they believed them to have the "necessary qualifications" for this "difficult and specialized work."[22]

Hartnett's Jesuit enemies remained utterly unmoved by his arguments. Ready now to take the battle into the public arena, they wrote to both the *Brooklyn Tablet* and the *New York Journal-American* (a pro-McCarthy Hearst publication) expressing their bitter disagreement with *America*. The *Tablet* and the *Journal-American* were only too happy to print the letters, since they were anxious to discredit the anti-McCarthy forces. One Jesuit from Wisconsin wrote that *America*'s editors represented only "a minority opinion," and besides, only Jesuit superiors "speak officially for American Jesuits."[23]

While the battle of the Jesuits was occupying the New York press, the Jesuit brethren were fighting it out in private as well. Some of the order's communities in New York City disagreed so violently over the McCarthy-*America* question that they finally decided, quite on their own, not to discuss the subject any more. Meanwhile, the superior of the New York Jesuits, the Reverend John McMahon, was coming under increasing and severe pressure to discipline *America*. The most impassioned letters he received came, not surprisingly, from other New York Jesuits who believed that the magazine's militant stand on McCarthy was bringing deep embarrassment to the order.[24] McMahon replied noncommittally to their pleas, as he did to similar missives from lay Catholics. (One layman even hinted that donations to the Jesuits might dry up if *America* did not change its tune.)[25]

As it happened, neither donations to the order nor complaints to *America* showed signs of diminishing. So many objections against the magazine came into St. Patrick's Cathedral that it cancelled its subscription.[26] More serious than that, however, were the violent and abusive telephone calls that inundated *America*'s switchboard. In the first few days immediately after the 22 May editorial, the McCarthyites bombarded *America* with angry calls, so many of them coming in that the editors had to take turns answering them. "The same Irish voices kept calling," one of the assistant editors recalls.[27] And as always, irate readers mailed their furious thoughts to the magazine: some seventy "shocked" and "outraged" letters arrived immediately after the publication of the now famous editorial.[28]

At the height of the uproar, someone shot a bullet through the front door of St. Ignatius Church, the Jesuit parish on Park Avenue in New York City. No one knows who shot the gun, or for what reason, but it was widely assumed that the 22 May editorial had caused the incident.[29] So anxious had the New York Jesuits become over the McCarthy crisis that they were ready to attribute even acts of violence to the McCarthyites.

It seemed that the furor over Hartnett's essay had begun to abate slightly when on 29 May *America*'s superiors suddenly silenced the magazine on the topic of Senator McCarthy. Nothing could have come as more of a shock to Hartnett, since he knew that his superiors had long resisted pressures to silence the journal. What had happened? Though the superiors had no intention of yielding to the power tactics of the Catholic McCarthyites, they were deeply worried about the way that the McCarthy dispute had divided the nation's Jesuits, and had done so in a public manner. The founder of the order, Ignatius of Loyoia, had repeatedly inveighed against public arguments between Jesuits, believing that unity in thought and action would be the key to their future success. Clearly the Jesuit debate over McCarthy violated this rule. Furthermore, *America* seemed to be breaking a long-standing command not to engage in "disputes among Catholics," a directive that went back to the founding of the periodical some fifty years earlier and that was still in effect. Finally, *America*'s superiors believed that in its zeal to pursue the McCarthy question, it had neglected other issues that were "hardly less important than the Army-McCarthy case." Thus on 29 May 1954 the magazine's superiors directed it to drop the McCarthy topic and to keep their directive strictly secret.[30]

Hartnett immediately protested the decision, as indeed the Jesuit rule allowed him to do. He argued not only that it would be impossible to keep the order a secret for long but that it violated the principle of freedom of expression, which he believed to be of paramount importance both to the magazine and to the church in America. If *America* were allowed to continue to speak its mind on McCarthy, he thought that everyone would see that the Catholic church believed in open debate and freedom of thought. He argued that if *America* had achieved any success at all, it was because of the latitude that it had always enjoyed, a freedom that the directive might destroy entirely.[31] Responding to Hartnett's pleas, the superiors modified their earlier order. They allowed *America*'s editors to write about McCarthy, provided that they acted as "censors" for each other and that they avoided the subject unless the "good of the Church" clearly required it.[32] Hartnett was in full agreement with the revised order and accepted it "with gratitude."[33] In effect, the magazine was free to say whatever it wished about McCarthy.

The problem would undoubtedly have ended at that point, if the Father General of the Jesuits in Rome had not intervened abruptly. The Reverend John Baptist Janssens, who had been following the *America*-McCarthy dispute with intense interest, in June 1954 ordered *America*'s superiors in the United States to take a hard line on the magazine:

I am deeply grieved that some of Ours [Jesuits] have chosen to express, in the public press, opposition to a periodical of the Society, and have done this bitterly. . . . Dissension, which St. Ignatius abhorred, has broken out among his sons, and in public at that. I am amazed that local Superiors and censors . . . have allowed a dispute of this kind to come to light.

But if we look for the deeper reason for this sad state of affairs, we find it in the failure of the Editor of *America* to follow the precepts which my predecessor has so clearly enunciated: 'Merely political or secular matters should not be a concern of our periodical. Bitter disputes among Catholics are to be avoided even more assiduously'. . . . Knowing these words, who can fail to see that this acrid dispute . . . should be excluded from the pages of this magazine? In fact, it should never have been discussed. I cannot fail to think that the Fathers Provincial [superiors], especially those assigned to the direction of the magazine, have failed somehow in their duty. Therefore, let the Fathers Provincial see to it that the Editor withdraws himself from this dispute immediately.[34]

In a later communication he expanded further on what seemed to bother him most of all, namely Hartnett's belief that the magazine ought to have complete freedom of expression. To Janssens this was errant nonsense: every Jesuit should understand that the order "gives no one a freedom to write which is not subject to strict censorship." He expected the superiors to make sure that in the future they exercised their function of censorship with the greatest zeal.[35] With the McCarthy question authoritatively settled by Rome, the Jesuit superiors relayed Janssens's unyielding order to Hartnett, who accepted it quietly and without protest.[36] *America* said nothing more about McCarthy until his death in 1957, when it noted the senator's demise almost in passing.[37]

Drained from the long battle with the McCarthyites and thoroughly "sick of the thing," as he said of the McCarthy affair, Hartnett took a long vacation. In September 1955 he retired from the editorship of *America*.[38] Rumors still persist that his superiors "fired" him from his post because of the McCarthy episode, but no documentary evidence exists to prove this. On the contrary, the voluminous evidence in the archives of the New York Jesuits shows that Hartnett retired because he was worn out, tired of the job, and believed that the magazine needed a new man at the helm.[39] Nor is it accurate to say that he was fired "in effect," since it is obvious that the letters from Rome (and from Hartnett's superiors in the United States) had nothing to do with the editor's retirement.

In looking back at the episode (one so painful that the editors of

America still wince when they talk about it), it seems clear that Janssens overreacted. The furor over the editorial was subsiding, Hartnett was ready to take a softer tone on McCarthy, and local superiors clearly had the situation well under control. Janssens's intervention therefore was precipitous, blunt, and peremptory. His letters to the American superiors showed his authoritarian and repressive tendencies at their worst: his high-handed regime as General of the Jesuits saw him cooperate zealously in efforts to suppress such leading Jesuit intellectuals as John Courtney Murray, Henri de Lubac, and the celebrated French anthropologist Pierre Teilhard de Chardin. Fearful both of innovations in the church and of Jesuit involvement in controversy, he worked tirelessly to form a body of men who asked no questions and did what they were told. One of the casualties of this approach was *America*, whose anti-McCarthy policy came to an abrupt and highly mysterious end. By contrast to Janssens, the magazine's superiors in the United States had acted with considerable flexibility, tolerance, and respect for intellectual freedom. Under intense pressure to silence the magazine, they had only asked for moderation in the face of an issue of immense dispute. The pity is that they did not get the chance to let *America* pursue it to the end.

Yet the McCarthy debate went on, largely because of McCarthy's obstreperous performance on television. For almost two months the nation watched him cavort before the cameras, seeming to confuse everything and settle nothing. If the army had failed to prove its charges of undue pressure on behalf of Private G. David Schine, the senator had yet to demonstrate the truth of his contention that security risks infested the United States Army. Though the Pentagon's witnesses and functionaries had sometimes appeared inept and confused, McCarthy had come across to the viewing public as bullying, sarcastic, and thoroughly destructive of the established order.

The emotional climax of the hearings came on 9 June, when McCarthy had a celebrated encounter with Joseph L. Welch, the counsel for the army. McCarthy had learned that a young lawyer in Welch's Boston law firm, one Frederick G. Fisher, had once belonged to a lawyer's association that subsequently had been accused of Communistic leanings. Though Fisher had long since left the organization and had maintained a record of impeccable loyalty, Welch decided to drop him from the case anyway, lest McCarthy be tempted to use Fisher's past associations in a way harmful to Fisher or to the army. Welch, however, had not adequately reckoned with Senator McCarthy.

In the middle of a heated exchange between Cohn and Welch, McCarthy suddenly interrupted the argument by charging that Fred Fisher "has been for a number of years a member of an organization which was named . . . years ago, as the legal bulwark of the Communist Party."[40] Welch stared in disbelief at McCarthy: "Until this moment, Senator, I think I never really gauged your cruelty or your recklessness. . . . Little did I dream you could be so reckless and so cruel as to do an injury to that lad. It is true he is still with Hale and Door [Welch's Boston law firm]. It is true that he will continue to be with Hale and Door. It is, I regret to say, equally true that I fear he shall always bear a scar needlessly inflicted by you. If it were in my power to forgive you for your reckless cruelty, I would do so. I like to think I am a gentleman, but your forgiveness will have to come from someone other than me."[41] Undaunted and unimpressed, McCarthy persisted with his pursuit of Fisher, but Welch cut him short: "Let us not assassinate this lad further, Senator. You have done enough. Have you no sense of decency, sir, at long last? Have you left no sense of decency?"[42] When McCarthy tried once again to raise an argument over Fisher, Welch put a definitive halt to the matter: "Mr. McCarthy, I will not discuss this with you further. You have sat within six feet of me, and could have asked me about Fred Fisher. You have brought it out. If there is a God in heaven, it will do neither you nor your cause any good."[43]

To be sure, the frenzied exchange over Fred Fisher had done McCarthy's cause no good at all. Many Americans who had been content to let the senator go his way, or who simply refused to take him seriously, suddenly found themselves in deep doubt about his actions. The results showed themselves in the Gallup poll for June, which revealed a continued erosion of his support. Although his strength among Catholics had risen four points (to 47 percent) since the previous month, so had the number of Catholics who expressed intense disapproval of him (they were up four points to 31.8 percent). Among Protestants the figures were about the same as in May, except that 6 percent of them said they strongly disapproved of McCarthy.[44] No matter how one interpreted the figures, it was apparent that he had continued to slip among all classes, Catholics not excepted.

Knowing this only too well, the anti-McCarthy forces in the Senate decided that the time was right for a concerted attack on his power in the upper house; if necessary, they would even try to cripple him entirely by stripping him of his committee chairmanships. The unlikely linchpin in this structure was the crusty, conservative Republican senator from Vermont, Ralph Flanders. Believing that the Senate had temporized far too long with its most troublesome member, he addressed the upper chamber on 1 June 1954, detailing McCarthy's destructive impact on the country. He took especially careful note of the way the senator had set "church against church" and even "Catholic against Catholic." Only recently, he pointed out, Cardinal Spellman had made an obvious political appearance at the New York police communion breakfast honoring McCarthy. "But soon, thank God," Bishop Sheil spoke out, telling the country that McCarthy was dividing it instead of uniting it. "Thus it became evident that Dennis the Menace had driven his blundering axe deep into the heart of his own church," he concluded.[45]

"Dennis the Menace" was quick to reply, angrily attacking Flanders for raising the religious issue at a time when it was thoroughly irrelevant to the question at hand.[46] A few days later Archbishop Richard Cushing of Boston commented on Flanders's statement: it was one of the vague, rambling, Eisenhoweresque comments that he loved to give when asked controversial questions. Queried about his reation to Flanders's speech, he said that McCarthy "certainly is not dividing the Church," because there is no such thing as a "Catholic attitude on McCarthy" and "Catholics can go the way they will."[47] What did he personally think about McCarthy? "The whole thing depends on how you look at communism. If you look upon it as one of the greatest evils that has attempted to undermine western civilization, naturally you do everything you can to save our way of life from the inroads of this evil." Asked if he meant that he sympathized with McCarthy, he said, "I sympathize with anybody interested in keeping communism in all its phases and forms from uprooting our traditions and our wonderful opportunity of assuming the leadership throughout the world that is the only hope of oppressed people."[48] Blessed with a convoluted syntax that only Eisenhower could match, Cushing showed his undoubted ability to slip nimbly down the middle path, all the while saying virtually nothing. Like many another Catholic American chary of the McCarthy issue, Cushing wanted to support the senator the same way that he would support any anti-Communist; yet he shrank back from endorsing him openly and unequivocally.[49] Still less did he assault Senator Ralph Flanders from Vermont.

No such compunctions restrained Cardinal Spellman. When told of Flanders's remark about McCarthy dividing Catholics, Spellman retorted, "Is Flanders uniting us? That's outside of his province. I'd stick to the welfare of the state." When reporters told him that Flanders had wondered if his presence at the police breakfast was a vote of support for McCarthy, he said that Flanders should "write me a letter if he wants to know." Spellman, a native of Massachusetts, said he was "surprised that a New Englander could be that naive."[50] Behind Spellman's riposte was more than simply a battle of words over Joe McCarthy; as an Irish Catholic from New England, he had little use for flinty WASPS like Flanders, and he wanted to make the most of a rare opportunity to denounce his kind.

With the opinion polls for the summer months showing the

McCarthy forces in a steep decline, the movement to censure him began to gain momentum. No group realized this more clearly than the Catholic McCarthyites in New York City, who intensified their efforts to defend the senator. As usual the *Brooklyn Tablet* led the attack, this time letting its rage fly at Frederick Woltman, who wrote a series of articles extremely critical of McCarthy in the *New York World-Telegram* (the Scripps-Howard newspaper in New York City). At one time a McCarthy supporter, Woltman reversed directions completely in the summer of 1954; one suspects that this change of heart, more than the articles themselves, is what enraged the *Tablet*. Whatever the reason, the paper lashed Woltman in a scathing editorial on 17 July, and on the following Sunday the *Tablet*'s supporters distributed copies of the editorial to Catholics attending Sunday Mass throughout the New York City area. Some Catholics tore out the editorial and mailed it to Woltman, adding what an observer from the *Nation* called "scabrous marginal notations."[51]

The New Yorkers suffered an even more formidable setback when McCarthy's opponents in the Senate forced Roy M. Cohn off the staff of his subcommittee. The *Tablet* warned that Cohn's removal would be "pleasing to Soviet Russia and her minions in this Country, but frightening, in its implications, to every informed, loyal American."[52] The "informed" and the "loyal," however, had their day of revenge on 28 July when Cohn's supporters gave him a testimonial dinner at New York's Hotel Astor. Although the event was truly the "rousing triumph" for Cohn that the *Tablet* said it was, some observers also thought that it had been a conspicuously "Catholic" demonstration as well. Catholic orators dominated the speech making of the evening, with the principal addresses coming from four members of that faith: William F. Buckley, Jr., Dean Clarence Manion of the University of Notre Dame's School of Law, Reverend James Gillis, and Professor Godfrey Schmidt of Fordham University. An Irish tenor, Mr. John Feeney, entertained the throng with patriotic and Irish songs, and copies of the *Irish Echo* were on the tables. In the opinion of the reporter from the *Commonweal*, it was a largely "Irish-Catholic gathering." He thought that the crowd looked like the kind one might see at the "graduation exercises of an Irish Christian Brothers' high school. I felt, with a chill, very much at home."[53] As expected, the Catholic War Veterans of Queens County, the Holy Name Society, and the Ancient Order of Hibernians had taken a leading role in the proceedings of the evening.[54]

The occasion was much more a celebration of McCarthyism than of Catholicism, however, and denominational affiliation really had little to do with the occasion. Yet to the throng present at the hotel that night, Cohn was right, McCarthy was right, and Cohn was only the first martyr with McCarthy sure to follow. Many Catholics in New York fervently shared the same thesis.

While the McCarthy censure movement was gaining day by day, the church's clerical and lay leadership in New York continued to propound the McCarthyite thesis, with only a handful of Catholic spokesmen defending the opposite cause. And it was surely no accident that many New York Catholics mobilized in defense of McCarthy. Nowhere in America did Catholic fraternal organizations have the combination of large numbers and conservative political power that they enjoyed in New York. The Catholic War Veterans had chapters all across the nation, but none as large, as efficiently organized, and as politically active as in Queens and Brooklyn. The Holy Name Society, the Knights of Columbus, the Ancient Order of Hibernians, and many similar groups rivalled the CWV in their right-wing sentiments and political activism. Orchestrating all of these militant efforts was the *Brooklyn Tablet*, which faithfully chronicled every Catholic political success, ascribed every failure to the deviltry of the opposition, and mapped out future plans of action. If conservative Catholicism's drive to "save McCarthy" seemed to center in New York, it was because it had the numbers, the organization, and the driving leadership. When the movement shifted into high gear in the autumn and winter months of 1954, the great strength of conservative New York Catholicism became even more apparent.

The *Brooklyn Tablet* spearheaded and marshaled the campaign to save McCarthy. Beginning in early May 1954 the paper intensified its coverage of the censure fight, putting a McCarthy editorial on the front page of almost every issue in addition to increasing its coverage of the Senate's actions against him. As the weeks passed by, its tone became increasingly shrill, viewing the senator's "enemies" in ever harsher terms, while McCarthy himself began to look more and more like a martyr. The *Tablet*'s thesis was familiar enough: the Communists were directing the anti-McCarthy drive, the press was carrying on a "shocking" and "scandalous" smear campaign against him, the Senate was stripping him of his constitutional rights, and a malevolent "conspiracy" was organizing the whole shoddy attempt to destroy him.[55] What was striking and new was the style of its writing, one that was far more strident than before and that betrayed a sense of desperation and even of impending defeat.

Fear struck the hearts of the Catholic McCarthyites when the Senate on 2 August appointed a "select committee" to examine the many charges that had been made against McCarthy's conduct. Chaired by the impeccably conservative and Republican Senator Arthur Watkins of Utah, the panel of three Republicans and three Democrats went about its business in a glacially impartial fashion that consoled McCarthy's enemies but infuriated the dedicated McCarthyites. One of the most enraged was the editor of the *Tablet*, Patrick F. Scanlan, who believed that the Watkins committee was "a loaded jury determined to 'get' McCarthy." He called the committee a "travesty of justice," and he accused the members of gross bias against the senator.[56] The *Commonweal*, on the other hand, thought that the group could not have been better; it especially liked the conservative makeup of the Watkins committee, since McCarthy represented "what can only be described as radicalism of the right."[57]

After two weeks of tense hearings that saw Chairman Watkins gaveling McCarthy into virtual impotence, the committee handed down its findings. In a unanimous report it recommended censure on two counts: first, his failure to cooperate with the Gillette-Hennings subcommittee that had tried to investigate his finances in 1952 and second, his abusive treatment of General Zwicker during the Army-McCarthy hearings. The Watkins report deeply alarmed the *Tablet*, which feared that it would lead to a "totalitarian policy of conformity of thought." The paper was concerned that future sessions of Congress might well censure their members simply for exercising their freedom of speech. If the paper's defense of civil liberties came as a surprise, its description of Watkins did not ("a calloused, unrelenting, biased prosecutor bereft of the quality of mercy") nor did its summation of the committee's work ("a preposterous, vindictive and disgraceful performance").[58]

The *Commonweal* showed unexpected magnanimity: it professed itself concerned about McCarthy's "present misfortunes," believing that "in the defeat even of demagogues there are elements of tragedy." Nevertheless, it believed that he had received what he had long and richly deserved—a "major, and historic, rebuke."[59] Democrats everywhere could agree with the *Commonweal* that the report had been a rebuke, but some Democrats in the Senate were unwilling to debate the report (fearing even at this late date the power of the McCarthyites), and many Republicans shared the same worries. Believing that it was the better part of prudence to leave the McCarthy bomb alone, the Senate voted to defer debate until after the November congressional elections. The elections of 1954, therefore, became the focus of attention, with the senator himself promising to become one of the major issues of the campaign. If the Senate had shorn him of much of his political power (and assuredly it had), he still remained a potent political issue, at least in the minds of many observers. But with his following dispirited and diminished, how strong would he be?

Chapter 9

Catholics and the McCarthy Censure Movement

Though the Senate had voted to defer formal debate on McCarthy until after the congressional elections in November, discussions of McCarthyism did not come to an end. Rather, the McCarthy question became one of the many issues in the campaign, just as it had entered the electoral contests of 1950 and 1952. The McCarthyites hoped desperately that the GOP might retain its slim control of the Congress, believing that with the Republicans remaining in power, McCarthy had a slim chance to stave off censure. It was a slight chance indeed, for he had become an albatross to his own party, with most Republicans refusing his help in the campaign. Should the Democrats succeed in winning back both houses (not an unlikely prospect in an off-year election), then the McCarthyites would face an exceedingly bleak future, for the "party of treason" (as McCarthy had styled it) would take the vote as a mandate to wreak vengeance on the junior senator.

Would Catholics vote the McCarthyism issue in the coming elections? If the question ever occurred to President Eisenhower, he gave no indication of it. Some of the Democrats, however, continued to monitor his Catholic followers with great care, hoping to find some indication of how Catholics would vote in November. In late August 1954 the CIO (acting in concert with the Democrats) commissioned a survey of both Catholic and non-Catholic opinion on McCarthy in ten key states—California, Illinois, Iowa, Massachusetts, Michigan, Minnesota, New Jersey, New Mexico, Ohio, and Oregon. Senator John Kennedy's staff took a long look at the polls, and undoubtedly other Democrats did the same. The most striking result of the sampling was the large number of both Catholics and non-Catholics who took no interest at all in the question of Senator Joe McCarthy. When asked whether the Senate ought to strip McCarthy of his committee chairmanship, 40 to 50 percent of the Catholics polled said that it was immaterial to them, and a slightly smaller proportion of the non-Catholics (35 to 45 percent) shared the same view. When asked if it made any difference to them whether McCarthy favored or opposed a given candidate, 50 to 60 percent said that it was immaterial; among the non-Catholics some 45 to 55 percent said the same thing.[1] It seemed clear that many Catholics, just as many non-Catholics, had decided that the McCarthy issue was dead, and they were ready to turn (probably with no regrets) to other problems.

Though the study showed unmistakably that Catholic McCarthyism was on the decline, it also revealed that the senator still possessed a reservoir of strength among the Catholics in Massachusetts. It was obvious, in fact, that his greatest strength by far lay in that state. The Bay State was the only one in which Catholics favoring a McCarthyite candidate outnumbered those who opposed such a candidate; in all the other states the larger group was the one that said that it would oppose a McCarthyite running for office. Massachusetts's Catholics also showed strong resistance to candidates who wanted McCarthy stripped of his chairmanship, with 40 percent opposing such a candidate and only 14 percent favoring him. The marked conservatism of the state's Catholics appeared in two other areas as well: more of them favored breaking off diplomatic relations with Russia than opposed such a move, and they were against trading with Russia and Red China.[2] Every possible indicator showed that McCarthy's Catholic support was stronger in Massachusetts than in any of the other nine states that the pollsters examined. The large number of Catholics with no opinion, however, showed that the issue of McCarthyism was declining in political significance. In short, Joe McCarthy had committed what John Roche called the "cardinal political sin, that of boring the populace."[3]

The CIO survey demonstrated that McCarthy's second largest pocket of Catholic strength was in New Jersey, though Catholics in that state lagged far behind their coreligionists of Massachusetts in their enthusiasm for the junior senator. The New Jersey Catholics, like those of Massachusetts, opposed candidates pledged to taking McCarthy's chairmanship away from him, but only by a slight margin. The state's Catholic voters joined Catholics in the other nine states, however, in opposing McCarthyite candidates for office. Since New Jersey was approximately 40 percent Catholic, the poll's findings gave no real encouragement to McCarthy's Catholic adherents in that state.[4]

In only two other states did McCarthy show even marginal Catholic support. They were Illinois (27 percent Catholic) and Ohio (19 percent Catholic). In both states one found a slightly larger number of Catholics who wanted McCarthy to keep his chairmanship, but far more important was the remarkable percentage of Catholics (from 40 to 60 percent) who showed no interest at all in the McCarthy problem. Furthermore, the number of Catholics opposing McCarthyite candidates was markedly larger than those in favor of them.[5] In the remaining states of the Middle West and Far West, McCarthy had no significant Catholic support at all, though it is worth noting that he was slightly more popular with Catholics in those states than with non-Catholics.[6] It would be wrong to place too much stress on this fact, however, since the number of Catholics who dismissed the McCarthy issue as insignificant was noticeably high, running from 40 to 60 percent. In sum, the nation's Catholics, like everyone else, were ready to wash their hands of Joe McCarthy. The senator's protracted wrangling with the army and the televised hearings had done their work: the people, tired of his endless indictments and spy hunts, longed for a change of headlines.

When the University of Michigan's Survey Research Center conducted a similar study in October 1954, it arrived at virtually the same results as the CIO poll taken in late August. A slightly larger number of Catholics opposed McCarthy than favored him, although almost half of the group polled (48 percent) remained steadfastly neutral. Though the study found that McCarthy's popularity was marginally greater among Catholics than among Protestants and Jews, the large number of Protestants remaining neutral on McCarthy (43 percent) showed that both Catholics and Protestants shared an utter indifference to McCarthy.[7]

With the drive to censure McCarthy gaining steadily in the fall and early winter months, Catholic sentiment on McCarthy continued to follow the national pattern of opinion. McCarthy's popularity with both Catholics and non-Catholics sank steadily in the monthly Gallup polls from June to September then rose slightly in November as the censure votes approached. Just as before, more Catholics than Protestants favored McCarthy (for example, in September 40 percent of the Catholics and 23 percent of the Protestants approved of him). However, the group of both Catholics and non-Catholics who had no opinion at all on the senator was large enough to keep either the McCarthyites or the anti-McCarthyites from gaining a clear majority.[8]

A glance at the opinion-poll figures reveals that McCarthy's Catholic following increased in the latter stages of the national discussion over McCarthy's censure: Catholics favoring McCarthy went from 47 percent in June to 40 percent in September and finally to 46 percent in November.[9] One can readily attribute this last gasp of increased support to the intensive efforts of the McCarthyites to save their man from the wrath of the Senate. Their frantic campaigning seems to provide the most obvious explanation for McCarthy's improvement among Catholics in November. Yet it is essential to avoid overemphasizing his last-minute Catholic support, since his national popularity also increased simultaneously (no doubt for the same reason). As before, the course of Catholic opinion exactly paralleled that of the rest of the country, falling when it fell and rising slightly at the end when it also rose slightly. Moreover, Catholic opposition to the censure never reached 50 percent, nor did it even approach the impressive Catholic approval of 58 percent that he had enjoyed in January 1954 or the 56 percent that he had received in February. Clearly his Catholic following had declined in an unmistakable manner. If the opinion polls foreshadowed the results of the November elections, then the Catholic McCarthyites had little cause for hope.

As the elections drew nearer, most observers concluded that if the McCarthy question were to have an impact on the Catholic vote, it would have to be in the four states where avowedly McCarthyite candidates or vehemently anti-McCarthyite ones had made an issue out of McCarthyism. Attention turned therefore to Maine, Massachusetts, Illinois, and Wisconsin.

In Maine the principal attraction was the Republican primary contest in June between the anti-McCarthy incumbent, Senator Margaret Chase Smith, and her opponent, Robert L. Jones, a stout supporter of McCarthy. Since McCarthy's strength was known to be greatest in the Northeast, the Jones-Smith struggle promised to be an interesting one. It failed to be anything of the sort, however. Smith won a smashing victory over Jones, beating him by a margin of nearly five to one.[10] Furthermore, Smith's victory was so massive that no amount of juggling the election figures could find a Catholic vote for McCarthy.

In Massachusetts the Republican Leverett Saltonstall was running for reelection as senator. Though Brahmin-like and possessing an impressive New England pedigree, he sported an enthusiastic following among the state's Irish Catholics. His enduring popularity, together with his successful efforts to evade the McCarthy issue, brought him a narrow victory over his Democratic opponent, Foster Furcolo. The failure of Senator John F. Kennedy to endorse Furcolo may also have aided Saltonstall's drive for reelection. Amazingly, he had managed somehow to work his way around McCarthy's Catholic minions in Massachusetts, where they were the most numerous and seemingly the most fervent in the nation.[11] How did Saltonstall manage this surprising feat? It may well be that he had less to manage than did others: though his constituents urged him to support McCarthy, they failed to pressure him in the truly formidable way they did John Kennedy. Perhaps Saltonstall's WASP and un-Catholic background made the difference. One suspects that the Boston Irish expected Kennedy to "conform" on McCarthy because, after all, he was Irish and Catholic, just as they and Senator McCarthy himself. Kennedy was "one of their own" in a special sense that was not at all true of Leverett Saltonstall. Perhaps they expected no more of Saltonstall than a benevolent neutrality. If so, that was exactly what they got.

The contest in Illinois pitted Senator Paul Douglas, a recent but rather restrained anti-McCarthyite, against the conservative Republican Joseph Meek. During the campaign Meek issued the McCarthyite statements that befitted one who was widely known as a McCarthy supporter. Fearing possible difficulty with the Catholic vote in Chicago, Douglas's staff took measures to shore up his image as a fighter of communism.[12] Candidate Meek, for his part, looked fondly toward McCarthy and Charles Kersten (McCarthy's friend and a conservative Republican Congressman from Wisconsin), believing that more open support from them would help him with the Catholic voters.[13] A poll taken in late August, however, revealed that Meek was so far behind with the Catholic voters that not even personal appearances by McCarthy or strenuous assistance from Kersten would make any difference. It showed that 50 percent of the prospective Catholic voters favored Douglas and only 20 percent planned to vote for Meek.[14] The results of the election seemed to bear out this dark portent; in Cook County, with its large numbers of Catholics, Douglas nearly doubled Meek's vote, tallying 884,000 votes to his opponent's 491,000. A postelection survey by the *Chicago Daily News* indicated that few voters had even thought of McCarthy when they cast their ballots.[15]

If Kersten had been slow to respond to Meek's pleas for help, the reason was no doubt that he faced an uphill fight against an openly anti-McCarthy candidate, the Democrat Henry Reuss. With his campaign under the management of a McCarthy lieutenant named Frederick Holtz, Congressman Kersten had to defend his record as a member of the "McCarthy trio" in the House of Representatives (Kit Clardy of Michigan and Fred E. Buseby of Illinois completed the threesome). All three faced defiant opposition in their districts, and all three went down to defeat. So desperate was Kersten that a week before the election he wired President Eisenhower, asking for a public statement of support from the White House. Kersten received the presidential support he wanted, but it came too late.[16] Reuss ran to an easy victory. The National Committee for an Effective Congress, an anti-McCarthy lobby in Washington, saluted the defeats of Kersten, Clardy, and Buseby as a setback for McCarthy's "three closest imitators."[17] Kersten's loss was clearly the most important of the three defeats because of his association with McCarthy, his public defense of the senator, the unavoidable fact that he came from McCarthy's home state, and his Catholicism.

The campaign and elections of 1954 demonstrated irrefutably that McCarthy was finished as a political force.[18] This must have been clear even to the senator himself, who suddenly found that no one was after his services as a political campaigner. Few Republicans, it seemed, wanted campaign assistance from a man who was under formal indictment by the Senate itself. His pull on the Catholic vote, always marginal at best, had virtually disappeared by the time of the elections of 1954. Democratic politicians never again had to worry about how many Catholic votes he would drag into the GOP. Most encouraging of all for the Democrats, they had gained control of both the House and the Senate in the coming Congress. Though the lame-duck Congress would vote on McCarthy, it seemed that conservative Republicanism was at least temporarily on the wane and that the Senate could at last get down to the odious task of dealing with its most troublesome member.

Senator McCarthy knew full well what the election returns meant. So desperate was he for help that he even made an attempt to enlist the assistance of the National Catholic Welfare Conference. During the height of the final censure debate in November, his office asked Monsignor John F. Cronin of the NCWC (who ironically had offered his help to McCarthy back during the days of the Tydings committee hearings) to meet with the senator to render him whatever aid he could. Cronin flatly refused, believing that McCarthy was so hopelessly disorganized, so chaotic in his methods of procedure, and so oblivious of the ordinary canons of truth that there was no point in trying to assist him.[19]

The senator's Catholic adherents, meanwhile, prepared to mount a final campaign to save their hero. They fired their opening shot on 8 November 1954, when Monsignor Edward R. Martin, the conservative pastor of a Catholic parish in New York City, addressed a gathering of the Catholic War Veterans in the same city. Speaking before an enthusiastic crowd of Catholic McCarthyites, Martin made the sensational announcement that McCarthy's enemies had collected over $5 million to kick him out of the Senate. Nor was that all: these very same forces were opposing McCarthy "solely because of his Catholic ideals." The monsignor exhorted his Catholic listeners to live up to the ideals of their church and to show real courage, "the same type of courage Senator McCarthy has. Joe is a really sincere Catholic—I know this." Martin failed to say how he knew that McCarthy was such a "sincere Catholic," and more mysterious still, he refused to answer questions about the $5 million that the anti-Catholics had raised to "get" McCarthy.[20]

Martin's dramatic charges, plus his refusal to explain or to document them, drew the expected barrage of criticism. The first to react was Father George Ford's Freedom House, which immediately denounced Martin's statement as a "fairy tale." Ford and his associates said they profoundly "resented" Martin's statement because they feared it would lead to the spread of bigotry and intolerance. At a time when all Americans needed to unite against the "designs of imperialistic communism," Martin's speech "bears false witness and breeds disunity," Freedom House said. A group of liberal professors at Colgate University joined Freedom House in denouncing Martin's comments and demanded to know whether Cardinal Spellman agreed with Martin.[21]

When asked what he thought about Martin's accusations, Spellman declined comment, insisting that it was "none of . . . [his] business." He added, however, "Everybody is a free American citizen and they can do what they want to do so far as I'm concerned."[22] Unfortunately, the incident was not quite as simple as he implied. Martin's appearance at the function as Cardinal Spellman's "personal representative"—something that did not escape the notice of Martin's critics—complicated the affair. The cardinal's critics were not reassured when they were told that such "personal representatives" had the function only of "conveying the greetings" and "nothing else."[23] This did not answer the central question at issue: did Spellman agree with Martin?

The Cardinal's Catholic subjects, however, took a much sterner view of Martin's address. The Catholics who wrote to Spellman opposed Martin's position almost five to one, and most of them said that as Catholics they were deeply embarrassed by Martin's intemperate remarks.[24] In a letter to Spellman, the wealthy Catholic hotel owner Conrad Hilton denounced Martin's comments as "wild statements that should not be made by a Catholic ecclesiastic."[25]

Senator McCarthy, showing once again his aversion for mixing religion and politics, seemed to side with those who disavowed Martin. When asked about the monsignor's speech, he replied that he knew of some groups who had "raised vast amounts of money to hamper my work," but he doubted that "religion enters into it."[26] One of the most ironic moments in the McCarthy era came when the stoutly anti-McCarthy *Christian Century* said virtually the same thing as McCarthy: it too condemned Martin's talk as an "effort to inject the religious issue" that was truly an "onerous assault on national decency."[27]

Martin's efforts were miniscule, however, compared to the truly impressive campaign that the Catholic War Veterans of Brooklyn and Queens were mounting on behalf of McCarthy. In late September the CWV announced a nationwide campaign to collect signatures for a "save McCarthy" petition that it planned to lay before the Congress as soon as final debate began on the Watkins Report. By early November it had collected 250,000 signatures, laboriously gathered from forty states.[28] In an emotional ceremony held on 8 November in Vice-President Richard Nixon's Senate office, the CWV gave the senator a set of twenty-two bound volumes containing the collected signatures. With the debate on the Watkins Report scheduled to begin immediately, the CWV hoped that the petitions would act as a kind of citizens' protest against the possibility of censure. Receiving the appeal with gratitude, McCarthy told the assembled Veterans that he would continue his work "even if the Senate censures me—and I think they will—for fighting the dirtiest fighters in the world, Communists. I will go on either until the Communists lose or we die."[29]

The CWV and the *Brooklyn Tablet* soon joined forces with a nationwide association calling itself Ten Million Americans Mobilized for Justice, which was also trying to forestall censure. In mid-November, when the crisis was reaching epic dimensions, the *Tablet* printed the organization's petition in its pages and entreated its readers to sign it and send it to their representatives in Congress. The *Tablet's* editor, Patrick Scanlan, boasts that the newspaper secured forty thousand signatures for the petitions.[30] (The Ten Million Americans drew much of its popular support from McCarthyite Catholics, but its leadership was mostly non-Catholic in character, with retired military men, wealthy businessmen, and extreme right-wingers making up the bulk of its hierarchy.)[31]

To the chagrin of the Catholic liberals, the save-McCarthy petitions made their way into the Catholic schools of the Brooklyn diocese. The anti-McCarthyites of course, denounced their presence, and the McCarthyites defended them with equal passion. At one grammar school McCarthy supporters handed out 110 petitions to the children and asked them to take them home for their parents to sign. The principal of the school announced with stunning naïveté that more petitions would be distributed as soon as they were available. The superintendent of Brooklyn's Catholic schools took a less benevolent attitude toward the petition, however. When told of what was happening, he said, "If it's been done, it's been done without the sanction of the superintendent of schools." McCarthyism as a "political matter" had no place in Catholic schools, he insisted.[32] Whether as a result of his warning or for other reasons, no more reports of such activity in the Brooklyn Catholic schools reached the press. Nevertheless, some of the petitions appeared again when Catholics went to Mass on Sunday morning. One Catholic man, accosted at the vestibule of his local parish church, wrote an impassioned letter to Cardinal Spellman asking him to put a stop to such proselytizing: "Let's keep politics on the soap box and not on the pulpit." The ever-vigilant *New York Times* heard about what was going on at the door of the city's Catholic churches and publicized it with its usual attention to detail.[33]

The climax of the save-McCarthy movement in New York came on 29 November, just three days before the censure vote, at a rally in Madison Square Garden. Though not advertised as a "Catholic" event, the presence of the New York Irish and many other Catholics was too strong to escape notice. The Ten Million Americans had planned the rally to announce the results of its nationwide drive to reach its goal of ten million signatures for McCarthy. In spite of the intensive publicity heralding the meeting, the crowd attending the rally was small, with only thirteen thousand showing up in a hall built to hold twenty thousand. Nevertheless, the audience responded enthusiastically to a brace of impassioned McCarthyite speakers and seemed especially pleased by the music of a forty-five-piece band that McCarthy's supporters had flown in from Wisconsin for the occasion. The high point of the evening was a surprise visit by Mrs. Jean Kerr McCarthy, wife of the senator, who told the crowd, "I want you to know how deeply touched Joe is by the tremendous fight you are waging." Gratifying as that message was, the best news of all was the announcement that the campaign for ten million signatures had "gone over the top."[34]

Both the *New York Times* and the *Christian Century* professed to find a certain "Catholic" note in the affair. The *Times* was especially intrigued by the presence of three Passionist fathers (a missionary and preaching order), who had come from the group's headquarters in Union City, New Jersey. One of them was the noted Bishop Cuthbert O'Gara, a survivor of two years in a Chinese Communist prison cell, who delivered a stirring conservative invocation that kicked off the rally. When the reporters asked the three Passionists if the members of the order stationed at the Union City headquarters had signed the McCarthy petitions, one of them replied, "I certainly did and plenty of us did. Aren't we American citizens?"[35] The *Century* estimated that the crowd had been "90 percent" Irish, though it did not say how it had arrived at this remarkable figure. It also noted the presence of large numbers of "fresh-faced girls in convent-school uniform."[36]

One of McCarthy's supporters, however, believed that the *Times* had far overestimated the Catholic dimensions of the event. Roy M. Cohn, one of the "surprise guests" of the evening, complained that the *Times* had given the impression that "there was some kind of religious significance to the rally." He thought that it had dwelled excessively on Bishop O'Gara's invocation without mentioning the benediction for the evening, which had come from a Jewish rabbi. (In making his point, Cohn seemed to be unwittingly substantiating the *Times*'s contention that organized religion had played a large role in the evening's activities.) He promised a further and "documented" attack on the *Times* when he addressed the Catholic Institute of the Press on 9 December. Cohn was true to his word, telling the Catholic editors that the *Times* had deliberately ignored the message that he and the rabbi had tried to make at the rally: the fight against communism "was being fought just as vigorously by Jews, Catholics, and Protestants all united together." Fortunately New York's newspaper readers did not have to rely solely on the *Times*, Cohn said. They also had such "great papers" as the *Brooklyn Tablet*, which "among others" gave "full accounts of anti-Communist activities."[37]

While the *Tablet*, the Catholic War Veterans, the Knights of Columbus, and the New York Holy Name Society were stirring up a storm in New York, a quieter but even more serious crisis was building up in Boston. The bitter conflict in Boston between the Catholic McCarthyites and the anti-McCarthyites attracted fewer headlines than the one occurring in New York because it was less open and organized. Nevertheless, the struggle in Boston was fully as important as the one in New York. Catholic McCarthyism in Boston failed to achieve the organizational sophistication of New York City McCarthyism because the archbishop of Boston equivocated magnificently on the McCarthy problem and the *Boston Pilot* refused to give aid and comfort to the McCarthyites. Nevertheless, the feelings of the city's Catholics on Joe McCarthy ran at a fever pitch. The Catholic McCarthyites seemed passionately convinced of the rightness of their cause, a feeling that they showed by the pressure they put on public officials, the letters of protest they sent to the local newspapers, and the strength they showed in local opinion polls.

Senator Saltonstall and Archbishop Cushing managed to slip clear of the wrath of the Massachusetts McCarthyites, largely by resorting to pious platitudes about the evils of atheistic communism and the glories of America.[38] The task was much harder, however, for that other political celebrity from Boston, young John Fitzgerald Kennedy, upon whose handsome head fell the full fury of the Catholic McCarthyites in Massachusetts.

John Kennedy's policy in 1952, when he had run for the Senate, had been to maintain a "low profile" in public on McCarthy; he adhered to the same tactic in 1953 and 1954. When with his intimates, however, he expressed his keen disgust with the senator. Lawrence Fuchs, for instance, remembers Kennedy's many "caustic" remarks about McCarthy. When Theodore Sorenson in early January 1953 responded to the senator's invitation to be his principal assistant, Sorenson expressed his fears that Kennedy favored McCarthy. The senator quickly dispelled his worries about McCarthyism, though he may have unsettled Sorenson a bit when he added that he still had his doubts about Owen Lattimore. To Arthur Meier Schlesinger, Jr., Harvard historian and friend, Kennedy indicated his "articulate dislike" for the McCarthy committee's operations, but he explained his failure to say anything publicly in the candid fashion he reserved for his closest associates: "Hell, half my voters in Massachusetts look on McCarthy as a hero."[39] He reflected the same thought in a speech that he wrote on the censure question (but never delivered): he said that he was "not insensitive to the fact that my constituents perhaps contain a greater proportion of devotees on each side of this matter than the constituency of any other Senator."[40] This was as close as he ever came to a frank and public expression of his feelings on the politics of McCarthyism, but it was one that he never gave.

All during 1953 and early 1954, as McCarthy had charged from sensation to exposé to headline, Kennedy had followed his moves with the keenest concentration, studying every step the senator made. Convincing evidence of this comes from Kenneth Birkhead, former political analyst for the Democratic National Committee. Birkhead had earned a reputation around Washington as one of the city's most knowledgeable McCarthy experts, he had been engaged in research on McCarthy since 1951. From time to time, Kennedy called Birkhead into his office, pummeled him with questions about the senator, and eagerly accepted all the materials on McCarthy that Birkhead had gathered for him. Birkhead doubts that any member of the Senate spent as much time talking to him about McCarthy as Senator Kennedy.[41]

The mail from Massachusetts was the first and most pressing problem Kennedy had to face. To the surprise of no one, the bulk of letters and telegrams proved to be overwhelmingly favorable to McCarthy.[42] Just as he had done in 1952, Kennedy moved warily, couching his replies in safe, cautious language designed to mollify his volatile constituents yet allowing himself the greatest possible room in which to maneuver on the McCarthy question. Typical was his reply to a man from suburban Boston who had asked him for his opinion of the senator. Kennedy replied vaguely that the Senate had recently completed its study of "various questions" having to do with McCarthy, and he assured the man, "I am giving attention to this situation, and I am hopeful that the outcome will be the one most desirable for the good of the Senate and the country."[43] Kennedy's answer was so nebulous that any member of the Senate, including both the most ardent McCarthyites and embittered anti-McCarthyites, could have subscribed to it. Clearly he was trying his best to avoid a politically lethal issue. His Catholicism seemed to make the problem even more difficult for him than for other senators. A woman from a western Massachusetts mill city reminded him forcefully of this when she wrote, "Surely when you received that degree from Notre Dame, the Holy Ghost should have descended upon you and enlightened you. Therefore I cannot understand why you are not completely behind Senator McCarthy and overjoyed at being able to work with him on a committee so vital to our nation's welfare."[44]

So many letters came into Kennedy's office asking for his views on the congressional investigating committees that he finally composed a form letter stating his position on them: "I do not think that anyone . . . doubts that committee investigations have from time to time exceeded the limits of fairness," he conceded with seeming candor. Witnesses had received unfair treatment, he noted, and committee chairmen had not conducted the hearings properly. To solve these defects he suggested stronger protections for witnesses: let them have due notification of charges, a chance to present evidence on their own behalf, an opportunity for rebuttal, and of course the assistance of legal counsel. When some of McCarthy's critics asked him why he had voted to fund the McCarthy subcommittee, he replied that Congress "should not abandon the very important instrument of full legislative inquiry." Moreover, he doubted that "opposition to the appropriation of funds to a standing committee of the Senate" would "solve any problem." (Most assuredly, Kennedy's evasions did not solve any problem that his liberal critics had raised.)

If congressional investigations had become irresponsible, then only public opinion and party responsibility would restrain them, he concluded.[45]

If Kennedy's letter sounded mealymouthed and equivocal to those who wanted him to take a strong stand against McCarthy, it also demonstrated a deep impulse in Kennedy that provided one of the keys to his position on McCarthy: he believed firmly that Mc-Carthyism was a legal problem, not a moral one. Had McCarthy broken any laws? If so, then let the court apply those laws to him with clear-eyed impartiality. Had McCarthy violated the rights of witnesses? If so, then let those witnesses have the protections that the Constitution guarantees them. Did the Senate want to "try" McCar-thy for his excesses? If so, then let the Senate take special care to protect McCarthy's own rights, seeing to it that he received the full and due process of the law. The McCarthy question, as his biographer has observed, was more a "procedural problem than a moral one" for John Kennedy.[46] His letters to his Massachusetts constituents fully reflected this view. Yet though he carefully straddled the fence, Kennedy never contradicted himself. Zealous above all to observe the restraints of the law, he hewed painstakingly to a narrow, exactly predefined course, one that never swerved (hence never controverted itself) and one that committed him in advance to as little as possible.

In 1960 when he sought the Democratic nomination for the presidency, and later on while in the White House, Kennedy's sup-porters made much of the several occasions when he had actually opposed McCarthy. One was his opposition to McCarthy's attempt to get his friend Scott McLeod appointed as ambassador to Ireland. (He told Theodore Sorenson, "I sympathize with their wanting to get rid of McLeod, but why pick on poor old Ireland?")[47] Speaking in a televised interview in February 1954, Kennedy said that McCar-thy and his associates in the Republican party were guilty of partisan excesses when they called the Democrats the "party of treason."[48] Later that same year Kennedy led the fight in the McCarthy commit-tee against the appointment of McCarthy's friend Owen Brewster to the position of chief counsel for the committee.[49] In the eyes of his admonitors, however, Kennedy destroyed whatever good he had accomplished with these moves by voting in early 1953 to fund the McCarthy committee's investigations.

If Kennedy's critics had found little to praise in his earlier handling of the McCarthy problem, they found even less to approve in the course of action that he took on the question of McCarthy's censure. To most of them, it seemed that he had chosen a policy that was elusive, devious, and temporizing. Most of all, they disliked his decision to vote in favor of the compromise motion that established a select committee (the Watkins committee) to study the charges against McCarthy. Kennedy explained his action in his usual oblique manner, saying that the "absolute necessity for a fair, unemotional procedure in the handling of the charges against Senator McCarthy" convinced him to vote for the select committee.[50] In fairness to Kennedy, it must be noted that he was one of seventy-five senators who voted for the amendment, and many of these were confirmed anti-McCarthyites like Wayne Morse. (The Oregon senator voted for the measure because he believed that McCarthy ought to have a chance to answer the charges with aid of counsel, something he could better accomplish before a small committee than before the full Senate.) Yet this argument had its weaknesses, too. Both Paul Douglas and Hubert Humphrey had to face election contests in November; yet they both voted against the Knowland compromise.[51]

Two years after Kennedy voted for the Knowland measure, the story appeared that he had been ready to deliver a speech against McCarthy as his part in the Senate's debate over censure.[52] The story (expounded principally by Theodore Sorenson) says that on the night of 31 July 1954 Kennedy was sitting in the Senate chamber, ready to give the speech, when Senator Morse's intervention pushed the debate in a new direction and the Senate soon afterward voted for the Knowland resolution establishing the select committee.[53] The undelivered speech announced that Kennedy would vote for censure, but on grounds peculiarly his own. McCarthy had attacked the "honor and the dignity of the Senate," he said. He described in detail how Roy Cohn had repeatedly abused the army's witnesses, always with the tacit permission of McCarthy. As chairman of the subcommittee investigating the army, McCarthy was clearly responsible for all of Cohn's actions.[54] He specifically rejected the charges of Senator Ralph Flanders and others who had attacked McCarthy for deeds he had committed before the present Congress had seated him. The preceding Congresses ought to have challenged those actions when they occurred, he insisted. He noted caustically that Flanders had supported McCarthy until only recently and had even defended the latter's charge that the Democratic party had perpetrated "twenty years of treason."[55] The Senate ought to base its censure proceedings on specific infractions of civil liberties, violations that clearly contravened the law and that this particular Congress had an unquestioned jurisdiction to judge.[56]

The Sorenson story abounds with difficulties. First of all, why did the world hear nothing about this speech until 1956 (two years later)? Second, why did no full copy of the text appear until 1959, when Kennedy was in the midst of campaigning for the presidency and when it was becoming clear that his nonstand on McCarthy might hurt his chances for the Democratic nomination? At that time the Kennedy office supplied to the historian James MacGregor Burns a photostatic copy of the speech, which it said had been somehow "misplaced" in the Kennedy office.[57] A recent search of the files at the Kennedy Presidential Library in Waltham, Massachusetts, has turned up neither the speech nor any copies of it nor even a record of its existence. Granted that Kennedy neither gave it nor released it to the press, where is it now? And why, finally, is Theodore Sorenson the only Kennedy aide with any recollection of the speech? (Sorenson has no copy of it, nor has Burns yet been able to locate his copy.)[58] One can hardly escape John P. Roche's conclusion: the speech was suppressed.[59] Either the Kennedy forces or John Kennedy himself concluded that the speech (truly a forthright condemnation of McCarthyism) was too hot to handle: better to take the safer approach and say nothing about it.

When John Kennedy entered the Senate chamber on that night of 31 July 1954, his speech ready for delivery, he made his way haltingly down the aisle, leaning heavily on crutches, his face and body wracked with intense pain. The wound that he had suffered in World War II had begun to act up again, forcing him into painful and immensely dangerous spinal surgery. On 22 October he underwent the first of two drastic operations, and for over two weeks afterward he fought a desperate battle for his life. Not until 11 November did the hospital in New York report that he was out of danger, and not until 21 December was he well enough to go to Florida to begin a long convalescence. From November until January, as Sorenson notes, Kennedy was absolutely incapable of doing any work at all.[60]

No one ever questioned whether he could have been present in the Senate chamber on 2 December for the final censure vote. But many observers wondered at the time, and continue to wonder still, why Kennedy did not pair or simply have his vote recorded? At this point Sorenson insists that the decision not to pair or be recorded was his, and his alone. Sorenson admits that he could have announced for Kennedy and "politically I would have saved his skin." He adds, however, "I'm a lawyer. And all I knew was that Kennedy was a member of the jury who was absent during the whole trial, [and] who had never heard any of the testimony. How could he, in all fairness, have voted as an absent juror? In all conscience, I just didn't see how he could vote." Sorenson has repeated his story several times, taking full responsibility for the move and insisting that he acted correctly.[61] On later occasions Kennedy himself gave virtually the same explanation, insisting that if the censure vote had come up in August he would have been prepared to vote for it, but by the time the vote came in December he had been out of touch with the issue so long that he could not possibly have paired on it.[62] (This was his familiar view that since the McCarthy debate had been essentially a judicial proceeding, he could not participate in the jury.)

The problem with Sorenson's (and Kennedy's) explanation is that the issue really had not changed much between August, when the select committee began its deliberations on McCarthy, and December, when the Senate finally voted to "condemn" McCarthy. McCarthy was still the same McCarthy, and the charges against him still dealt with the same transgressions of law, the right to reputation, and Senate decorum. It was truly nitpicking to say that Kennedy's absence from the Senate during the November debate on the Watkins Report had made him an "absent juror." He had been present in the Senate for all of the senator's activities since January 1953; moreover he was exceptionally well informed about everything McCarthy had done before that time. This is not to say that Sorenson acted out of cynicism, deliberately choosing to keep Kennedy out of the voting because he had an eye on the 1958 elections in Massachusetts. One may accept his thesis that he had acted on technical and legal grounds. One may also question the relevancy of those grounds, in the face of what McCarthy was and what he stood for.

The heart of Kennedy's struggle with McCarthy, as with the larger problem of McCarthyism itself, was the issue of civil liberties. If Kennedy saw McCarthyism as a legal problem exclusively, it was because his background was legal and political and he had yet to develop the sensitivity to civil liberties that characterized his later years. Kennedy was "shaping his liberalism by fits and starts," as James MacGregor Burns writes. "He had been willed the heritage of economic liberalism, 'the groceries,' but not the heritage of liberty."[63] To the members of the ADA, Kennedy's failure to denounce McCarthy was unforgivable because the McCarthy issue was (to them at least) a clear choice between freedom and totalitarianism.[64] Not only did Kennedy fail to see it that way, he thought that a lot of "emotionalism" had beclouded the libertarian position. He told one reporter in 1956 that when it came to the McCarthy issue, he could not "get as worked up as other liberals did."[65] In a later period of his life he not only got "worked up" over the problem of personal freedom but admitted that he had been insensitive to the havoc McCarthy had wreaked on personal reputations.[66] But all of that came later.

Besides lacking the civil-liberties ethic that might have pushed him into a strong stand against McCarthy, he always had the influence of his family pulling him in the opposite direction. Kennedy himself noted this (perhaps somewhat ruefully) when he told a reporter, "To understand my situation you must remember that my father was a friend of Joe's, as was my sister Eunice, and my brother Bobby worked for him. So I had all those family pressures."[67] The family problem was, as he put it inelegantly to Burns, "really the guts of the matter."[68] If the Kennedy's had been an ordinary family, the problem might not have been so acute, but they were a remarkably close-knit group (some said "clannish") who kept their squabbles strictly to themselves and put immense stock in a unified appearance.

In the years after the censure, Kennedy's interpreters and Kennedy himself commented at length on his behavior during the censure debate. Kennedy repeatedly insisted that he had favored censure all along and that he would have voted for it if the question had come to a vote in August. During the presidential campaign of 1960, his critics threw the McCarthy question at him again and again, sometimes to his vast distress. He had explained himself before; he explained yet another time. Why did he have to keep defending himself, he asked wearily? (One reason, of course, was that he had written a volume called *Profiles in Courage* which moved his liberal preceptors to carp at him for having shown so much profile and so little courage himself.)[69] He wanted nothing so much as an end to the whole discussion about Joe McCarthy.

Seen in retrospect, the censure affair does not emerge as one of John F. Kennedy's better moments. With his reelection fully four years away, he took the most evasive of all possible courses. He never acknowledged the slightest distress over McCarthy's persistent mauling of witnesses, his misuse of evidence, his intemperate attacks on his "enemies," or his abuse of senatorial privilege. Only the narrowest possible legal considerations seemed to impress Kennedy at all, and thoughts of the "moral issue" of McCarthyism left him glacial and unmoved. Liberals were slow to forget, though they began to forgive him when he entered the White House and began tendering presidential favors to some of McCarthy's former targets (J. Robert Oppenheimer, for instance). For the long-suffering liberals in the ADA, John Kennedy acted none too soon.

One could hardly say that Kennedy's response to the McCarthy matter illustrated the pattern of American Catholic reaction to McCarthyism. For one thing, his own attitude toward the senator had virtually nothing to do with Catholic teachings or principles (either liberal or conservative). His belief that McCarthyism was a "legal" problem probably derived from his close association with Theodore Sorenson and his own shrewd perception that the legal approach was the safest one to take. Nor were his Catholic constituents in Boston, Worcester, and the other Catholic enclaves of the state the paradigm of American Catholic response to McCarthy. Massachusetts's Catholic population demonstrated a deeper conservatism than Catholics in the rest of the country (and even in the remaining northeastern states), and they gave evidence of a stronger propensity toward McCarthyism and its associated conservative positions than Catholics in other parts of the nation.

Furthermore, Kennedy's Catholic constituents in Massachusetts seemed slower than the rest of the country to tire of Joe McCarthy. Long after the rest of the nation had turned toward other questions and other politicians, the Boston Irish seemed to retain a special interest in McCarthy. Products of an environment that was heavily Catholic, tightly insulated, and rigidly authoritarian, Boston Catholics were slow to forget their knight-in-shining-armor from Wisconsin. Indeed, some of his Catholic admirers are with us still, holding forth in the Irish precincts of South Boston, Forest Hills, and Dorchester.

Though McCarthy's Catholic followers everywhere grew more

anxious in the waning days of the censure fight, nowhere did they take the struggle more seriously than in Boston. They remained loyal to McCarthy after the hearings ended in September, during the debate over Flanders's resolution of censure, while the Senate conducted hearings over the Watkins Report, and in the final tense days of debate in the Senate at the end of November. None of this growing feeling of desperation was lost on that other junior senator, the one from Massachusetts, John Fitzgerald Kennedy. The McCarthyite fervor of his Catholic constituents continued unabated as he lay in his hospital bed, fighting a grim battle for his life. The Boston McCarthyites believed that Joe McCarthy was fighting for his life, too, and their hearts went out to him—perhaps not as demonstrably and in such an organized fashion as the Catholics in New York, but they went out to him nonetheless. John Kennedy would survive his ordeal of November and December 1954; Joseph Raymond McCarthy would not.

Chapter 10

The End of Senator McCarthy

The end came suddenly for Senator Joe McCarthy on 2 December 1954. To the surprise of no one at all, not even the senator himself, the Senate voted to "condemn" him for his abuse of the Gillette-Monroney subcommittee that had investigated his finances in 1952, as well as for his contemptuous treatment of the Watkins committee. The vote was an overwhelming one, 67 to 22, with only McCarthy, John Kennedy, and Alexander Wiley (the senior senator from Wisconsin) remaining unrecorded.[1]

Among the Catholic senators the vote was six against McCarthy, two for him. The six voting for condemnation (Burke of Ohio, Chavez of New Mexico, Mansfield of Montana, Murray of Montana, Pastore of Rhode Island, and O'Mahoney of Wyoming) were all Democrats, and the two voting against (Purtell of Connecticut and Barrett of Wyoming) were Republicans. An examination of the votes cast by the Catholics in the Senate revealed that they had voted along strict party lines, as did the rest of the Senate. (The Democratic Minority Leader, Lyndon Johnson, had lobbied so strenuously behind the scenes that every Democrat in the Senate voted against McCarthy.) The attempts of several political commentators to discern a Catholic vote against McCarthy fell far short of the mark: Catholic senators voted their party, not their religious affiliation.[2]

The vote of the Catholics in the Senate aptly symbolized the whole story of Catholic response to Joe McCarthy. It was apparent that the Catholic senators (Democrats all) viewed him as a threat to the health of their party and to the liberal ideology they had all espoused over their whole careers. They remembered his characterization of the Democratic party as the "party of treason," his condemnation of the "Truman-Acheson-Marshall gang" as "soft on communism," and the eagerness with which the Republicans (middle-of-the-road as well as conservative) used him to smear the loyalty record of all of the Democrats. With good reason they voted their party, needing little of the energetic prodding that Lyndon Johnson was quite willing to provide.

The Catholic Republicans also voted their party, following the lead of the Knowland-Jenner-Mundt conservative Republicans. (The GOP divided evenly in the McCarthy vote, 22 siding with the conservative Taft forces who were strongest in the West and 22 voting with the more moderate Eisenhower Republicans concentrated along the eastern seaboard.) They saw McCarthy as their last best hope against the Democrats, believing that with his help they stood a fair chance of attaining their long-cherished goals: retrenchment in social welfare policy, isolationism in foreign affairs, and a tough stand against communism at home and abroad. They too voted their party, joining with other conservative Republican stalwarts like Roman Hruska, Barry Goldwater, and William Jenner. From the start of his crusade, McCarthy had been a pawn in the power struggle between the two parties; he remained the same until the end. In sum, the Catholic senators voted their party's ideological stand on subversion; religious considerations seemed to have little to do with the matter.

Although almost everyone in Washington had expected McCarthy's downfall, the Senate's move came as a shattering blow to his loyal Catholic admirers. In the eyes of the *Wanderer*, the censure vote showed a "world in revolt against God and His Law, a world not only locked in mortal conflict between East and West, but savagely at war with itself and with all that remains of what was once Christendom."[3] Less apocalyptic but fully as anguished was the *Brooklyn Tablet*. It labeled the Senate's action "hypocritical" (because McCarthy had never been as harsh against his fellow senators as they were toward him) and "farcical" (because most of the senators had neither read the Watkins Report nor heard the Senate's debate on it). The day would come, the *Tablet* warned, when the Senate would have to admit that it had made a mistake "akin to that of giving lend-lease to Russia."[4] Under mandate from its superiors to stay out of the McCarthy mess, *America* adopted a ho-hum approach, saying that since the public had lost interest in the McCarthy question, it had become "an intra-GOP controversy."[5] The *Commonweal* savored its ultimate triumph. It noted that despite all of the forces working against censure—the religious issue, the legions of fanatical McCarthy supporters, the Senate's traditional reluctance to condemn its own—the Senate had nevertheless taken the "astonishing" step of voting to discipline McCarthy. "Social responsibility asserted itself to rebuke the destructive Adventurer," it concluded with satisfaction.[6]

A few political observers tried to soften McCarthy's defeat by pointing out that the Senate had "condemned" him rather than "censured" him. (Through an oversight the Senate had labeled it the former.) Everyone agreed, however, that McCarthy's political power was gone for good. With its passing went the bogey of Catholic McCarthyism, that durable myth that had stirred up many a controversy and had caused repeated anguish over the previous five years.

But if Joseph McCarthy had finally died politically, his devoutly committed followers had not. Anticensure petitions continued to circulate around the Catholic environs of New York City, and Catholic priests continued to give sermons defending McCarthy, much to the disgust of the *Commonweal*, which called such efforts a "scandal."[7] Equally shocked were the liberal-minded student editors of the Fordham University newspaper, *The Ram*. They were so deeply annoyed by the tactics of the Catholic McCarthyites in New York that they wrote an open letter protesting them to the *New York Times*. The *Times* printed their missive without delay. The letter, signed by 101 members of the Fordham senior class, expressed shock at the notion that "to be a good Catholic one must necessarily support the senator." The implication of such a thesis, the seniors believed, was that Catholics who did not support him were "somehow beyond the pale of truly good Christian practice, and are in some way suspect." Although they defended the right of Catholics to support McCarthy, they vehemently rejected the doctrine that "faith is in any way increased" because one defends his cause. Thus they condemned "the slurs so often made against another segment of the Catholic press whose members have their religious sincerity questioned because of their opposition to the cause of McCarthy." As practicing Catholics, the Fordham seniors opposed "this attempt to yoke our Faith to a transient political doctrine."[8]

The *Brooklyn Tablet*, no doubt hoping to embarrass the editors of the *Ram*, noted that only a small minority of Fordham seniors had signed the letter; 265 others had failed to approve of it. In addition, the *Tablet* said, an opinion poll taken at the school in October 1952 had revealed that the Fordham student body favored McCarthy by over five to one.[9] (The *Tablet*'s point was almost meaningless, however, since the political situation had changed so much since McCarthy's triumphant days of 1952.) The *Tablet*'s readers naturally agreed. One Italian gentleman wrote that he had never had a chance to go to college because the depression had forced him to go to work. "Nevertheless, I have the temerity to disagree" with "these intellects." Another man condemned what he called these "prize hypocritical attacks on the senator. And I am thinking as I write of Our Blessed Lord vis-a-vis the Pharisees, as He bent His Sacred Body to write in the sands . . . 'He that is without sin among you, let him cast the first stone.'" Most of the letters that came to the editorial offices of the *Tablet* showed a virulent strain of antiintellectualism: if the students were so smart, the writers said repeatedly, then why did they show such stupidity on the subject of communism? Surely "these intellects ought to know better than to give aid and succor to the Marxists," the *Tablet*'s followers said again and again.[10] The letters revealed unmistakably that McCarthyism was far from dead in Catholic Brooklyn.

But impressive as it was, the flurry of letters appearing in the *Tablet* did not point to a growing movement; they rather signaled the beginning of the end for Catholic McCarthyism in New York City.

The *Tablet* itself gave evidence of this trend: it continued to lament the condemnation vote and to damn McCarthy's critics as enemies of the Republic, but it did so less frequently as the months passed by. The Catholic War Veterans, gathered in 1955 at their national convention in New York, voted a resolution applauding McCarthy's "fight against atheistic communism," but they too had begun to turn toward other issues.[11] The next two years marked further Catholic attempts to restore McCarthy's sagging fortunes—even Robert F. Kennedy came out publicly for him—but they were fading echoes, symbolic reminders of a parade that had long since passed by.[12]

McCarthy himself receded into anonymity, increasingly isolated from political life and declining both physically and emotionally. He made two final visitis in late 1956 to his alma mater, Marquette University, but hardly anyone noticed him.[13] Seldom in American history has a major political figure descended into oblivion as quickly and with such finality. Even the *Commonweal* seemed bored with him, and after routinely condemning some of the reckless statements he made against Eisenhower in 1955, it ceased covering his activities at all.[14]

It seemed that the nation had no sooner forgotten Joe McCarthy than he died suddenly on 2 May 1957. His death and the lengthy obsequies that followed caused a renewal of the controversies that had surrounded his entire life, serving once more to divide the nation into McCarthyites and anti-McCarthyites. The senator's death itself proved to be an occasion for debate, since the tale spread around Washington that he had died of alcoholism.[15] The navy doctors at Bethesda Naval Hospital who performed the autopsy seemed to give the report some credence (though no real proof) when they said that he had died of a "liver ailment." *America* passed discreetly over this delicate problem, noting simply that his last years "were clouded, as we know now, by ill-health." (As expected, McCarthy had received the church's anointing, or "last rites," as it was then called, shortly before his death.)[16]

The End of Senator McCarthy

An orgy of lamentations followed the senator's death. Although the funeral and burial services passed largely without incident, something approaching the glorification of a martyr followed the ceremonies. It all started out quietly enough, with an official funeral on 6 May at St. Matthew's Catholic Cathedral in Washington, D.C. Archbishop Patrick O'Boyle of Washington conducted the obsequies, attended by a throng of friends, admirers, and political leaders. The eulogist, Monsignor John K. Cartwright, saluted the senator as one of the few men of the times who had seen that communism was "an evil with which there can be no compromise."[17] The *Tablet* described the funeral services as a solemn tribute to the senator's greatness and noted that eight "stalwart Marines" had carried his casket down the steps of the cathedral.[18]

The next day a second funeral service took place in the senator's home parish of St. Mary's Church in Appleton, Wisconsin. It was fitting that the Knights of Columbus and the Catholic War Veterans, two of the staunchest pro-McCarthy groups in American Catholicism, were with him to the end: they formed an impressive honor guard around his coffin and acted as ushers during the funeral Mass. A packed congregation listened intently as McCarthy's pastor, the Reverend Adam Grill, eulogized McCarthy as "a dedicated man, not a fanatic. He gave his whole heart and soul to the successful completion of his work. The guidance of our beloved land is under the guidance of human beings," and as humans "we are all fallible," he said tactfully. With the ceremonies completed, a throng of mourners flocked to the Catholic cemetery in Appleton, where Father Grill sprinkled the casket with water, blessed it, and presided at the lowering of the coffin.[19] No incidents marred the services.

The first of a long series of memorial masses took place soon afterward at St. Patrick's Cathedral in New York City. Irish fraternal groups, the Knights of Columbus, and the Catholic War Veterans once again took prominent part in the ceremonies, as they did in the years that followed when the annual McCarthy Mass at St. Patrick's became a fixture of Catholic life in that city.[20] In other parts of the country, Catholics attended religious services in honor of the late senator, as was usual and fully expected.

Neither usual nor expected, however, was the manner in which many Catholic ethnic and patriotic groups began to shower special awards on the senator's widow, Mrs. Jean Kerr McCarthy. The first of these came a month after the senator's passing from the American Order of General Pulaski, a Polish-American patriotic society, which tendered her a scroll in honor of her late husband. The speakers at the award ceremony described the senator as one who had made "the supreme sacrifice" in defense of "his country, civilization, and Christianity."[21]

It seemed supremely appropriate, however, that the most important and highly publicized award should come from the Catholic War Veterans of New York. At an elaborate ceremony held in Forest Park, Long Island (a large Catholic McCarthyite enclave), the CWV gave Mrs. McCarthy a plaque whose inscription deliberately compared the senator to the crucified Savior: it said that when God "saw fit to send us Joseph R. McCarthy, He showed His love for us." Like Jesus the senator had "emptied himself, by undergoing every kind of personal humiliation and condemnation" so that the world might know "the menace of Atheistic Communism." The Veterans therefore offered "a pledge of gratitude and fealty to this man who was not content with giving anything less than life itself as the measure of his love and devotion." Lest anyone miss the comparison between McCarthy and Jesus, the citation concluded resoundingly, "Greater love than this no man hath—that a man lay down his life for his friends." In the sermon Father Edward Lodge Curran (who had often sniped at Eleanor Roosevelt) pursued the theme of the day by saying that McCarthy had "laid down his life" for the protection of "our beloved country and our beloved Church against the forces of atheistic communism forever."[22] In truth, the Catholic War Veterans and Curran turned Joseph Raymond McCarthy into a kind of second

Jesus Christ, one who had come in complete innocence to save all men but instead had suffered ignominy, rejection, and ultimate martyrdom.

The eulogies began appearing almost as soon as the senator had yielded his last breath. Not unexpectedly, the themes of persecution and murder dominated the tributes that came from his Catholic admirers. *Columbia*, the journal of the Knights of Columbus, averred that "the Senator was killed—the victim of the most shameful, deliberately contrived and unrelenting attack ever directed against a loyal citizen of the United States." The *Tablet* agreed, arguing that "no individual in our day has borne the brunt of as much mad, unreasoned hatred." The *Wanderer* took the same line, complaining bitterly that McCarthy had been "subjected to the most withering persecution ever heaped on one person."[23]

What did the anti-McCarthyite publications say? The *Commonweal* made a fine distinction between McCarthyism, which it had "unalterably" opposed, and McCarthy the man, for whom it could only offer its humble prayers.[24] We are all beset with weaknesses, wrote the executive editor, John Cogley, and sometimes we forget those limitations when we find ourselves in the midst of the "storm of controversy."[25] And yet the *Commonweal*, even in this difficult moment, vehemently had rejected those misguided supporters of the senator who tried to belittle the destructive forces he had unleashed against the American political system. This minimalist attitude made "too little of a person and a phenomenon that severely tested the fabric of our democratic society," it believed.[26] A writer for the *Catholic World*, which had tried (mostly without success) to give both sides of the McCarthy issue, condemned those conservatives who foolishly confused McCarthy's brand of anticommunism with "legitimate" anticommunism. The article said that McCarthy had too often been "rash" in his judgments against suspected Communists to deserve the title of legitimate foe of communism. Had he lived longer, McCarthy would have attacked social legislation as well, the *World* believed, for his voting record and his political temperament were ample indications of what he believed.[27] In sum, the Catholic press remained consistent to the end: not even McCarthy's death could shake the Catholic editors from the viewpoints they had chosen over seven years earlier.

Though McCarthy died on 2 May 1957, his Catholic admirers saw that his immortal spirit, like that of the great John Brown, went marching resolutely on. The Catholic War Veterans, as always, spearheaded the movement to keep alive the memory both of his work and of his followers' devotion to his cause. In the fall of 1957, the CWV established its annual Senator Joe McCarthy Gold Medal Americanism Award, to be given to a Catholic War Veteran who was outstanding for his patriotism. The winner of the award for 1957 confessed that he was "humbled" at the thought of receiving an award named after the "patriotic" Senator McCarthy.[28] The winner for the next year was a veteran who had taken it upon himself to ransack the stacks of the Baltimore City High School library in search of subversive and obscene books. When he found a distressing number of such volumes, he organized a vigorous citywide campaign to strip the library's shelves immediately of all such pernicious books.[29] It seemed that hyperpatriotism, devotion to McCarthy, and repression of forbidden books all went together, at least in the minds of the Catholic War Veterans. In recent years, as the CWV has declined in membership and as dedication to McCarthyism has faded, the group has discontinued both the gold medal and the annual New York City Mass for Senator McCarthy.[30] Among the older and surviving veterans, however, the memory of the senator remains strong and fresh.

Some of his Massachusetts supporters also remained loyal to his cause, at least in the affluent Boston suburb of Winchester. A study in 1958 of the townspeople's feelings about McCarthy showed that the Catholics (making up almost half of the population) favored McCarthy by 54 percent and that only 32 percent of the Protestants took a positive attitude toward him. (The survey also found that as the Catholics moved out to Winchester from the inner city they tended to change their voting habits from Democratic to Republican; this was especially noticeable among Catholics who had received a college education.)[31]

In 1959 the diminishing band of McCarthy supporters organized the most widely publicized of all of the attempts to preserve his memory, the annual "pilgrimage," as they call it, from Milwaukee to his grave in Appleton.[32] (The journey and the concluding ceremony usually take place around 2 May, the date of the senator's death.) Although the pilgrimage and graveside services occur under "Catholic" auspices, their tone is more one of extremely conservative Republican politics than of Catholicism. After their departure from Milwaukee, the McCarthy pilgrims usually gather at St. Mary's Church in Appleton for a memorial Mass. The church services finished, they make their way to the senator's grave, where a priest delivers a few remarks reminiscent of John Birchite ideology, and one or two conservative politicians from Milwaukee give short speeches reflecting the same philosophy. The recitation of the rosary around the grave generally concludes the day's memorial services.

Since the members of the John Birch Society make up a large proportion of the mourners, it is not surprising that the speeches of the afternoon dwell on the continuing menace of communism, the presence of the malignant Communist "conspiracy" in America, and the viciousness and depravity of Senator McCarthy's "murderers."[33] Typical was the graveside prayer of the Reverend Lawrence Brey, a recent chaplain for the group, at the ceremonies held in 1966:

We thank Thee, O Lord, for giving us this great warrior, who so truly gave his life fighting the powers of darkness. Be merciful to his soul, and at the same time forgive those who through shortsightedness or ignorance joined his enemies in thwarting his efforts. FINALLY, O LORD, in this hour of grave national peril give us more brave men like 'Joe' to carry on his work . . . . O Mary, Virgin Mother of God

... save America from Marxian communism; free those nations who have succumbed to the Red Beast ... support our young men in service, especially those
who are this very moment risking their lives in battle to hold back the tide of the
ravaging Red monster. Amen.[34]

The Catholic McCarthyites scattered across the land had their
last chance to vent their feelings in an organized way in August 1958
when Richard Rovere, liberal political columnist for the *New Yorker*,
published a celebrated article in *Esquire* on the senator's last days.[35]
A candid and almost embarrassingly detailed account of the senator's decline and death, it shocked the McCarthyites into angry
retaliation. A swarm of furious letters, some from writers with Irish
names (though few correspondents identified themselves as Catholics), descended on *Esquire*'s editorial offices.[36] The next year, when
Rovere published his now famous biography of the senator, Catholic conservatives once again denounced his slashing criticisms of
McCarthy. The Knights of Columbus seemed especially upset by his
acerbic treatment of the senator, and so too was Mrs. McCarthy,
who said that Rovere had made a "vicious, lying attack upon . . .
[her] husband." Rovere was exactly like all the other people who had
attacked her husband when he was still alive, she said—they all
opposed him because he was against communism. Rovere was no
different at all, she angrily insisted. Showing that she had picked up a
trick or two from her late husband, she noted in conclusion that
Rovere had once served as an associate editor of the *New Masses*, a
publication that the attorney general had officially described as a
"Communist periodical."[37] (Mrs. McCarthy's McCarthyism carried
her away at this point: Rovere had long since declared his defiant
opposition to communism.)

Though McCarthy is dead, his memory unquestionably lives
on in the hearts and minds of his devoted followers, dwindling
though their numbers be. Chief among these is of course his Catholic widow, who continues her stern efforts to protect her husband's
reputation (as well as his private papers) against all marauders. Age is

taking its toll on the rest of the faithful, but bands of Catholic McCarthyites still gather in Brooklyn and Queens, in the affluent suburbs of Washington, in Wisconsin, and in Southern California to honor his name and to continue the fight against the menace of atheistic communism. They dare not rest from their efforts, since they believe emphatically that the survival of America, the Catholic church, and the senator's good name are all at stake.

Chapter 11

Catholics and the Politics
of McCarthyism

"Catholics are free to back McCarthy to the hilt or to the wall," a Catholic editor wrote in late 1954.[1] Catholics did precisely that—both to McCarthy and to one another. With unmitigated fury they lacerated each other's political opinions and impugned the intelligence, integrity, patriotism, and even the religious fidelity of their Catholic opponents. Though American Catholics had never hesitated to go to war with one another when the "truth" was at stake, they seemed to enter the McCarthy fray with most unwonted enthusiasm. They were indulging themselves in a vicious family quarrel and little cared who knew it.

Since Catholics made no attempt to hide their differences (and, indeed, went out of their way to insist that they were *not* like other Catholics), it seems strange that so many commentators credited McCarthy with massive Catholic support. The sheer volume of angry argumentation, alone, ought to have been enough to convince the skeptics. Many observers, nonetheless, remained hard to persuade. For example, Richard L. Strout of the *New Republic* (who wrote under the pseudonym of T.R.B.) said that McCarthy had a "tremendous gravitational pull on [the] Catholic masses." Senator Charles Potter noted ominously that "many Catholics are behind him and so is the Ku Klux Klan." A year after McCarthy's death an otherwise sophisticated observer of the political and religious scene concluded that Catholics had shown an "almost monolithic uniformity" on the McCarthy question. And as recently as 1971 Fred Cook wrote darkly that a "large and powerful segment" of the church shared Cardinal Spellman's favorable assessment of McCarthy.[2]

Yet a number of authors were shrewd enough to perceive the split in the Catholic community, and they concluded rightly that Catholics were anything but "monolithic" on McCarthy. Even T.R.B. (perhaps trying to have it both ways) eventually discovered the "deep fissure" that McCarthy had created among Catholics.[3] A number of Catholic liberals saw the rift with equal clarity, and repeatedly proclaimed that Catholics were as divided on McCarthy as everyone else.[4] There was no more a "Catholic position" on McCarthy than there was a "Protestant" or "Jewish" one on him, they insisted. Donald McDonald, for instance, believed that the Catholic McCarthyites had never formed more than a "hard and bitter minority," and John Cogley denied that McCarthy had ever achieved the "sweeping Catholic acceptance" that careless writers often assumed he enjoyed.[5] The more perceptive writers of recent years, scholars such as James MacGregor Burns, for example, have made considerable efforts to delineate the rift in Catholic ranks over the senator.[6]

The opinion polls had always complicated the picture and at first glance made it seem that McCarthy enjoyed a "massive" Catholic following. Beginning in early 1954 the Gallup agency published several of its surveys of national opinion on McCarthy, carefully including Catholic opinion in the sample; it noted that Catholics seemed more solidly behind McCarthy than did the rest of the populace.[7] A closer examination of those same polls, however, would have revealed a certain softness in McCarthy's Catholic strength: although Catholics usually were eight to ten points more in favor of McCarthy than other Americans, the questions used in the polls were somewhat misleading. The pollsters usually asked, "Do you support Senator McCarthy?" This query was so vague in its phrasing that many people, Catholics included, could easily answer "yes" without meaning anything more than opposition to communism. In the fanatically anticommunistic atmosphere of the 1950s, anyone who seemed to be "doing something" about communism was guaranteed a good following: the public presumed that he was performing a worthwhile public service until the opposition emphatically proved otherwise. Finally, the questions that the pollsters asked seldom discriminated between McCarthy's *methods* and his ostensible *goal* of rooting Communists out of the government. Many Americans could have subscribed to the *goal* out of a desire to check the advance of the Communists, but they might have balked at the *methods* if asked specific questions about them. More precise questioning might have revealed a stronger reservoir of anti-McCarthy sentiment than seemed immediately apparent.

The polls unmistakably revealed a remarkably large body of vague opinion on McCarthy, with few Americans having deep feelings of either hostility or approval. Over the course of McCarthy's five years of crusading, the Gallup and Roper agencies conducted thirty-three samplings of national opinion on the senator, and on twelve different occasions they asked respondents to describe the intensity of their opinion. After examining three of these surveys, the author found that each of them showed a sizable group of people who entertained only mild feelings of approval or disapproval. The truly vehement McCarthyites and anti-McCarthyites made up only a small portion of each sample. Thus the Catholics who expressed intense approval of McCarthy never registered over 21 percent of the sample and once fell as low as 11 percent; those who expressed intense disapproval of McCarthy ranged from 14 percent to 25 percent. In the same three polls the group of Catholics with only very mild feelings or with none at all ranged impressively in size from 55 percent to 74 percent. (The number of Protestants with similarly moderate opinions was slightly smaller.)[8] These figures seemed to reveal a large mass of opinion on McCarthy that was mildly committed or virtually uncommitted; this characteristic spanned both the Catholic and the non-Catholic communities.

If most Catholics showed a marked tendency (shared by the rest of the country) to avoid taking a strong stand on McCarthy, a number of them refused to go even that far, rendering a no-comment or an I-don't-know answer when queried about him. The uncommitted portion of the Catholic community bulked as large as 56 percent (in March 1953) and as small as 8.7 percent (in December 1953) but usually ran about 20 percent.[9] At no time was the Catholic group that expressed no comment much different in size from that of the Protestants.

Even if one takes the polls at face value, they give evidence of a Catholic population not radically different from the rest of the nation in its views of the senator. Can one seriously argue that a spread of eight to ten points constitutes a major difference? Does it posit the existence of a body of Catholic opinion fundamentally different from the rest of the nation? More important still, what is one to say of the fact that Catholic support for McCarthy rose and fell in exact harmony with the rise and fall of national opinion? When the Army-McCarthy hearings destroyed McCarthy's national following, they destroyed his Catholic support as well. After the senator's disastrous bout with the Pentagon, Catholics stopped carrying the torch for McCarthy (except for the hard core of his admirers, epitomized best by the *Brooklyn Tablet* and its followers). And the rest of the country followed the same course. In similar fashion the Catholic vote on McCarthy, like the polls of Catholic opinion, showed a divided response. When Catholics voted in the elections in which McCarthyism was a factor, they generally voted like the other voters in their region (as in Appleton, Wisconsin, where McCarthy swept the electorate) or like the other voters in the wing of the political party to which they belonged.

The profound split in the Catholic ranks becomes even clearer when we examine the Catholic Americans in terms of their geographical location, organizational affiliation, educational level, occupational status, and political party affiliation. New York City is a case in point. Though it emerged as the area in which Catholic McCarthyism showed its greatest political strength (it boasted the *Brooklyn Tablet*, Cardinal Spellman, the Catholic War Veterans, and the Holy Name Societies), the McCarthyites also had to contend with the *Commonweal*, *America*, the Association of Catholic Trade Unionists, and the city's Catholic advocates of social justice. Gotham's

Catholics showed no real consensus on McCarthy, even though the Catholic McCarthyites clearly dominated the headlines, the political rallies, and the parades down Fifth Avenue.

McCarthy probably enjoyed his greatest popular strength in John Kennedy's Boston, though even there the legions of Catholic liberals rose in wrath to oppose the senator and his "ism." It seems clear, however, that McCarthy's most widespread grass-roots support among Catholics was in Boston. A 1954 survey of opinion on McCarthy in ten key states showed Massachusetts with the highest proportion of Catholic McCarthyites.[10] Other studies showing similar findings, plus the evidence of the intensive pressure that Massachusetts Catholics put on John Kennedy to force him into supporting McCarthy, seemed to underline the 1954 survey's findings. Boston's Catholic McCarthyism failed to take organized form, however, thanks to the efforts of the city's Catholic liberals and intellectuals, as well as the refusal of the hierarchy and Catholic press to lead an avowed McCarthyite crusade.

Chicago gave McCarthy his fiercest Catholic opposition, though he appears to have enjoyed a measure of popular support in that city as well. Overt Catholic McCarthyism had no chance at all in Chicago, however, due to Bishop Bernard J. Sheil, who vehemently opposed McCarthy, and because of the neutrality of both Cardinal Samuel Stritch and the *New World*, the archdiocese's official newspaper. In addition, the archdiocese had carefully nurtured a tradition of Catholic liberalism that effectively blocked right-wing movements like McCarthyism. It had long supported a variety of liberally oriented Catholic institutions such as labor-management study groups, interfaith clubs, youth associations, and civil-rights programs. Finally, the Democratic voting habits of Chicago's Catholic ethnic groups and the Catholic liberals' virtual monopoly of pulpit and press destroyed what little chance McCarthyism ever had to spread in Catholic Chicago.

Wisconsin's Catholics (making up about one-third of the state's population) seemed neither very fond of McCarthy nor much disturbed by him. For the most part those who were Democrats simply joined the rest of the state's Democrats in opposing him, with the Republican Catholics taking the opposite course. Neither side showed much interest in organizing themselves as Catholics-for-McCarthy or Catholics-against-McCarthy. The reasons for this are readily apparent: ironically enough, Wisconsin saw much less of the senator than did the Northeast, where he gave most of his speeches and carried on his anti-Communist crusades. The senator gave almost no attention to Communist suspects in Wisconsin, probably because his Red hunting in Washington was spectacularly successful at garnering the publicity he apparently wanted so badly. Why beat the Wisconsin woods for Communists when so many seemed to be lurking in Washington, where reporters were hungry for inside information and headlines came so quick and so cheap? To many Wisconsinites (Catholics included) McCarthy seemed a remote and almost irrelevant phenomenon.

In the remaining areas of the Midwest, and in the South as well, both Catholic McCarthyism and Catholic anti-McCarthyism were weak and widely diffused. Catholics had always formed a tiny minority in the rural sections of the central states and the South, and this fact, plus the failure of the populace to take a keen interest in the affairs of McCarthy, prevented outbreaks of serious Catholic activity either for the senator or against him. Not even in Louisiana, the most Catholic state in the South, did one find serious Catholic interest in the matter of McCarthy. The archbishop of New Orleans took no stand on the senator, nor did the rest of the clergy or the diocesan press or the Catholic laity. In brief, McCarthyism was a nonissue in Louisiana, as it was in all of the Catholic South. Undoubtedly one of the reasons for this was the tendency of the South to take a dimmer view of McCarthy than did the rest of the country. (For instance, the Gallup poll for June 1954 showed a larger percentage of the South registering intense disapproval of McCarthy than any other sector of the country.)[11] Once again it appears that Catholics simply followed the pattern of the region in which they lived, in this case tending either to ignore him or to look disparagingly on his crusade.

Nor did McCarthyism ever become an issue in the Far West, except for a few pockets of southern California where conservative Catholics valiantly carried the torch of McCarthyism. The living embodiment of this kind of conservative Catholic McCarthyism was the cardinal archbishop of Los Angeles, James Francis McIntyre. Though he scrupulously avoided making public statements about McCarthy, the cardinal's feelings about him appeared repeatedly in the editorials in the *Los Angeles Tidings*, the official organ of the archdiocese. (Under McIntyre's autocratic rule, the *Tidings* faithfully reflected his every opinion.) The paper took an especially strong stand for McCarthy during the tense days of the Army-McCarthy hearings, no doubt reflecting the McCarthyite views of its mentor.[12] McIntyre notwithstanding, southern California Catholics failed to canonize McCarthy. No doubt one of the reasons for this was the extraordinary expansion that the church in southern California was undergoing during the postwar years, a phenomenon that occupied most of the time, talents, and energies of the Catholics in that region.

The major organizations of the Catholic laity in America reflected the bitterly divisive feelings on McCarthy. The Catholic War Veterans, numbering over 200,000 by 1954, boasted an energetic leadership that made no attempt to hide its affections for the senator, believing his cause to be eminently Catholic and American. Though a few of the Catholic veterans expressed dissent with the CWV's official stand, the former National Commander of the CWV, Robert Goff, is probably correct when he says that most members favored McCarthy and only a few ever questioned his methods.[13] Nevertheless, when it came to active participation in McCarthyism, most of the CWV's members seemed content to let the National Commander and his local assistants carry on the bulk of the crusade. McCarthy's "mass support" with the veterans seems to have remained largely passive and inchoate, though it was unquestionably present within the membership.

The Knights of Columbus, enjoying a national membership of over 920,000 in 1954, carefully avoided a formal endorsement of McCarthy. The fact remains, however, that many Knights supported him nonetheless.[14] To illustrate: the monthly journal of the Knights, *Columbia*, published a series of editorials praising the exploits of a mythical Communist investigator named "O'Clavichord" who used "tough" methods (called "O'Clavichordism") to rout the Communists out of the government. O'Clavichordism was precisely what the country needed, the editors of *Columbia* averred.[15] The mythical O'Clavichord was, of course, nothing but a thinly disguised Joe McCarthy. A majority of the Knights who wrote to *Columbia* about the O'Clavichord editorials approved of the magazine's pro-McCarthy policy, though a vociferous minority condemned him as a reactionary demagogue, disapproving especially of his book-burning tactics and his efforts at thought control.[16]

The Knights took their boldest stand for McCarthy in August 1954, just before the Watkins committee began its hearings. Meeting at their annual convention, they passed a resolution calling for continued congressional investigations into the problem of Communist subversion. Coming during the national debate then raging over McCarthy, the resolution could only represent a vote of confidence in his activities.[17] The Knights' pro-McCarthy policy was completely congruent with their long history of political conservatism, their failure to support civil rights and social legislation, their flag-waving patriotism, and their abiding distaste for Protestants, liberals, and intellectuals of every religion.

Catholic labor groups, on the other hand, violently opposed McCarthy, calling his style of anticommunism counterproductive and condemning his actions as bogus politics of the worst sort. In New York City, when the International Ladies Garment Workers' Union took a defiant stand against McCarthy, the many Italian

Catholics active in the union supported its policy. The Association of Catholic Trade Unionists would have moved more decisively against McCarthy if it had possessed enough funds and membership to wage a full-scale, nationwide campaign. Lacking such resources, ACTU leaders in Boston, New York, Detroit, and Chicago lobbied as actively against him as they could, making especially vigorous efforts to publicize his antilabor voting record. Meanwhile, ACTU's principal publications—*The Wage Earner*, *The Labor Leader*, and *Work*—denounced McCarthy repeatedly and often with great bitterness.[18]

What *kinds* of Catholics liked McCarthy? Were they the masses of Catholic workers, the less educated, the poor, the Irish, the Italians? Or did McCarthy draw his Catholic strength from the newly rich, the upward bound, and the Catholics who were beginning to switch their traditional political affiliation from the Democrats to the Republicans? These are some of the questions that the two leading schools of McCarthyite historiography have attempted to answer. The earlier, or "pluralist" school (as it is often called) numbering Seymour Martin Lipset, Daniel Bell, Richard Hofstadter, and others concluded that McCarthy appealed to those Catholics who were anxious about their status—to Catholics who felt their social and economic position threatened by upper-class WASPS, for instance, or by a vaguely defined Eastern "establishment." (It is apparent that the pluralist theorists were thinking about the discontented agrarian protesters of the late nineteenth century as they developed their hypothesis.) Since they believed that most cold-war Catholics fell into the status-threatened category, they tended to find that McCarthy enjoyed strong support among Catholics.[19] The more recent school of Nelson Polsby, Michael Paul Rogin, and others has also tended to conclude that McCarthyism was intense among Catholics but has found that it was limited mostly to conservative Republican Catholics.[20] Consequently, they have proposed a *political* interpretation, one that stands at variance with the earlier theories based on class consciousness or patterns of psychological distress (such as paranoia and schizophrenia).

Which theory holds up better in the light of the evidence currently available? Both schools of thought believed that McCarthyism flourished among the less-educated classes.[21] Was this true for Catholics as well? Of the three existing studies that attempt to answer this problem, two find that McCarthyism declined as the educational level of Catholics rose. An examination conducted in 1954 of Catholic opinion on McCarthy in Bennington, Vermont, showed that the more education a Catholic had received, the less chance he had of favoring McCarthy. Thus although Catholics who had completed only a grammar-school education approved of McCarthy by 68 percent, the number of McCarthyites decreased as the educational level rose: for instance, only 38 percent of the Catholic college graduates opted for McCarthy. (Among Protestants the same pattern prevailed, though his support was smaller at every stage.)[22]

The Bennington study also attempted to find a correlation between Catholic McCarthyism and the respondents' occupational levels and educational attainment. The survey revealed that among Catholics, at least, sentiment for McCarthy fell noticeably as educational and occupational levels rose. Thus among the manual workers, some 57 percent favored McCarthy; among those with a high school education or more, the same number, 56 percent, also favored him. But among the salaried workers, only 36 percent of those without as much education still took his side. Finally, those employed in small business showed the greatest disparity: 37 percent of the better educated favored him, while 88 percent of the lesser educated opted for McCarthy.[23] Not only did a short education seem to breed McCarthyites, but the combination of poor education and a successful climb out of the ranks of the manually employed seemed to increase the chances that a Catholic would favor McCarthyism. The data from the Gallup polls, however, presented a quite different picture.

An analysis of the Gallup poll on McCarthy for January 1954 showed that McCarthy had a majority of support among Catholics in every educational category save one, that of the Catholics whose education had stopped between grades one through six (45 percent of this group favored McCarthy). In all the other educational levels he enjoyed support ranging from 50 percent to 57 percent. The only anomaly one can notice is that college graduates were slightly less favorable to McCarthy than those with an incomplete college education (50 percent for the graduates and 51.6 percent for the rest); the same pattern holds true for high-school graduates as compared with those who did not complete their high-school education.[24] (Data for Protestants and Jews are not yet available.)

Clearly, we need much more evidence if we are to solve the puzzle of what educational attainment had to do with Catholic McCarthyism and anti-McCarthyism. For one thing, McCarthy's strong showing in the Gallup data may reflect nothing more than the fact that his fortunes were at high tide in January 1954; surveys taken over the whole five years of his career as a Red hunter may reveal a sharper differentiation between the better-educated Catholics and those with shorter educational backgrounds.

Did age have a bearing on the way Catholics felt about McCarthy? The Gallup data for January 1954 present no truly convincing correlates between age and McCarthyism. The pollsters tested every age group from twenty to eighty years of age and found that a majority of all but two of the categories favored McCarthy by 50 percent or more:

Age Level of Catholics and Opinion of McCarthy

Age	% Favoring McCarthy	% vs. McCarthy	% with No Opinion
20–29	52.5	20.0	27.4
30–39	55.2	26.0	18.5
40–49	50.0	29.6	20.2
50–59	46.4	30.3	23.1
60–69	73.6	15.7	10.5
70–79	40.0	26.6	33.2

A glance at the figures shows that McCarthy's popularity declines from category 30 to 39 through the 40s and 50s until category 60 to 69.[25] Is the moral of the story that the older one got, the wiser one got about McCarthy? Perhaps so, though the sudden rise to 73.6 percent favoring McCarthy among the Catholics in their 60s raises an immediate problem, the solution of which does not readily appear. Once again, McCarthy studies need much more data than is presently available.

If educational level and age do not yield very certain insights into the structure of Catholic McCarthyism, then perhaps income level (or at least occupational status) provides one. A study of the upper-class Catholics in Winchester, Massachusetts, revealed a pronounced ground swell for McCarthy, with 54 percent of the Catholics approving of him as compared to 32 percent of the Protestants.[26] It is noteworthy that the Winchester Catholics not only made up the largest religious group in the city and 46 percent of the population, but they constituted some of the wealthiest Catholics in the state.[27]

The study of the Catholics in Bennington described earlier shows similar findings for labor-class Catholics. The survey revealed that Catholic workers were noticeably stronger in their admiration for McCarthy than were Protestant laborers: thus 41 percent of the Protestants liked McCarthy, and 52 percent of the Catholics leaned the same way. Among middle-class Catholics, by contrast, almost twice as many opposed him as favored him, though the remarkably large number of Catholics with only mild feelings of approval or disapproval reduces the significance of the anti-McCarthy group.[28]

The Bennington and Winchester studies, taken together, show majority support for McCarthy among upper-class and working-class Catholics, but middle-class Catholics seemingly avoided taking a strong position on the senator. A long list of further questions needs to be answered when the materials become available: did upward-bound Catholics favor McCarthy? Did lower-class manual workers, trapped in a system of short schooling and low socio-economic achievement, also turn to McCarthy? Perhaps so, but the evidence available at this point is too small to permit firm judgments. Michael Paul Rogin confidently asserted that successful businessmen, professionals, and the better-educated classes all opposed McCarthy, but that Catholics, lower socio-economic groups, and the poorly educated all favored him.[29] Was he right? He may well have guessed correctly, but it is little more than a guess, and his speculations need empirical verification.

The most revealing and convincing evidence appears when one looks at the party preferences of the Catholic McCarthyites and anti-McCarthyites. For example, the study of the Catholic workers in Bennington demonstrated that only a minority of the Catholic Democrats (48 percent) favored McCarthy; yet the Catholic Republicans and independents supported him by 68 percent and 64 percent respectively. It is immediately apparent that party preference was a major factor in determining how Catholic workers (at least in Bennington) felt about McCarthy. (Since the Democrats outnumbered the Republicans almost three to one and equalled the Republicans and independent workers taken together, the significance of these findings can hardly be overestimated.)[30]

When researchers from the University of Michigan examined prospective Catholic voters in 1954, they found results strikingly similar to those of the Bennington study cited above. Thus among strong Democrats (by far the largest group of Catholics), some 33 percent opposed McCarthy and only 18 percent favored him. Equally important was the size of McCarthy's margin among strong Republican Catholics: 39 percent of them said they liked McCarthy, compared to 23 percent who opposed him.[31] In short, among Catholics who expressed a political preference, Democratic allegiance definitely weakened McCarthy's strength, and Republican affiliation sharply intensified it.

The study of the upper-class Catholics in Winchester, Massachusetts, seems to lead toward the same conclusions. It found that as Catholics moved to that affluent suburb, they tended to switch their vote to the Republican party.[32] (Since the survey failed to break down the Catholic McCarthyites according to party, we cannot conclude with certainty that his findings supported the studies of the Bennington Catholics and the University of Michigan analysis cited earlier. Nevertheless, they seem to verge in that direction since the study found that the Winchester Catholics were both McCarthyite and Republican.) In addition, Professor Rogin has correctly noted that for strong party identifiers, party seemed to have more impact on opinion about McCarthy than did religion.[33]

All of this seems to show that the newer political interpretation gives a much better explanation of Catholic McCarthyism than does the earlier pluralist approach with its emphasis on status anxieties, authoritarian personality types, and distaste for the Eastern establishment.

Both schools of thought agreed on one conclusion, however: they concurred that the Catholic Irish had given fervent support to McCarthy. Whether correct or wide of the mark, the point is worth examining in detail, for the Irish constituted the politically dominant force in the American church and made up one of its largest bodies as well. Thus Seymour Martin Lipset found that Irish (as well as Italian) Catholics "were among the most pro-McCarthy groups," and Rogin said the same.[34] More prosaic statements of the same thesis have come from Allan Nevins, who believed that "Irish Catholics . . . admired Joe as a fighting Hibernian," and Kevin Phillips, who wrote that the "typical Irish plumbing contractor and his work crew shared hearty amusement over McCarthy's yanking of the English moustache of Secretary of State Dean Acheson."[35]

Does the theory stand the test of empirical analysis? A Roper poll for 1952 showed that 18 percent more Irish supported McCarthy than rejected him.[36] However, two problems arise immediately. First, the authors who cite the poll do not say how many Irish remained uncommitted on McCarthy; if the group was large, then the significance of the 18 percent who favored him declines greatly. Secondly (as Lipset himself notes), a second poll conducted in 1954 by the International Research Associates showed the pro-McCarthy Irish edging out the anti-McCarthyites by only 5 percent.[37] Lipset does not account for the discrepancy between these two polls, which indeed is crucial to his thesis that the Irish "disproportionately backed" McCarthy.[38] His study of Italian Catholics shows a similar clashing of figures between the 1952 and 1954 polls and hence suffers from the same weakness.[39] Only when more data becomes available will it be clear precisely how large a portion of the Irish Catholics in the nation truly took McCarthy's side and how many of them took up arms against him. Certainly the Irish *leadership* was as fully divided on McCarthy as any other segment of the American church: liberal Irish educators and publicists matched wits with their conservative Irish counterparts in the press—as did Irish priests, bishops, educators, etc. One suspects that the masses of Irish Catholics, who took a less public and active role in the controversy, reflected the nationwide split on McCarthy.

What about the other three large bodies of Catholic ethnics—the Germans, the Poles, and the Italians? None of these Catholics took any significant part in the McCarthy debate, either as advocates of the senator or as challengers to his thesis. One looks in vain at the Italian precincts in Boston (the North End, for instance) to find evidence of interest in Joe McCarthy; one finds the same absence of political activity in the Polish wards of Milwaukee, as well as in the German Catholic farming communities of Wisconsin and Minnesota. Everywhere it was the same: the Catholic ethnics, though unquestionably anticommunist, were more concerned with the bread-and-butter issues of employment, welfare, education, farm prices, housing, and world peace. To be sure, when the Poles of Milwaukee and Madison were confronted directly with the issue of McCarthyism, as they were in the election of 1952, they voted overwhelmingly against the senator. But not even the Wisconsin Democrats who engineered the victory could claim that McCarthyism had been the overriding issue of the campaign. In fact, it had been a secondary issue.

Our conclusion therefore is that Catholics divided on McCarthy fully as much as the rest of the country, though their support for him was broader than among other population groups. That is to say, the Catholic McCarthyites outnumbered the anti-McCarthy Catholics, and his popularity with Catholics was slightly stronger than with the rest of the population. Still, the eleven polls of national opinion made available to the present writer show that McCarthy captured a majority of the Catholics in three months only: December 1953, January 1954, and March 1954. Moreover, it is clear that only a small minority took up his cause in a vocal and active way. The remaining Catholic McCarthyites gave him passive and silent support until they finally drifted away under the pressure of the TV hearings. Although Catholic support for him was "broad," it was nevertheless "thin" as well, tending to break down when put to the test.

The debate over McCarthyism was thus predominantly an affair of elites—of conservative editors, politicians, educators, business leaders, and leading clergymen—all ranged against liberals drawn largely from the same ranks. Only in New York and Boston did the Catholic masses actively support his campaign, and even in those cities a conservative elite pushed the McCarthy bandwagon fully as much as the masses followed it. Within the Catholic elites, however, a savage battle raged over McCarthy. The conflict grew worse as the issue progressed because it inevitably got caught up with that most volatile of political issues, the love of country. Both sides made repeated and strident appeals to patriotism, the McCarthyites insisting that love of one's homeland meant unqualified acceptance of McCarthy, since he alone was attacking the root of everything that menaced America, the specter of atheistic communism. The anti-McCarthyites in the Catholic community made a similar appeal to patriotism (though perhaps a little less stridently) by claiming that the preservation of the Republic depended on the destruction of McCarthyism, because it threatened the democratic procedures that lay at the heart of the American system. Both sides looked upon themselves as fully American and fully patriotic. Each side felt no scruples at all about casting doubts on the loyalty of the opposition, though each did so in different ways. The conservatives constantly impugned the Americanism of the anti-McCarthyites, saying that as liberals they stood ready to do business with Communist sympathizers and that the Communists had not better friends than these liberals who cynically called themselves "Catholics." They made an open and emotional appeal to love of country, insisting that the virtue of unalloyed Americanism belonged to them alone. The liberals (though not without their own emotionalism) indirectly attacked the Americanism of the conservatives by calling them "undemocratic." With the advent of Joe McCarthy in the fifties, the liberals had a new enemy of civil liberties to worry about, and they attacked his Catholic admirers with renewed zeal, seeing them as his helpmates in the war against freedom and democracy.

The searing argument over patriotism, therefore, was the one that made Catholics angry. Why was this so? The answer probably lies deep in the history of American Catholicism, in that long chronicle of a foreign-born people who fought for three centuries to shed their immigrant status but never seemed fully Americanized. For nearly three hundred years their critics accused them of owing allegiance to a foreign power (the pope), of speaking strange languages, of practicing exotic religious rituals, of maintaining their own peculiar system of morals, and worst of all, of supporting their own private schools at the expense of the public-school system. They always appeared to be a people apart and seemed to resist becoming a part of the great American melting pot. By the late 1950s, it seemed that in many ways Catholics were finally entering into the American social fabric. They were making a long-delayed entrance into the suburbs, the professions, and the "good life." They were beginning to have an impact on national politics, and the memory of their devotion to the American effort in the Second World War was still fresh. To many non-Catholics it seemed that they were less of a menace to the American democratic system than they had seemed to be thirty or forty years earlier.

Catholics and McCarthyism

With the advent of the Communist-hunt era, Catholics had a chance to eliminate all doubt about their patriotism. Americanism in the 1940s and 1950s came more and more to mean anticommunism, since external and domestic communism were clearly the gravest problems besetting the Republic (or so many believed). Many American Catholics were beginning to argue that anticommunism was not only true Americanism, it was authentic Catholicism as well. With a relish born of their centuries-long status as a despised minority, Catholics eagerly took upon themselves the mantle of patriotism. It was an impregnable cloak, they soon found out, and one perfectly suited to the political climate prevailing in the postwar years. At long last, their critics would be unable to question their Americanism. They would be above suspicion, for they had become the most fully American of the Americans.

It was probably inevitable that the McCarthy contest would poison the relationship between Catholics and non-Catholics. Many Protestant leaders, convinced that they saw the specter of Catholicism lurking behind Joe McCarthy, feared that the church was using him to club the rest of the nation into submission. If this argument seems fanciful now, it was painfully real at the time and was a clear product of the emotionalism born of the epoch. The *Commonweal* and the *Nation*, for instance, shared a common distaste for McCarthy; they also had a mutual loathing for each other, one that surfaced every time the *Nation* printed another article by Paul Blanshard or ran an editorial accusing Spanish Catholics of denying religious freedom to Protestants in Spain.

Yet in spite of the efforts of Paul Blanshard, the *Nation*, and the *Christian Science Monitor* to make a Catholic issue out of McCarthyism, Catholics generally avoided turning the McCarthy dispute into a religious affair. By and large they looked on McCarthyism as a political question, with the Catholic opponents of McCarthy continuing to side with the Democrats (as they had always done) and the Catholic conservatives continuing to find their McCarthyite moorings in the legions of the Republican right. Though a few Catholics did at times evoke the religious argument, the occasions that they did so stood out as exceptions, not as the rule. They showed little patience with political commentators and Protestant divines who found the shadow of the pope lurking furtively in the wings, and of course they had no patience at all with other Catholics who tried to invoke arguments from sacred writ or Catholic tradition, either in defense of the senator or in condemnation of him.

All of this seemed to show that Catholics had assimilated themselves rather well into the political system; at times they seemed barely distinguishable from other Democrats and other Republicans. An examination of the position of the Catholic liberals on *other* issues besides McCarthyism shows them consistently following the Democrats (or occasionally the liberal Republicans). Not surprisingly, they admired and supported the Fair Deal just as they had earlier upheld the cause of the New Deal. But the Catholic conservatives had become an integrated part of the Republican family as well. By the decade of the fifties, they stood shoulder to shoulder with their fellow Republicans in support of the Taft-Hartley Act, in denouncing Harry Truman's social welfare schemes, and in opposing massive assistance to the war-torn European nations. Catholics more and more tended to follow the mainstreams of American political life, choosing the left current or the right, as the political mood suited them.

This is not to say that Catholics were assimilated totally into American political life. Far from it. Sometimes, the process had gone no further than common agreement on a set of rhetorical statements; a fine example was the great American doctrine of the separation of church and state. Both Catholics and non-Catholics could concur on the reasonableness of this high-sounding principle, but they differed sharply on its application. Did separation of church and state exclude government assistance to Catholic parochial schools? Catholics thought not, but Protestants emphatically believed that it did, drawing their support from a far wider source than lobbying groups like the Protestants and Other Americans United for Separation of

Church and State. Catholics had come a long way, nevertheless; by and large the Catholic Democrats showed little difference from Protestant Democrats, as did Catholic Republicans when compared to Protestant Republicans.

When one looks back on the Catholic experience with McCarthyism, one is also struck by the *lack* of churchly influence on the nation's Catholics. Put in its simplest terms, Catholics failed to follow the direction of the church in the matter of McCarthy because that direction was muted and ambiguous at best. Furthermore, Catholics were determined to follow their ecclesiastical leaders only in the most strictly defined religious areas, such as attendance at church on Sunday, the requirement of marriage before a Catholic priest, or the maintenance of the parochial school system. Whether by default, by accident, or by design, Catholics were in the habit of finding their own answers to most day-to-day questions (and in virtually all intellectual, cultural, and political matters) without the help of the duly appointed and official leaders of their church. It was not simply that Catholics chose their occupations without the advice and consent of the local bishop. Virtually the entire scope of their lives existed outside the direct influence of the church.

A survey of Catholic reading habits taken in 1954 dramatically illustrated this phenomenon. When the pollsters asked Catholics how many of them regularly read a Catholic newspaper or periodical, only 44 percent of them said that they customarily did so.[40] Is it any wonder, then, that the overwhelmingly McCarthyite Catholic press failed to have so little influence on the Catholic readership in America? If Catholics paid little attention to papal statements on capitalism, peace, and the errors of recent heretics, they seemed equally uninterested in the annual statements of the American bishops on similar topics. As early as the Spanish Civil War (1936–39), a majority of Catholics polled in national surveys indicated that they disagreed with the American hierarchy in its public stand on the war (in this case, the pro-Franco position that the bishops had adopted).[41] Repeated calls of the hierarchy and the lower clergy for the masses of lay Catholics to join in crusades against abortion, pornography, or Paul Blanshard had met an indifferent reception. Only in New England or New York City could Catholics shake off their political passivity long enough to pass laws against birth control or to remove "anti-Catholic" books from the shelves of public libraries. If the Catholic church was an authoritarian institution, the masses of lay Catholics seemed resolutely determined to confine that authority to a set of narrowly defined religious functions. The bishops might well urge Catholics to support the civil-rights movement for blacks, but many lay Catholics would wonder out loud if the prelates had spoken out of turn. The activist-minded Catholic liberals, to be sure, defended the bishops' right to speak out in favor of black equality (or on any other moral issue) because they believed most vehemently in the thesis that Catholic belief ought to have an impact on all of one's actions. They detested the tendency of many Catholics to think that their religion began and ended with Mass on Sunday. A popular poem of the period, one that the liberals liked to quote, described a Catholic businessman who refused to let the church interfere with his daily life:

> Mr. Business went to church,
> He never missed a Sunday.
> Mr. Business went to hell,
> For what he did on Monday.

Viewed in retrospect, Mr. Business and Joe McCarthy seemed to share much in common. Though chary of making a public display of their religiosity, both were loyal Catholics: they carefully obeyed the rules of their religion, nor would they ever have thought seriously about abandoning Catholicism for another church. A streak of anti-intellectualism, however, also ran through them: they tended to look with suspicion on scholars, experts, professors, and, above all else, the critics of the church and the nation. The church was good enough as it stood, since its only real function was to prevent sin in this life and lead to glory in the next. The nation was also good enough as it stood, since it had won two wars in a half century and stood as the last remaining obstacle against atheistic communism. (The very phrase *atheistic communism* indicated how devotion to church and loyalty to country had become so closely intertwined.) If the fidelity of Mr. Business and Joe McCarthy to religion and Republic seemed knee jerk and unreflective, it was nevertheless sincere and deeply felt.

Though serious about Mass on Sunday, both Mr. Business and Joe McCarthy put severe limits on the *moral* authority of the church: the church had no business "butting in," as they liked to say, on affairs that it called moral questions but that were nevertheless none of its concern. Such topics included open housing, the closed shop, child-labor legislation, civil rights and civil liberties, and the moral conduct of politicians holding elective office. All of these were strictly political questions in which the church had no real competence. Many churchmen (and most Catholic liberals), by contrast, argued that such questions were moral as well as political and hence fell most properly within the domain of the church. The split between the advocates of the hands-off school of thought (perhaps typified best by William F. Buckley, Jr., who averred that the church was a "mother" but not a "teacher") and the interventionist school (perhaps exemplified best by John Cogley of the *Commonweal*) constituted one of the deepest divisions in the church. Furthermore, the rift was a historic one that went back to the earliest days of the church in the New World. Catholics had long split their ranks between the interventionists who wanted to remake American society because they believed it tainted with immorality and the antiactivists who believed that the church ought to stay in church and leave the rest of the world to the men of the world. By and large Catholics wanted to leave the matter of McCarthy to the men of the world.

If American Catholics chose to define their church's task in the narrowest possible terms, focusing myopically on Sunday things and Sunday problems, part of the reason undoubtedly lies in that remarkable American institution known as the "civil religion." Though not an organized or even a visible entity, the American civil religion is nevertheless most real and all-pervasive. It is that body of religious beliefs and moral values that undergirds American life, to which all (or nearly all) Americans give specific assent, and that forms an enduring staple of the rhetoric of American politics. The closest student of the phenomenon, Robert Bellah, has identified some of the salient doctrines that make up the civil religion: the belief that God has called America to be a "new Israel" (an example to the rest of the world of a God-fearing and law-abiding nation); the conviction that God will stay with America in times of trial but that at the end of time America, too, must face a stern judgment; the notion that democracy, individual freedom, and religious pluralism are all ordained by God for America's benefit; the thesis that God has made America to be an asylum for the oppressed; the doctrine that God made all men equal in America and gave them all an equal chance in this "new" country that He established for the edification of the rest of the world.[42] In Bellah's view the civil religion does not replace the established religions but runs parallel to them, embodying what all Americans, nonchurchgoers as well as churchgoers, have come to believe. Religious cynics like Benjamin Franklin can subscribe to it, as well as mystic-martyrs like Abraham Lincoln and righteous churchmen like John Foster Dulles.

The civil religion was alive and well in the McCarthy era (as it still is). When President Eisenhower talked about America as the world's last bastion against "atheistic communism," he was merely voicing a new form of the old axiom that America is the "last best hope" of mankind. (It was as traditional a viewpoint as John Winthrop's prayer of 1630 that the Commonwealth of Massachusetts Bay would be a "city on a hill," giving the rest of the world an example of a godly community, of the only community left on the globe that held out the promise of salvation and order.) When politicians of both parties and all faiths scored the Communists for their irreligion, their antidemocratic practices, and their plain indifference to personal freedoms, they struck chords that went back beyond the Founding Fathers and lay at the heart of the civil-religious ethic. When the nation opened its doors to the refugees from the Communist states (and opened its hearts to ex-Communists like Whittaker Chambers and Louis F. Budenz), it was following a tradition as old as the nation and one aptly symbolized by the words of Emma Lazarus engraved on the Statue of Liberty, "Give me your tired, your poor, your huddled masses, yearning to breathe free."

In short, the McCarthy era brought about a renewal and an intensification of the civil religion. In doing so, the civil religion did what it always does: it stripped the established churches of much of their power, it deflected religious energies in other directions, and it called attention more to "this nation under God" than to God himself. Nevertheless, it showed once again that America was in some sense a profoundly religious enterprise, that it went to church in ways peculiar to itself (but nevertheless it *went*), and that it was still a "nation with the soul of a church."

But if most Catholics turned a deaf ear to the political arguments arising over McCarthyism, a few of them did not. The Catholic liberals were especially active during the McCarthy episode, striving to articulate an ethic both of Catholic civil libertarianism and of reasonable anticommunism. These concepts helped form the foundation of the "Catholic renaissance" of the 1960s—a period that witnessed the Second Vatican Council and a growing Catholic emphasis on personal freedom, on religious toleration, and on the right of the individual (even the Catholic individual) to a personal expression of his own opinions. Most important of all, however, the decade brought the inauguration of the first Catholic president, for whose acceptance the Catholic liberals had helped pave the way by demanding religious freedom for all. Many thoughtful Americans began to question the need of worrying about a Catholic in the White House, with Catholics insisting vigorously on freedom of religion for everyone. Is it too much to say that out of the conflicts of the McCarthy era came the ecumenical promise of the Kennedy years, that out of the trauma of the early fifties came the promise of the sixties?

Notes

1. *Brooklyn Tablet*, 10 June 1950.

2. Roy Deferrari, *The Sources of Catholic Dogma*, pp. 429–37, 461–64.

3. Henry J. Browne, "Catholicism in the United States," in James Smith and A. Leland Jamison, eds., *The Shaping of American Religion* (Princeton: Princeton University Press, 1961), p. 98.

4. George N. Shuster, *Religion Behind the Iron Curtain* (New York: Macmillan Co., 1954), pp. 16–17; Alberto Galter, *The Red Book of the Persecuted Church* (Westminister, Md.: Newman Press, 1957), pp. 44–46; D. J. White, "Union of Soviet Socialist Republics, Since 1917," in *New Catholic Encyclopedia*, 14:410.

5. On Ryan, see Francis Broderick, *Right Reverend New Dealer* (New York: Macmillan Co., 1963); David O'Brien, *American Catholics and Social Reform*, chap. 6 and pp. 37–40, 72–74, 175–77; on Day, see Dorothy Day, *The Long Loneliness* (New York: Harper and Bros., 1952), pp. 169–263.

6. O'Brien, *American Catholics*, pp. 81–83.

7. Ibid., pp. 79–80.

8. For a reliable study in English of the war, see Gabriel Jackson, *The Spanish Republic and the Civil War, 1931–1939* (Princeton: Princeton University Press, 1965).

9. O'Brien, *American Catholics*, pp. 86–89; Donald Crosby, "Boston's Catholics and the Spanish Civil War," pp. 82–100.

10. J. Lerhinan, "Divini Redemptoris," in *New Catholic Encyclopedia*, 4:924.

11. O'Brien, *American Catholics*, p. 96.

12. *National Catholic Almanac, 1942*, p. 762.

13. Ibid., *1944*, p. 723.

14. *New York Times*, 18 February 1945, p. 24; *Almanac, 1946*, pp. 689, 704–5. Gillis is quoted in Peter H. Irons, "America's Cold War Crusade," p. 170.

15. *New York Times*, 18 April 1945, p. 25; *Almanac, 1946*, pp. 703, 714.

16. *New York Times*, 27 May 1945, p. 11; *Almanac, 1946,* pp. 722, 735, 772.

17. Quoted in Irons, "America's Cold War," p. 318.

18. *New York Times*, 19 October 1946, p. 6.

19. Ibid., 2 December 1946, p. 14.

20. *Boston Pilot*, 8 March 1947, 8 August 1947.

21. Robert I. Gannon, *The Cardinal Spellman Story*, p. 338.

22. *Almanac, 1948*, pp. 727, 800; *New York Times*, 10 February 1947, p. 19; 5 October 1946, p. 3; 7 October 1946, pp. 5, 7; 12 October 1946, p. 7.

23. *Almanac, 1949*, p. 793.

24. *New York Times*, 26 June 1946, p. 6; *Boston Pilot*, 8 February 1947; *Almanac, 1950*, p. 784.

25. *Almanac, 1948*, p. 783; *Almanac, 1950*, p. 748.

26. Gannon, *Spellman*, pp. 340–46.

27. *New York Times*, 7 February 1949, pp. 1, 3.

28. Ibid., 6 January 1949, p. 18.

29. Ibid., 10 February 1949, p. 4.

30. Ibid., 16 May 1949, p. 13.

31. Ibid., 7 October 1946, p. 5; Eric Goldman, *The Crucial Decade—and After*, p. 130.

32. *New York Times*, 25 October 1946, p. 48; Gannon, *Spellman Story*, pp. 336–37.

33. Goldman, *Crucial Decade*, p. 130.

34. *New York Times*, 25 September 1948, p. 32; 10 February 1941, p. 1; Goldman, *Crucial Decade*, pp. 130–31.

35. Francis Cardinal Spellman Papers, St. Joseph's Seminary, Dunwoodie, N.Y.

36. See especially Fulton J. Sheen, *Communism and the Conscience of the West*; Sheen, *Philosophy of Religion*.

37. *New York Times*, 25 March 1946, p. 6.

38. See especially Louis F. Budenz, *This Is My Story*; Budenz, *The Bolshevik Invasion of the West*.

39. *New York Times*, 26 June 1946, p. 6; *Boston Pilot*, 8 February 1947; *Almanac, 1950*, p. 784.

40. *New York Times*, 22 March 1948, p. 41; 23 March 1948, p. 27; 24 March 1948, p. 5; 31 March 1948, p. 1; 27 April 1948, p. 5.

41. Ibid., 24 March 1949, pp. 1, 2; 27 March 1949, p. 47.

42. Ibid., 20 March 1946, p. 8; 24 March 1947, p. 23; 27 March 1947, p. 2; 14 October 1947, p. 29.

43. Ibid., 12 June 1946, p. 3; 23 August 1946, p. 38; 11 March 1948, p. 9.

44. Ibid., 17 July 1948, p. 28.

45. Ibid., 8 November 1949, p. 13.

46. *Boston Pilot*, 15 March 1947.

47. *Almanac, 1949*, p. 788.

48. *New York Times*, 9 September 1947, p. 19.

49. Goldman, *Crucial Decade*, p. 131.

50. Interview with James O'Gara, 17 February 1972.

51. Christopher Emmet, "Mundt-Nixon Bill" pp. 253–56; "Civil Liberties and Mundt-Nixon," 306–7, 354, 423; 13 August 1948, p. 23; John C. Cort, "Mundt-Nixon Bill," pp. 285–86.

52. *New York Times*, 16 October 1945, p. 15.

53. Aaron I. Abell, *American Catholicism and Social Action*, pp. 275–78.

54. Interview with James O'Gara, 17 February 1972.

55. Ernest Havemann and Patricia West, *They Went to College* (New York: Harcourt, Brace & Co., 1952), pp. 192, 194.

56. Angus Campbell, Gerald Gurin, and Warren E. Miller, *The Voter Decides*, p. 71; Angus Campbell and Robert L. Kahn, *The People Elect a President*, p. 36.

57. *Commonweal* 49 (14 January 1949): 345.

58. *Public Opinion Quarterly* 11 (Winter 1947–48): 643.

59. Ibid. 13 (Winter, 1949–50): 712.

60. Robert Griffith, *The Politics of Fear*, pp. 48–51.

Chapter 2

1. Jack Anderson and Ronald May, *McCarthy*, p. 8.

2. Ibid., p. 11.

3. Interviews with the Reverend James Orford, 15 November 1971; the Reverend Raphael Hamilton, 16 November 1971; the Reverend Perry Roetz, 13 November 1971.

4. Interview with Arlo McKinnon, 16 November 1971.

5. Allen Matusow, ed., *Joseph R. McCarthy*, p. 11.

6. Richard Rovere, *Senator Joe McCarthy*, p. 91.

7. See Quickie Divorce folder, National Committee for an Effective Congress Papers, National Committee for an Effective Congress, Washington, D.C. See also Oliver Pilat and William V. Shannon, "The One-Man Mob of Joe McCarthy," *New York Post*, 6 September 1951.

8. Anderson and May, *McCarthy*, p. 70.

9. Robert Griffith, *The Politics of Fear*, p. 9.

10. *Antigo* (Wis.) *Daily Journal*, 4 June 1945.

11. Interview with Charles Kersten, 15 November 1971.

12. Griffith, *Politics*, p. 11.

13. *Madison* (Wis.) *Capital-Times*, 23 October 1946.

14. *Appleton* (Wis.) *Post-Crescent*, 2 November 1946. For more on the Catholic issue in the 1946 campaign, see Michael O'Brien, "Senator Joseph McCarthy in Wisconsin," p. 322.

15. James M. O'Neill, *Catholics in Controversy*, pp. 173–74.

16. *Time*'s descriptions of McCarthy's physical appearance were particularly vivid. See especially, 55 (10 April 1950): 17–19; 56 (25 December 1950): 11; 58 (22 October 1951): 21–24. See also Rovere, *McCarthy*, chap. 2, as well as Anderson and May, *McCarthy*, pp. 3–4, 23–24, 358–59. For a description of the McCarthy that most Americans came to recognize best, the senator of the Army-McCarthy hearings, see the standard work by Michael Straight, *Trial by Television*.

17. Interview with Arthur Watkins, 4 January 1968, Oral History Collection, Dwight D. Eisenhower Papers, Dwight D. Eisenhower Presidential Library, Abilene, Kans.

18. Interview with Theodore Hesburgh, 6 January 1972.

19. Interview with Charles Kersten, 15 November 1971.

20. Interview with Clarence Manion, 5 January 1972.

21. Anderson and May, *McCarthy*, pp. 61–62.

22. Ibid., pp. 58–61.

23. Griffith, *Politics*, pp. 48–60.

24. Rovere, *McCarthy*, pp. 109–10.

25. Kersten interview. See also Personal Notes on McCarthy folder, National Committee for an Effective Congress.

26. Robert Schwartz to Barron Beshoar, 14 October 1951, Robert Fleming Papers.

27. Kersten interview.

28. Interview with Patrick F. Scanlan, 22 February 1972.

29. Interview with Clement Zablocki, 10 February 1972.

30. Interview with the Reverend Robert Sampon, 15 November 1971.

31. Confidential source.

32. Senate and House, *Memorial Services Held in the Senate and House . . . in Eulogy of Joseph Raymond McCarthy*, pp. 47, 50, 88, 89.

33. *Time* 58 (22 October 1951): 22.

34. James Gillis, "Sursum Corda," *San Francisco Monitor*, 5 September 1952.

35. Kersten interview.

36. Interview with Joseph P. McMurray, 1 March 1972. (At the time of the McCarthy controversies, McMurray was staff director of the Senate Banking and Currency Committee; he was thus able to observe McCarthy at close range.)

37. Interview with Miles McMillin, 22 November 1971; John Cogley, "Behind the Many Faces," p. 182; interview with James O'Gara, 17 February 1972.

38. Anderson and May, *McCarthy*, p. 364.

39. Interviews with Kersten and Cohn; interview with William F. Buckley, Jr., 16 May 1972.

40. Oliver Pilat and William Shannon, "Smear Incorporated," *New York Post*, 5 September 1951.

41. *New York Times*, 15 November 1954, p. 26.

42. Zablocki interview. A similar opinion comes from Congressman (and ex-Speaker of the House) John McCormack. Interview with John McCormack, 15 December 1972.

43. "Deposition of Joseph R. McCarthy" and "Wisconsin State Tax Returns," William Roberts Papers, State Historical Society of Wisconsin, Madison, Wis.

44. *Brooklyn Tablet*, 30 May 1953; Scanlan interview; Helen Williams, "Never Sound Retreat!" p. 88.

45. *Brooklyn Tablet*, 3 October 1953.

46. *Washington Star*, 19 September 1953; *Washington Post*, 30 September 1953; *New York Times*, 30 September 1953, p. 15.

47. *Congressional Report* 2 (16 October 1953): 3.

48. See especially *Memorial Services . . . McCarthy*, pp. 172, 251–52, 261–62; Richard Ginder in *Our Sunday Visitor*, 19 May 1957.

49. *Boston Pilot*, 3 October 1953.

50. *Davenport* (Iowa) *Catholic Messenger*, 30 October 1952.

51. Rovere, *McCarthy*, p. 49.

52. Warren Vinz, "Protestant Fundamentalism and McCarthy," p. 319.

Chapter 3

1. For an exhaustive study of the Wheeling speech, including all its problems, see Robert Griffith, *The Politics of Fear*, pp. 48–51.

2. For detailed accounts of the crises leading to the McCarthy era, see Allen J. Matusow, ed., *Joseph R. McCarthy*, pp. 1–10; Griffith, *Politics*, pp. 30–48.

3. See Athan Theoharis, *Seeds of Repression*.

4. Matusow, *McCarthy*, p. 5.

5. *Washington Post*, 14 March 1950.

6. *Madison* (Wis.) *Capital-Times*, 19 April 1950.

7. *Washington Post*, 29 November 1951, 7 May 1957.

8. Jack Anderson and Ronald May, *McCarthy*, pp. 172–73.

9. I. F. Stone, *The Haunted Fifties* (New York: Random House, 1963), p. 39; "The Present Danger," p. 495.

10. Richard H. Rovere, *Senator Joe McCarthy*, pp. 122–23.

11. Eric Goldman, *The Crucial Decade–and After*, pp. 139–40.

12. Cabell Phillips, *The Truman Presidency*, pp. 378–79; Alan D. Harper, *The Politics of Loyalty*, p. 126; Burt Hirschfeld, *Freedom in Jeopardy*, pp. 44–45; Fred J. Cook, *The Nightmare Decade*, pp. 139–41; David Halberstam, *The Best and the Brightest*, pp. 117–18.

13. Michael J. O'Brien, "Senator Joseph McCarthy and Wisconsin," p. 97.

14. Edmund A. Walsh Papers, Georgetown University, Washington, D.C.

15. The Reverend Louis Gallagher to author, 19 October 1971. (N.B.—Gallagher was Walsh's lifelong companion and closest friend.) Other accounts of Walsh's challenge to Pearson come from the following Jesuits at Georgetown, both immediately acquainted with Walsh: the Reverend Dan Power (interviewed 4 February 1972) and the Reverend Brian McGrath (interviewed 8 February 1972).

16. Julia J. McCormick to Guthrie, 20 April 1950, Walsh Papers; Guthrie to McCormick, 24 April 1950, ibid.

17. Interview with George Higgins, 11 February 1972.

18. Edmund A. Walsh, *Total Empire*, p. 95.

19. Griffith, *Politics*, p. 49.

20. Interview with Eugene McCarthy, 3 February 1972.

21. Gallup poll No. AIPO 454 (March 1950), Rober Public Opinion Research Center, Williamstown, Mass.

22. *Brooklyn Tablet*, 4 March 1950, 25 March 1950.

23. *Boston Pilot*, 1 April 1950. For similar opinion, see *Milwaukee Herald-Citizen*, 15 April 1950; *Sign* 29 (April 1950): 8.

24. Christopher Emmet, "McCarthy Muddle," p. 674.

25. "Congress Looking for Facts," pp. 6–7.

26. Cronin to author, 2 June 1972; interview with Cronin, 7 February 1972.

27. "Confidential Preliminary Report," William A. Roberts Papers, State Historical Society of Wisconsin, Madison, Wis.

28. Cronin interview.

29. *Milwaukee Journal*, 2 April 1950.

30. Griffith, *Politics*, pp. 71–77.

31. Interview with Charles Kersten, 15 November 1971.

32. Owen Lattimore, *Ordeal by Slander*, p. 120.

33. U.S., Congress, Senate, Committee on Foreign Relations, *State Department Loyalty Investigations*, 81st Cong., 2d sess., 1950, pp. 487–98.

34. Interview with Louis F. Budenz, 14 April 1972.

35. Ibid.

36. U.S., Congress, *State Department Loyalty Investigations*, p. 629; Budenz interview.

37. *Ave Maria* 72 (20 September 1950): 419.

38. Ibid. For similar comment see "The Budenz Testimony," p. 129; *Wanderer*, 8 April 1950.

39. Elmer Davis, *But We Were Born Free*, p. 189.

40. *Washington Post*, 16 April 1950.

41. Interview with Maurice Rosenblatt, 1 February 1972.

42. U.S., Congress, Senate, *Congressional Record*, 81st Cong., 2d sess., 1950, pp. 6969–75.

43. (New York City) *Catholic News*, 20 May 1950.

44. *Wanderer*, 18 May 1950; "Chavez Muddies the Waters," p. 229.

45. Joseph A. Breig in *Los Angeles Tidings*, 26 May 1950.

46. Budenz interview.

47. *Milwaukee Journal*, 26 May 1950. See also *Boston Pilot*, 20 May 1950.

48. Rosenblatt interview; Rosenblatt to author, 22 December 1972.

49. For Protestant opinion see "McCarthy and the Catholics," p. 667.

50. George Higgins in "The Yardstick," NCWC News Release, week of 5 June 1950. Copy in Mullen Library, Catholic University of America, Washington, D.C.

51. Interview with Monsignor John Randall, 25 February 1972.

52. *Rochester* (N.Y.) *Courier-Journal*, 2 June 1950; *New York Times*, 18 May 1951, p. 25.

53. *Rochester* (N.Y.) *Times-Union*, 26 May 1950; *Milwaukee Herald-Citizen*, 3 June 1950.

54. *Chicago Tribune*, 26 May 1950.

55. Religious News Service release, 26 May 1950, Religious News Service Papers, National Conference of Christians and Jews, New York, N.Y.

56. *Milwaukee Journal*, 26 May 1950.

57. "The McCarthy Question," p. 53.

58. Interview with James Doyle, 17 November 1971. Mr. Doyle was a member of the *Milwaukee Herald-Citizen*'s staff during the McCarthy era.

59. *Brooklyn Tablet*, 3 June 1950; interview with Patrick Scanlan, 28 February 1972.

60. *Milwaukee Journal*, 10 June 1950.

61. *New York Times*, 18 July 1950, pp. 1, 16.

62. "Senator McCarthy's Big Show," p. 381.

63. *Brooklyn Tablet*, 2 September 1950; 4 August 1951; 6 October 1951; 12 April 1952; 20 December 1952.

64. *Sign* 30 (October 1950): 9; *Sign* 31 (October 1951): 6; Richard Stokes in *Los Angeles Tidings*, 4 August 1950; *Milwaukee Herald-Citizen*, 22 July 1950; "Letter to Senator Tydings," *Ave Maria*, 72 (12 August 1950): 195.

Chapter 4

1. *New York Times*, 21 May 1950, sec. 4, p. 7.

2. *Milwaukee Journal*, 8 November 1950.

3. Interview with Clemzablocki, 10 February 1972.

4. *Milwaukee Journal*, 8 November 1950; interview with Charles Kersten, 15 November 1971.

5. J. J. Tierney, "Maryland," *New Catholic Encyclopedia*, 9: 400.

6. Robert Griffith, *The Politics of Fear*, p. 130.

7. *New York Times*, 24 September 1950, p. 76.

8. Griffith, *Politics*, p. 127.

9. Ibid., p. 129.

10. "Cadets and Campaigners," *Commonweal* 54 (17 August 1951): 445.

11. Griffith, *Politics*, pp. 129–31.

12. Louis Bean, *Influences in the 1954 Mid-Term Elections*, p. 28.

13. State Administration Board of Election Laws, State of Maryland, to author, 17 January 1973. The most recent assessment of the Catholic vote suggests that Catholicism was not a major factor in the vote. See Richard M. Fried, *Men against McCarthy*, pp. 138–39.

14. Ibid.

15. *New York Times*, 12 November 1950, sec. 4, p. 8.

16. *Our Sunday Visitor*, 26 November 1950.

17. Griffith, *Politics*, p. 131.

18. Spingarn to Administration, 22 May 1950, Stephen Spingarn Papers, Harry S. Truman Presidential Library, Independence, Mo.; Matthew J. Connelly to Donald Dawson, 25 January 1951, Harry S. Truman Papers, ibid.; Bishop Emmet Walsh to Truman, 7 February 1951, ibid.; John H. Lemon to Truman, 28 February 1951, ibid; Spingarn memorandum to administration, 19 November 1952, Spingarn Papers.

19. Quotation cited in Vincent A. Lapomarda, "Maurice Joseph Tobin, 1901–1953," pp. 445–46.

20. *Christian Science Monitor*, 12 October 1951; copy of Tobin speech in Maurice J. Tobin Papers, National Archives, Washington, D.C.

21. U.S., Congress, Senate, *Congressional Record*, 82d Cong., 1st sess., 1951, pp. 6556–6603.

22. Richard Rovere, *Senator Joe McCarthy*, p. 177.

23. Interviews with Brian McGrath, 8 February 1972, and Daniel Power, 4 February 1972.

24. Vincent S. Kearney, "Wedemeyer Versus McCarthy," p. 323. See also *America* 85 (29 September 1951): 614.

25. *Milwaukee Journal*, 16 June 1951.

26. Francis Downing, " 'Patriots' and 'Controversial Figures,' " p. 91.

27. *Wanderer*, 30 October 1952.

28. *Brooklyn Tablet*, 4 August 1951.

29. *Commonweal* 55 (19 October 1951): 36.

30. For a full discussion of the Benton-Hennings-Gillette affair, see Griffith, *Politics*, pp. 152–84.

31. Benton to Harold E. Fey, 29 August 1951, William Benton Papers, State Historical Society of Wisconsin, Madison, Wis. (hereafter cited as SHSW).

32. Robert C. Hartnett, "Benton-McCarthy Show-Down?" p. 660. See also *America* 87 (12 April 1952): 32.

33. Gustaf Anderson to Benton, 7 August 1951, Benton Papers, SHSW.

34. Copy in National Conference of Catholic Bishops Papers, United States Catholic Conference, Washington, D.C.

35. Speech to Holy Name Society, Waterbury, Conn., copy in Benton Papers, New York City; Benton to Catherine M. Flynn, 8 December 1951, Benton Papers, SHSW; Flynn to Benton, 5 February 1952, ibid.

36. *Madison* (Wis.) *Capital-Times*, 20 November 1951.

37. *Washington Post*, 29 November 1951.

38. Jack Anderson and Ronald W. May, *McCarthy*, p. 395.

39. John B. Oakes, "Report on McCarthy and McCarthyism," p. 28. The *New York Times* printed the full text of the bishop's statement on 18 November 1951, pp. 1, 68.

40. *Madison* (Wis.) *Capital-Times*, 20 November 1951.

41. Vincent P. DeSantis, "American Catholics and McCarthyism," p. 8.

42. Bishop Karl Alter to author, 19 February 1972; Bishop Thomas Gorman to author, 28 February 1972.

43. Interview with George Higgins, 11 February 1972.

44. Interview with John F. Cronin, 7 February 1972.

45. Roper poll, No. RCOM 59, May 1952, Roper Public Opinion Research Center, Williamstown, Mass.

Chapter 5

1. *New York Times*, 28 October 1952, p. 30.

2. Ibid.

3. Ibid.

4. Michael O'Brien, "Senator Joseph McCarthy in Wisconsin: 1946–1957," pp. 298–99.

5. *Milwaukee Journal*, 29 June 1952.

6. *Christian Science Monitor*, 8 September 1952.

7. *Madison* (Wis.) *Capital-Times*, 15 October 1951.

8. Schmitt to author, 9 June 1972.

9. Karl Ernest Meyer, "The Politics of Loyalty," p. 168.

10. Ibid., pp. 188–91.

11. John B. Oakes, "Report on McCarthy and McCarthyism," p. 28. See also, Miles McMillin in *New York Times*, 21 September 1952, sec. 4, p. 5.

12. *Green Bay Press-Gazette*, 10 September 1952.

13. *Brooklyn Tablet*, 13 September 1952.

14. Helen Williams, "Never Sound Retreat!" pp. 86–87. For similar viewpoints, see *Wanderer*, 11 September 1952; *Our Sunday Visitor*, 28 September 1952.

15. *Davenport* (Iowa) *Catholic Messenger*, 9 October 1952.

16. Interview with Patrick F. Lucey, 2 December 1971.

17. Interview with Clement Zablocki, 10 February 1972.

18. Interview with Charles Kersten, 16 November 1971.

19. Interview with James E. Doyle, 30 November 1971.

20. Lucey interview.

21. *1954 Wisconsin Blue Book* ([State of Wisconsin], Madison, Wis., 1954), pp. 477 ff. Figure for 1946 taken from Fred J. Cook, *The Nightmare Decade*, p. 110.

22. Meyer, "Politics of Loyalty," pp. 207–10.

23. David Oshinsky, "Joe McCarthy (Revisited)," p. 119.

24. David Oshinsky, "Senator Joseph McCarthy and the American Labor Movement," pp. 253–57, 263.

25. Louis Bean, *Influences in the 1954 Mid-Term Elections*, pp. 14–15.

26. Ibid.

27. Zablocki interview.

28. Figures supplied by Manuscript Division, State Historical Society of Wisconsin, Madison, Wis. Hereafter cited as SHSW.

29. Manuscript Division, SHSW; *1954 Wisconsin Blue Book*, p. 757.

30. *1954 Wisconsin Blue Book*, p. 757.

31. Interviews with Zablocki, Lucey, and Doyle.

32. Michael P. Rogin, *The Intellectuals and McCarthy*, p. 246.

33. Robert C. Hartnett, "Pattern of GOP Victory," p. 209.

34. McCarthy to Hartnett, *America* 88 (13 December 1952): 316.

35. Robert C. Hartnett, "Daily Worker on Stevenson," pp. 302–3.

36. Robert C. Hartnett, "Documents and Innuendoes," pp. 327–28. See also "Detecting Subversives," *America* 88 (3 January 1953): 370.

37. McCarthy to Hartnett, 6 January 1953. Stencilled copy in Patrick McCarran Papers, College of the Holy Names, Oakland, Calif.

38. Ray Kiermas [for McCarthy] to McMahon, 13 January 1953, Jesuit Archives, Fordham University, New York, N.Y.; McMahon to McCarthy, 15 January 1953, ibid.

39. *Washington Post*, 4 January 1953.

40. *New York World-Telegram*, 6 November 1952.

41. Interview with William F. Benton, 25 February 1972.

42. *New Catholic Encyclopedia*, 4: 178. The most Catholic state was Rhode Island, with a Catholic population of 58.6 percent; Massachusetts was second with 48.5 percent, ibid., 7: 460, 9: 429. These figures are based on a study compiled by the National Council of the Churches of Christ in 1952 and published in 1956. The study is proba-

bly the most accurate one ever made of church membership in the United States.

43. See especially *Congressional Report* 1 (25 October 1952): 3.

44. Bean, *Influences*, p. 24.

45. Sidney Hyman, *The Lives of William Benton*, p. 481.

46. Figures supplied by Registrar of Voters, City of Waterbury (Thomas J. McLarney to author, 17 November 1972).

47. Benton oral history interview, 18 July 1964, Oral History Collection, John F. Kennedy Presidential Library, Waltham, Mass. Hereafter cited as JFKL.

48. Roy Cohn, *McCarthy*, p. 16.

49. *New York Post*, 30 June 1956.

50. Robert Thompson and Hortense Myers, *Robert F. Kennedy*, p. 96.

51. See interviews with James M. Burns, 14 May 1965; Leonard Bernstein, 21 July 1965; William O. Douglas, 9 November 1967; and George Smathers, 10 July 1964—all in Oral History Collection, JFKL.

52. For Joseph P. Kennedy's relationship with McCarthy, see Irwin Ross, "Joseph P. Kennedy, The True Story," *New York Post*, 6 January 1961; Margaret Laing, *The Next Kennedy*, p. 140; Theodore C. Sorenson, *Kennedy*, p. 46; Jean Stein, *American Journey*, p. 49.

53. For Robert Kennedy's relationship with McCarthy, see Edwin Guthman, *We Band of Brothers*, pp. 12–26; Robert F. Kennedy, *The Enemy Within*; Laing, *The Next Kennedy*, pp. 138–46; Jack Newfield, *Robert Kennedy*; William V. Shannon, *The Heir Apparent*, pp. 55–57; Nick Thimmesch and William Johnson, *Robert Kennedy at 40*, pp. 25, 52–64; Thompson and Myers, *Robert Kennedy*, pp. 98–122.

54. John Mallan, "Massachusetts," p. 12. See also James M. Burns, *John Kennedy*, p. 138.

55. U.S., Congress, House, *Congressional Record*, 81st Cong., 1st sess., 1949, pp. 532–33.

56. Copy of speech in box 25, JFK Pre-Presidential File, John F. Kennedy Papers, JFKL.

57. Arthur Schlesinger, Jr., *A Thousand Days*, p. 13.

58. Statement made in speech of 21 April 1951 before a Boston taxpayers group. See copy in box 25, JFK Pre-Presidential File, Kennedy Papers, JFKL.

59. Paul F. Healey, "Galahad in the House," p. 11.

60. Burns, *Kennedy*, p. 133.

61. Mallan, "Massachusetts," p. 110.

62. Schlesinger, *Thousand Days*, p. 12.

63. Ibid.

64. For the two occasions when McCarthyism emerged as an issue, see Richard J. Whalen, *The Founding Father*, p. 426; Ralph Martin and Ed Plaut, *Front Runner, Dark Horse*, p. 203.

65. See campaign literature in "1952 Senate Campaign" File, boxes 1–27, Pre-Presidential File, Kennedy Papers, JFKL.

66. See press release for 30 October 1952, "1952 Senate Campaign" File, box 24, Pre-Presidential File, ibid.

67. See "Nationalist Groups Files" folder, "1952 Senate Campaign" File, box 17, Pre-Presidential File, ibid.

68. Copy in "1952 Senate Campaign" File, box 1, Pre-Presidential File, ibid.

69. Mulkern interview of 27 May 1964, Oral History Collection, JFKL; author's interview with Powers, 3 March 1972.

70. Burns, *Kennedy*, p. 108.

71. William F. Benton interview of 18 July 1964, Oral History Collection, JFKL.

72. Westbrook Pegler column, *New York Journal-American*, 9 December 1960; Whalen, *Founding Father*, pp. 427–28.

73. Burns, *Kennedy*, pp. 109–110.

74. Irwin Ross, "Joseph P. Kennedy, The True Story," *New York Post*, 12 January 1961.

75. Commonwealth of Massachusetts, *Election Statistics, The Commonwealth of Massachusetts, 1952*, Public Document No. 42, p. 357.

76. Eric Sevareid, *Candidates 1960* (New York: Basic Books, 1969), pp. 202–3. See also Emmet John Hughes, *The Ordeal of Power*, p. 355.

77. Schlesinger quoted in Martin and Plaut, *Front Runner*, p. 203.

78. INRA State Poll, 1954, "Massachusetts," p. 44, in box 591, Pre-Presidential File, Kennedy Papers.

79. Interview with Harold Miller, 10 February 1972. (Miller was Kilgore's administrative assistant at the time of the 1952 election.) Figures on West Virginia's Catholic population from J. L. Morrisson, "West Virginia," in *New Catholic Encyclopedia* 14: 881.

80. Bean, *Influences*, pp. 24–25.

81. Miller interview.

82. Interview with Kenneth Birkhead, 2 February 1972.

83. *Washington Post*, 3 November 1954; Thompson and Myers, *Robert Kennedy*, p. 109.

84. Angus Campbell, Gerald Gurin, and Warren E. Miller, *The Voter Decides*, p. 71; Morris Janowitz and Dwaine Marvick, "Competitive Pressure and Democratic Consent," p. 385.

85. Campbell, Gurin, and Miller, *Voter Decides*, p. 77.

Chapter 6

1. Interview with Emmet John Hughes, 20 April 1972.

2. Gallup poll No. AIPO 513, March 1953, Roper Public Opinion Research Center, Williamstown, Mass. Unfavorable Protestant opinion of McCarthy stood at 15.9 percent; unfavorable national opinion was 17.8 percent.

3. Robert Griffith, *The Politics of Fear*, pp. 200–204, 212–16.

4. See, for instance, "Voice of America," p. 567; Donald McDonald in *Davenport* (Iowa) *Catholic Messenger*, 9 April 1953; *Brooklyn Tablet*, 28 November 1953; on the famous "bookburning" issue see "'Book-Burning'" p. 371; *Brooklyn Tablet*, 20 June 1953; *Boston Pilot*, 20 June 1953.

5. For bibliography on Robert Kennedy and McCarthy, see chapter 5, note 53.

6. Mike M. Masaoka to Shuster, 21 January 1953, and Shuster to Masaoka, 30 January 1953, George N. Shuster Papers, University of Notre Dame, South Bend, Ind.; Irma Piepho to Shuster, 22 January 1953, and Shuster to Piepho, 4 February 1953, ibid. Text of Shuster speech in *New York Times*, 20 March 1953, p. 12.

7. *Madison* (Wis.) *Capital-Times*, 20 March 1953; "The Bohlen Affair," p. 279; Max Lerner in *New York Post*, 22 March 1953; *Washington Post*, 20 March 1953; *New York Times*, 20 March 1953, p. 12.

8. Shuster's mail ran about four to one in his favor. See Shuster Papers, and George N. Shuster, *The Ground I Walked On* (Notre Dame: University of Notre Dame, 1969), p. 186.

9. See Religious News Service Release for 3 June 1953, Religious News Service Papers, National Conference of Christians and Jews, New York, N.Y. (hereafter cited as NCCJ); see also *Washington Post*, 11 June 1953.

10. "Draw Your Own Conclusions," pp. 29–30; "Senator McCarthy Replies," p. 190.

11. "Senator McCarthy Replies," p. 190.

12. Lerond Curry, *Protestant-Catholic Relations in America*, p. 44.

13. See especially the weekly column of James Gillis, "Sursum Corda," in such Catholic newspapers as the *Boston Pilot*, *Los Angeles Tidings*, and *San Francisco Monitor*, and the weekly editorials of Patrick F. Scanlan in the *Brooklyn Tablet*, all for 1945 to 1955. See also *New York Times*, 1 March 1954, p. 13, and 5 December 1954, p. E3; *Wanderer*, 7 January 1954; William R. Bechtel, "Protestants and Catholics," pp. 11–12; "McCarthy in the White House?" p. 675; "What Are the Facts?" p. 5; "Loss of the South," p. 6; James M. O'Neill, *Catholics in Controversy*, pp. 186–93.

14. See especially two works by Paul Blanshard, *American Freedom and Catholic Power* (Boston: Beacon Press, 1949) and *Communism, Democracy, and Catholic Power*. See also "McCarthy and the Catholics," p. 667; "Trying to Make McCarthy a Catholic Martyr," p. 1420; "Should Catholics Approve McCarthy for President?" p. 531; TRB [Richard L. Strout], "Washington Wire," *New Republic* 130 (11 January 1954): 2; *The Churchman*, July 1955, p. 9; Curry, *Protestant-Catholic Relations*, pp. 36–60; Bechtel, "Protestants and Catholics," pp. 11–12; *New York Times*, 16 December 1953, p. 21; Ralph Lord Roy, *Communism and the Churches*, p. 261.

15. Blanshard, *Communism, Democracy*, pp. 298–99.

16. "McCarthy Resorts to Religious Test," p. 311.

17. The Reverend Lee P. Farrell to Truman, 11 January 1950, box 351, Official File, Harry S. Truman Papers, Harry S. Truman Presidential Library, Independence, Mo.

18. John V. Mulvihill to Truman, 5 July 1951, box 881, Official File, ibid.

19. The Reverend Timothy Stockmeyer to Lehman, 20 September 1952, McCarthy File, Herbert H. Lehman Papers, Columbia University, New York, N.Y.; Lehman to Stockmeyer, 3 November 1952, ibid.

20. *Our Sunday Visitor*, 26 July 1953; *Boston Pilot*, 6 June 1953.

21. John Hoving, "My Friend McCarthy," p. 31.

22. Interview of McCarthy by Roy L. Matson in *Madison* (Wis.) *State Journal*, 23 April 1953.

23. "Should Catholics Approve McCarthy for President?" p. 531.

24. "McCarthy in the White House?" p. 675.

25. Joseph B. Matthews, "Reds and Our Churches," p. 3.

26. Interview with John A. O'Brien, 5 January 1972; interview with James M. Eagan, 29 February 1972; O'Brien explained his motives in *Our Sunday Visitor*, 13 September 1953.

27. Hughes interview.

28. John A. O'Brien, Rabbi Maurice Eisendrath, and John S. Bonnell to Eisenhower, 9 July 1953, and Eisenhower to O'Brien, Eisendrath, and Bonnell, 9 July 1953, all in *New York Times*, 10 July 1953, pp. 1, 6. On Hughes and the White House events, see Emmet John Hughes, *The Ordeal of Power*, p. 95.

29. Letters in box 660, 133–E–1, Official File, Dwight David Eisenhower Papers, Dwight D. Eisenhower Presidential Library, Abilene, Kans.

30. O'Brien interview.

31. *New York Times*, 6 July 1953, 11 July 1953; Drew Pearson column in *Madison* (Wis.) *Capital-Times*, 11 July 1953.

32. *Los Angeles Tidings*, 10 July 1953.

33. *Our Sunday Visitor*, 19 July 1953.

34. *Brooklyn Tablet*, 18 July 1953.

35. Richard Ginder, "The Matthews Case," p. 662.

36. Louis F. Budenz, *Techniques of Communism*, p. 324. James Gillis's column in *Los Angeles Tidings*, 31 July 1953; Richard Ginder, "Twenty Years of Coincidence?" p. 679.

37. *New York Times*, 12 July 1953, sec. 10, p. 3.

38. Pearson column in *Madison* (Wis.) *Capital-Times*, 11 July 1953.

39. James Doyle to Herbert Lehman, 30 March 1954, in "McCarthy-HHL" folder, Lehman Papers; Donald McDonald in *Davenport* (Iowa) *Catholic Messenger*, 16 July 1953.

40. "McCarthy, Matthews, and the Protestant Clergy," p. 384.

41. "Matthews Will Return," p. 455.

42. *Boston Pilot*, 11 July 1953.

43. Roy, *Communism*, pp. 9–10, 422–25.

44. "Senator McCarthy's New Critics," p. 3; *Congressional Report* 2 (22 July 1953): 3; "McCarthy, Matthews and the Protestant Clergy," p. 384.

45. Interview with George Ford, 18 February 1972.

46. *Madison* (Wis.) *Capital-Times*, 6 August 1953.

47. *Los Angeles Tidings*, 30 October 1953.

48. *New York Times*, 25 October 1953, p. 20.

49. Ibid., 27 October 1953, p. 17.

50. Interviews with George Ford; George Shuster, 4 January 1972; Joseph McMurray, 2 March 1972; Monsignor Eugene Clarke, 28 February 1972. Msgr. Clarke not only knew Spellman intimately but is widely considered an authority on him.

51. *New York Times*, 3 November 1953, p. 20.

52. Roy, *Communism*, p. 261.

53. *New York Times*, 16 December 1953, p. 21.

54. Dulles to Margaret Edwards, 4 November 1953, John Foster Dulles Papers, Princeton University, Princeton, N.J.

55. *New York Times*, 1 March 1954, p. 13.

56. Donald McDonald in *Chicago New World*, 19 March 1954.

57. Vincent P. DeSantis, "A Catholic View of McCarthy," p. 22.

58. *New York Times*, 22 March 1954, p. 21.

59. *Washington Post*, 21 March 1954.

60. *Western Michigan Catholic*, 25 March 1954.

61. *Brooklyn Tablet*, 27 March 1954; "Drs. Pike and Sayre Refuted," p. 5; *Columbia* 33 (May 1954): 1.

62. *New York Times*, 26 March 1954, p. 8.

63. Ibid., 29 March 1954, p. 12.

64. Ford interview.

65. Ford interview; George Ford, *A Degree of Difference*, p. 150.

66. Copy of film in archives of Freedom House, New York City. Brief notice of film in *New York Times*, 5 May 1954, p. 45.

67. Ford interview; Ford, *Degree*, p. 150.

68. Interview with John C. Cort, 1 November 1971.

69. *Boston Evening Globe*, 1 December 1954; Cort interview; Cort to author, 1 November 1971.

70. Hazel G. Erskine, "The Poll: Religious Prejudice, Part I," *Public Opinion Quarterly* 29 (Fall, 1965): 489.

71. Ibid., p. 491.

72. Ibid., p. 493.

Chapter 7

1. *New York Times*, 21 February 1954, pp. 1, 2.

2. Robert Griffith, *The Politics of Fear*, p. 278.

3. U.S., Congress, Senate, Committee on Government Operations, Permanent Subcommittee on Investigations, *Communist Infiltration in the Army*, 83d Cong., 2d sess., 1954, p. 153.

4. Senate, Committee on Government Operations, Permanent Subcommittee on Investigations, *Special Senate Investigation on Charges and Countercharges Involving: Secretary of the Army Robert T. Stevens . . . and Francis P. Carr*, 83d Cong., 2d sess., p. 2155.

5. Gallup poll No. AIPO 524, December 1953, Roper Public Opinion Research Center, Williamstown, Mass.

6. Gallup poll for January 1954, cited in William V. Shannon, *The American Irish* (New York: Macmillan Co., 1966), p. 381; Vincent P. DeSantis, "American Catholics and McCarthyism," p. 2.

7. Gallup poll for April 1954, *Washington Post*, 4 April 1954.

8. *New York Times*, 31 January 1954, p. 57; *Brooklyn Tablet*, 30 January 1954.

9. *Marquette* (Univ.) *Tribune*, 22 January 1953.

10. *Wanderer*, 25 March 1954.

11. Gillis column, *Los Angeles Tidings*, 19 March 1954.

12. Gallup poll, *Los Angeles Times*, 14 March 1954.

13. Poll cited in *Boston Post*, 21 March 1954.

14. Mitchell to Grace Tully, 10 October 1953, box 12, Stephen Mitchell Papers, Harry S. Truman Presidential Library, Independence, Mo. (Hereafter referred to as HSTL.)

15. *New York Times*, 27 February 1954, p. 6.

16. *Chicago Daily News*, 27 February 1954.

17. *Boston Daily Globe*, 27 February 1954.

18. *Chicago Daily News*, 27 February 1954.

19. Ibid.; *Chicago Tribune*, 27 February 1954.

20. *Chicago Tribune*, 18 March 1954.

21. Ibid.

22. Ibid.

23. Ibid. Saul Alinsky reported (without evidence) that Bishop Bernard Sheil of Chicago was infuriated by McCarthy's speech. See Saul Alinsky, "The Bishop and the Senator," p. 6.

24. Copy of Mitchell address in "McCarthy-Dixon-Yates" folder, Mitchell Papers, HSTL. See also *New York Times*, 18 March 1954, p. 18.

25. *New York Times*, 19 March 1954, p. 18.

26. *Wanderer*, 1 April 1954; "Catholics, Non-Catholics, and Senator McCarthy," p. 639.

27. Mitchell to James P. Conway, 31 March 1954, box 8, Mitchell Papers, HSTL.

28. *Georgetown* (Univ.) *Hoya* 35 (18 March 1954):3.

29. Gallup poll of April 1954, *Washington Post*, 4 April 1954.

30. "Joe Must Go," p. 427; see also Leroy Gore, *Joe Must Go*, pp. 176–77.

31. Michael J. O'Brien, "Senator Joseph McCarthy in Wisconsin, 1946–1957," p. 327.

32. Ibid., p. 327.

33. *New York Times*, 5 April 1954, p. 12.

34. Ibid.

35. Ibid.

36. Ibid.

37. Ibid. See also, *New York Post*, 5 April 1954.

38. Senator McCarthy folder, Francis Cardinal Spellman Papers, St. Joseph's Seminary, Dunwoodie, N.Y.

39. *New York Post*, 6 April 1954.

40. Murray Kempton column, *New York Post*, 6 April 1954.

41. "Catholic Police Cheer for McCarthy," p. 483.

42. Interview with George Higgins, 11 February 1972.

43. The story of Spellman, the Catholic police, and McCarthy appeared for instance in the *Washington Post*, 5 April 1954; *Chicago Tribune*, 5 April 1954; *Boston Globe*, 5 April 1954; and many others.

44. On Spellman and Eisenhower, see *New York Times*, 1 September 1952, p. 1. On Spellman and MacArthur, see *New York Times*, 24 April 1951, p. 5.

45. Interview with James O'Gara, 17 February 1972. (O'Gara was managing editor of the *Commonweal*.)

46. Interview with John Cogley, 4 August 1971.

47. Copy of speech in Bernard J. Sheil Papers, Chicago Historical Society, Chicago, Ill. See also, *New York Times*, 10 April 1954, p. 8.

48. *New York Times*, 10 April 1954, p. 8.

49. Ibid.

50. *Chicago Daily News*, 9 April 1954.

51. *New York Post*, 12 April 1954.

52. Ibid. The text also appeared in the *Chicago Daily News*, 9 April 1954; long quotations appeared in *Time* 63 (19 April 1954): 22–23, and *New Republic*, 130 (19 April 1954): 4.

53. *Madison* (Wis.) *Capital-Times*, 13 April 1954; *Boston Globe*, 9 April 1954; *Chicago Sun-Times*, 9 April 1954; *Milwaukee Journal*, 9 April 1954; *Washington Post*, 10 April 1954; *Washington Star*, 13 April 1954.

54. Alinsky, "Bishop and Senator," p. 6.

55. *Boston Globe*, 12 April 1954.

56. Alinsky, "Bishop and Senator," p. 8.

57. *New York Post*, 12 April 1954; *New York Times*, 12 April 1954, p. 11.

58. *Brooklyn Tablet*, 17 April 1954; *Wanderer*, 15 April 1954, 9 September 1954.

59. "Fortieth Anniversary Symposium," p. 265.

60. *Boston Pilot*, 2 April 1954.

61. Alinsky, "Bishop and Senator," p. 9.

62. *New York Times*, 3 September 1954, p. 9; *Chicago New World*, 10 September 1954.

63. *New York Times*, 3 September 1954, p. 9.

64. "Bishop Sheil's Resignation," pp. 573–74.

65. *Time* 64 (20 December 1954): 55; *New York Times*, 3 September 1954, p. 9.

66. Interview with Saul Alinsky, 21 December 1971; interview with John Cogley, 4 August 1971. A former Sheil assistant published an explanation of his resignation: see Mary Elizabeth Carroll, "Bishop Sheil," pp. 45–51.

67. Interview with Monsignor John Egan, 5 January 1972. (Egan had a long and intimate association with Sheil and also knew Stritch very well. He, too, is certain that Sheil's financial woes formed the reason for his resignation.)

Chapter 8

1. *Boston Evening Globe*, 6 May 1954.

2. Gallup Poll No. AIPO 531, May 1954, Roper Public Opinion Research Center, Williamstown, Mass.

3. *Brooklyn Tablet*, 8 May 1954; 15 May 1954; 22 May 1954.

4. See Bulk Mail, McCarthy, Central File, Dwight D. Eisenhower Papers, Dwight D. Eisenhower Presidential Library, Abilene, Kans.

5. *New Hampshire Sunday News*, 2 May 1954.

6. Steve Connor to *Davenport Catholic Messenger, Messenger*, 6 May 1954.

7. *Ave Maria* 79 (29 May 1954): 6.

8. "The Hearings," p. 134.

9. Dorothy Day, "Theophane Venard and Ho Chi Minh," p. 1; Anthony Aratari, "And Pilate Wondered . . . ," p. 7.

10. *Work*, June 1954, p. 1.

11. *Boston Pilot*, 22 May 1954.

12. "The Purloined Letter," pp. 165–66.

13. Gillis column, *Boston Pilot*, 3 July 1954; *Los Angeles Tidings*, 18 June 1954.

14. "We Can Do Better Than This," p. 585; Robert Hartnett, "Presidential Leadership vs. Senate Hegemony," pp. 621, 623; "Fighting Communism," p. 34; Robert Hartnett, "Congress, Communists and the Common Good," pp. 677–79.

15. Hartnett to Wilfred Parsons, 7 April 1954, Parsons Papers, Georgetown University, Washington, D. C.

16. "Feature X," *America* 91 (17 April 1954): 71.

17. Joseph T. Prentiss to *America, America* 91 (10 April 1954): 44.

18. " 'Peaceful Overthrow' of the U.S. Presidency," pp. 210–11.

19. The article went out over the AP wires on 18 May 1954. (The 22 May issue of *America* appeared several days before the date shown on the magazine.) The AP article appeared in *Boston Daily Globe*, 18 May 1954; *Washington Post*, 18 May 1954; *Baltimore Sun*, 18 May 1954; and many other newspapers as well.

20. *Brooklyn Tablet*, 21 May 1954.

21. See, for example, *Denver Post*, 22 May 1954; *Washington Post*, 22 May 1954; *New York Journal American*, 22 May 1954.

22. "Freedom of Catholic Opinion," p. 261.

23. The Reverend Robert H. Millmann to *Brooklyn Tablet, Tablet*, 29 May 1954; the Reverend Patrick F. Hurley to *Tablet, Tablet,* 29 May 1954; the Reverend J. A. Lennon to *New York Journal-American, Journal*, 27 May 1954. (The letter from Lennon was reprinted in the *Tablet*, 29 May 1954.)

24. On agreement not to discuss McCarthy issue: interview with Thurston N. Davis, 21 February 1972. Jesuit McCarthyites complain to their superior: Joseph McGowan to McMahon, 25 May 1954, in "McCarthy editorial" folder, Jesuit Archives, Fordham University, New York, N.Y.; McMahon to McGowan, 25 May 1954, ibid.; Joseph A. Lennon to McMahon, 25 May 1954, ibid.; John F. Hurley to McMahon, 25 May 1954, ibid.; McMahon to Hurley, 26 May 1954, ibid.

25. Daniel K. Shanley to McMahon, 26 May 1954, ibid.

26. Bishop Joseph F. Flannelly to Hartnett, 29 May 1954, ibid. Flannelly to McMahon, 20 May 1954, ibid. For McMahon's reply to the Bishop, see McMahon to Flannelly, 21 May 1954, ibid.

27. Interview with Thurston N. Davis, 21 February 1972.

28. Hartnett wrote that the magazine had received seventy letters for McCarthy and six for *America*. See Hartnett to Parsons, 21 May 1954, Parsons Papers, Georgetown University, Washington, D.C.

29. Davis interview.

30. McMahon, William E. Fitzgerald, and William F. Maloney to Hartnett, 29 May 1954, "McCarthy Editorial" folder, Jesuit Archives, Fordham University, New York, N.Y. In a covering letter McMahon wrote Hartnett, "We do not wish you to interpret this Directive as a vote of no confidence. It is not that. You still have our support. But in the present heated state of public opinion, particularly among Catholics, we think silence for two months will be golden . . . P.S. If some extraordinary and crucial situation should develop which you and the Staff think should warrant an editorial or comment, you may represent this to me and I shall take it up with the Committee." McMahon to Hartnett, 29 May 1954, ibid.

31. Hartnett to Vincent McCormick, 31 May 1954, "America" box, ibid. Hartnett to McMahon, 2 June 1954, ibid.

32. McMahon, Maloney, and Fitzgerald to Editors of America, 3 June 1954, ibid.

33. Hartnett to McMahon, 4 June 1954, ibid.

34. Janssens to McMahon, 2 June 1954, "America" box, ibid.

35. Janssens to McMahon, 17 June 1954, ibid.

36. Fitzgerald, Maloney, and McMahon to Hartnett, 23 June 1954, ibid.; Hartnett to Thomas E. Henneberry, 27 June 1954, ibid.; Henneberry to Hartnett, 3 July 1954, ibid.

37. "The Passing of Senator McCarthy," p. 223.

38. Hartnett to Wilfred Parsons, 30 September 1954, Parsons Papers, Georgetown University, Washington, D.C. On 17 September 1955 Thurston N. Davis took over as the new editor of America.

39. On Hartnett's personal reasons for leaving: author's interview with Hartnett, 9 September 1971. For documentary evidence on Hartnett's departure, see Jesuit Archives, Fordham University, New York, N.Y.

40. New York Times, 10 June 1954, p. 15.

41. Michael Straight, Trial by Television, p. 251.

42. New York Times, 10 June 1954, p. 15.

43. Ibid.

44. Gallup poll No. AIPO 532, June 1954, Roper Center.

45. U.S., Congress, Senate, S.R. 301, Hearings Before a Select Committee to Study Censure Charges, 83d Cong., 2d sess., 1954, pp. 308–9.

46. Senate, 83rd Cong., 2d sess., Committee on Government Operations, Special Subcommittee on Investigations, Special Senate Investigation of Charges and Countercharges Involving: Secretary of the Army Robert T. Stevens . . . Francis P. Carr, p. 1920.

47. Boston Pilot, 12 June 1954.

48. Los Angeles Tidings, 11 June 1954. See also New York Times, 5 June 1954, p. 10; Boston Post, 5 June 1954.

49. Interview with the Reverend Francis Lally, 27 October 1971; Joseph Dever, Cushing of Boston, pp. 172–73.

50. New York Times, 17 June 1954, p. 25.

51. Brooklyn Tablet, 17 July 1954; Nation 179 (31 July 1954): 85–86.

52. Brooklyn Tablet, 24 July 1954. See also Tablet, 31 July 1954.

53. Frank Gibney, "After the Ball," p. 532.

54. Ibid., p. 533.

55. *Brooklyn Tablet*, July to September, passim. For a similar view see *Wanderer*, 9 September 1954; *Georgetown* (Univ.) *Hoya* 35 (30 September 1954): 2, 4.

56. *Brooklyn Tablet*, 4 September 1954. See also *Tablet*, 18 September 1954.

57. "The McCarthy Committee," p. 478.

58. *Brooklyn Tablet*, 2 October 1954, 30 October 1954.

59. "The Watkins Report," p. 4.

Chapter 9

1. INRA State Polls 1954, in box 591, JFK Pre-Presidential File, John F. Kennedy Papers, John F. Kennedy Presidential Library, Waltham, Mass. (hereafter cited as JFKL.)

2. INRA State Polls, 1954, "Massachusetts." pp. 38, 44, ibid. Forty percent opposed a candidate pledged to strip McCarthy of his chairmanship, and 14 percent favored such a candidate.

3. John P. and Constance L. Roche, "The McCarthy Issue," in *Shadows and Substance* (London: Macmillan Co., 1969), p. 335.

4. INRA State Polls 1954, "New Jersey," pp. 50, 54, and Table B–9, in box 591, JFK Pre-Presidential File, Kennedy Papers, JFKL.

5. INRA State Polls 1954, "Illinois," pp. 37, 40; "Ohio," pp. 32, 40, ibid.

6. INRA State Polls 1954, "Oregon," "California," "New Mexico," "Minnesota," "Michigan," "Iowa," ibid.

7. Angus Campbell and Homer C. Cooper, *Group Differences in Attitudes and Votes*, pp. 146, 149.

8. Gallup poll No. AIPO 533, June 1954, Roper Public Opinion Research Center, Williamstown, Mass.; Gallup poll No. AIPO 537, September 1954, ibid.; Gallup poll No. AIPO 539, November 1954, ibid.

9. Ibid.

10. *New York Times*, 23 June 1954, p. 14.

11. For Saltonstall's attempt to avoid the McCarthy issue, see Robert J. Donovan, *Eisenhower*, p. 255. For McCarthy's popularity in Massachusetts, see Cabell Phillips in *New York Times*, 20 June 1954; John P. Mallan, "Massachusetts," pp. 10–12; and Lawrence Fuchs, *John F. Kennedy and American Catholicism*, p. 127.

12. Frank W. McCulloch to Edward Marciniak, 19 November 1953, Paul H. Douglas Papers, Chicago Historical Society, Chicago, Ill. (McCulloch was administrative assistant to Douglas.)

13. Memorandum of Irl Marshall to himself (c. October) 1954, Joseph T. Meek Papers, Chicago Historical Society, Chicago, Ill. (Marshall was Meek's campaign manager.)

14. INRA State Polls 1954, "Illinois," Table C–9, box 591, JFK Pre-Presidential File, Kennedy Papers, JFKL.

15. *Chicago Daily News*, 3 November 1954.

16. Kersten to Bryce Harlow, 25 October 1954, Official File 138–A–4, box 701,

Dwight D. Eisenhower Papers, Dwight D. Eisenhower Presidential Library, Abilene, Kans. (hereafter cited as DDEL); Eisenhower to Kersten, 26 October 1954, Official File 138–A–4, box 701, DDEL.

17. *Congressional Report* 3 (19 November 1954): 2.

18. The feminine viewpoint was instructive here: when asked "Is what McCarthy has done good for our country?" the women of the nation said "Yes" 44 percent and "No" 48 percent. Copy of poll in Official File 138–A–4, box 700, Eisenhower Papers, DDEL.

19. Interview with John F. Cronin, 7 February 1972.

20. *Boston Daily Globe*, 8 November 1954; *New York Times*, 9 November 1954, p. 17.

21. *New York Times*, 9 November 1954, p. 17, and 10 November 1954, p. 18; *Boston Daily Globe*, 9 November 1954.

22. *New York Times*, 17 November 1954, p. 17.

23. "McCarthy's Ten Days," p. 3.

24. Senator McCarthy folder, Francis Cardinal Spellman Papers, St. Joseph's Seminary, Dunwoodie, N.Y.

25. Hilton to Spellman, 11 November 1954, ibid.

26. *Boston Daily Globe*, 8 November 1954.

27. "Trying to Make McCarthy a Catholic Martyr," p. 1420. See also Drew Pearson column in *Madison* (Wis.) *Capital-Times*, 16 November 1954.

28. *New York Times*, 28 September 1954, p. 19; *Boston Daily Globe*, 8 November 1954.

29. *New York Times*, 9 November 1954, p. 16; *Brooklyn Tablet*, 13 November 1954.

30. *Brooklyn Tablet*, 20 November 1954 and 27 November 1954; interview with Patrick F. Scanlan, 28 February 1972.

31. Paul E. Breslow, "The Relationship between Ideology and Socio-Economic Background in a Group of McCarthyite Leaders," p. 41; out of the nine top leaders of the organization listed in the *Chicago Tribune* (15 November 1954), only one was a Catholic: John Francis Neylan, a right-wing Republican from California. Ibid., p. 101. It is significant that in a long article on the association's leadership, the National Committee for an Effective Congress made no mention of Catholic participation in the movement. See *Congressional Report* 3 (1 December 1954): 1–3.

32. *New York Times*, 18 November 1954, p. 19, and 28 November 1954, p. 38.

33. Peter J. Kelly, Jr., to Spellman, 21 November 1954, in "Senator McCarthy" folder, Spellman Papers; *New York Times*, 3 December 1954, p. 17.

34. *New York Times*, 29 November 1954, p. 12, and 30 November 1954, pp. 1, 22.

35. Ibid., 30 November 1954, p. 22.

36. Alson J. Smith, "The McCarthy Falange," p. 1582.

37. *New York Times*, 1 December 1954, p. 19, and 10 December 1954, p. 31.

38. Ibid., 12 November 1954, p. 11; *Boston Daily Globe*, 14 November 1954; *Boston Pilot*, 11 December 1954; Elmer Davis, *But We Were Born Free*, p. 49.

39. Fuchs, *Kennedy and Catholicism*, p. 213; Theodore C. Sorenson, *Kennedy*, p. 12; Arthur M. Schlesinger, Jr., *A Thousand Days*, p. 12.

40. Speech quoted in James M. Burns, *John Kennedy*, p. 142.

41. Interview with Kenneth M. Birkhead, 1 July 1964, in Oral History Collection, Kennedy Papers, JFKL.

42. Interview with David Powers, 3 March 1972.

43. Kennedy to John E. Burchard, 2 February 1953, copy in General Files, box 291, Pre-Presidential File, Kennedy Papers, JFKL.

44. Letter quoted in Burns, *Kennedy*, p. 138.

45. Copy of form letter in box 449, "Legislative File, 1953–1955," Pre-Presidential File, Kennedy Papers, JFKL.

46. Burns, *Kennedy*, p. 151.

47. Sorenson, *Kennedy*, p. 46.

48. Ibid., p. 47.

49. Burns, *Kennedy*, p. 142. See also *New York Times*, 4 August 1954, p. 8.

50. Form letter of Kennedy to constituents (c. August 1954), in box 449, "Legislative File, 1953–1955," Pre-Presidential File, Kennedy Papers, JFKL.

51. U.S., Congress, Senate, *Congressional Record*, 83d Cong., 2d sess., 1954, p. 12989.

52. Irwin Ross column, *New York Post*, 30 July 1956.

53. Sorenson, *Kennedy*, p. 47; Theodore C. Sorenson, *The Kennedy Legacy*, pp. 41–42.

54. Speech quoted at length in Burns, *Kennedy*, pp. 145–46.

55. Sorenson, *Kennedy*, pp. 47–48.

56. Ibid., p. 48.

57. Burns, *Kennedy*, p. 292.

58. Sorenson to author, 14 November 1972; Burns to author, 23 October 1972.

59. John P. Roche, "On the Kennedy Library," *New Leader* 68 (20 December 1965): 17–18.

60. Sorenson, *Kennedy*, p. 49.

61. Sorenson quoted in Ralph Martin and Ed Plaut, *Front Runner, Dark Horse*, pp. 204–205; Sorenson, *Kennedy*, p. 49.

62. Joseph F. Dineen, *The Kennedy Family*, pp. 219–20; Kennedy to Robert C. Ross, 28 March 1960, in "McCarthy" folder, box 523, "Legislative Files 1960," Pre-Presidential File, Kennedy Papers, JFKL.

63. Burns, *Kennedy*, p. 155.

64. Interview with Robert Nelson, 9 June 1967, in Oral History Collection, Kennedy Papers, JFKL.

65. Irwin Ross column, *New York Post*, 30 July 1956.

66. Sorenson, *Kennedy*, p. 26.

67. Irwin Ross column, *New York Post*, 30 July 1956.

68. Burns, *Kennedy*, p. 152.

69. Kennedy to Leo Kahian, 8 May 1958, in "McCarthy" folder, box 485, "Legislative Files, 1958," Pre-Presidential File, Kennedy Papers, JFKL; interview with Patrick F. Lucey, interview of 1 August 1964, in Oral History Collection, ibid.; interview with Cyrus Rice, interview of 7 December 1965, in Oral History Collection, ibid.

Chapter 10

1. U.S., Congress, Senate, *Congressional Record*, 83d Cong., 2d sess., 1954, pp. 16329, 16335–36, 16340, 16370, 16380–81, 16392. See also *New York Times*, 3 December 1954, p. 1.

2. See, for instance, Drew Pearson column in *Madison* (Wis.) *Capital-Times*, 3 December 1954; William S. White, "McCarthy's Future Now Lies Outside the Senate," *New York Times*, 5 December 1954, p. E3; TRB [Richard L. Strout], "Washington Wire," *New Republic* 131 (6 December 1954): 2.

3. *Wanderer*, 9 December 1954.

4. *Brooklyn Tablet*, 4 December 1954.

5. "McCarthy Censure," p. 309.

6. Francis J. Keenan, "The Censure of Senator McCarthy," pp. 355–56, 358.

7. "Catholics and McCarthy," p. 276. For a similar opinion see "McCarthy's Ten Days," p. 3.

8. *New York Times*, 17 December 1954, p. 20.

9. *Brooklyn Tablet*, 25 December 1954; Jack Shanahan to *Brooklyn Tablet*, *Brooklyn Tablet*, 8 January 1955.

10. Salvatore Panzarella to Editor, *Brooklyn Tablet*, 1 January 1955; Edward I. Fenlon to Editor, *Brooklyn Tablet*, 8 January 1955. For remainder of letters, see *Brooklyn Tablet*, 15 January 1955, 22 January 1955.

11. *New York Times*, 20 August 1955, p. 18.

12. Ibid., 16 April 1956, p. 23; Margaret Laing, *The Next Kennedy*, p. 146.

13. *Marquette* (Univ.) *Tribune*, 28 November 1956, 8 May 1957.

14. "The Decline of McCarthy," p. 325; "'Who Promoted Belsky?'" p. 517; "Senator McCarthy's Refund," p. 117; "The Broken Record," p. 484.

15. Recent authors on McCarthy have put McCarthy's drinking problem into print, whereas it had previously been only a matter of gossip and rumor. See, for instance, Fred J. Cook, *The Nightmare Decade*, pp. 538–40. The present writer interviewed a number of McCarthy's closest friends, and they all agreed that "Joe really hit the bottle near the end." All concurred that the problem began much earlier but took on epic proportions with his emotional decline following his condemnation by the Senate. Understandably, McCarthy's associates insisted that their names be left out of this essay.

16. *New York Times*, 3 May 1957, pp. 1, 15; "The Passing of Senator McCarthy," p. 223; *Los Angeles Tidings*, 10 May 1957.

17. Roy M. Cohn, *McCarthy*, pp. 265–66.

18. *Brooklyn Tablet*, 11 May 1957.

19. *Appleton* (Wis.) *Post-Crescent*, 7 May 1957; "Watchman of the Citadel," *Columbia* 37 (June 1957): 2; *New York Times*, 8 May 1957, p. 37; *Milwaukee Journal*, 7 May 1957.

20. *New York Times*, 12 May 1957, p. 86.

21. Ibid., 29 June 1957, p. 9.

22. U.S., Congress, *Memorial Services Held in the Senate and House . . . in Eulogy of Joseph Raymond McCarthy*, p. 263; photographic copy of plaque sent to author by Robert Goff, past National Commander of CWV.

23. *Columbia* 37 (June 1957): 22; *Brooklyn Tablet*, 11 May 1957; *Wanderer*, 9 May 1957.

24. "Joseph R. McCarthy," p. 174.

25. John Cogley, "The Death of Joe McCarthy," p. 206.

26. "Joseph R. McCarthy," p. 174.

27. Herbert A. Kenny, "Senator McCarthy," p. 451.

28. *The Cathvet*, September 1957, p. 5.

29. Catholic War Veterans of U.S.A., *Americanism Bulletin No. 1* (15 October 1958), pp. 1–3.

30. Goff to author, 28 February 1972. (Goff is a former National Commander of the CWV.)

31. Robert Sokol, "Power Orientation and McCarthyism," p. 448; Robert Sokol, "Status Inconsistency," pp. 69, 73, 75, 80.

32. *Appleton* (Wis.) *Post-Crescent*, 4 May 1959; *Madison* (Wis.) *Capital-Times*, 2 May 1959.

33. *Milwaukee Journal*, 7 May 1962; *Milwaukee Metro*, 15–17 May 1964; *Chicago Tribune*, 3 May 1965; *Madison* (Wis.) *Capital-Times*, 3 May 1966.

34. Copy of prayer sent to author by Brey. See also *Milwaukee Journal*, 2 May 1966.

35. Richard H. Rovere, "The Last Days of Joe McCarthy," pp. 29–34.

36. See, for instance, the Reverend Lawrence Cronin to *Esquire*, 21 August 1958, in box 10, Richard Rovere Papers, State Historical Society of Wisconsin, Madison, Wis. Cronin wrote: "May I recall that the late Senator, in death, was honored by the United States Marine Corps, the Senate and his Church. They should have consulted Rovere and Esquire first."

37. For critique of Knights, see "Harper's and the Knights," *Commonweal* 73 (7 October 1960): 29; for widow's comments see her letter in *Milwaukee Journal*, 17 July 1959.

Chapter 11

1. John B. Sheerin, "Senator McCarthy," p. iii.

2. TRB [Richard L. Strout], "Washington Wire," *New Republic* 130 (11 January 1954): 2; Charles E. Potter, *Days of Shame*, p. 22; Leo Pfeffer, *Creeds in Competition*, p. 14; Fred J. Cook, *The Nightmare Decade*, p. 289.

3. TRB [Richard L. Strout], "Washington Wire," *New Republic* 130 (3 May 1954): 2.

4. See especially Vincent P. DeSantis, "A Catholic View of McCarthy," p. 22; and the same author's later monograph, "American Catholics and McCarthyism," pp. 1–30.

5. Donald McDonald in *Davenport Catholic Messenger*, 16 December 1954; John Cogley, "Two Images of One Man," p. 233.

6. James M. Burns, *John Kennedy*, p. 154. For a balanced and recent assessment by a Catholic author, see T. O. Hanley, "Joseph Raymond McCarthy," p. 6.

7. Gallup poll for January 1954, *Time* 63 (25 January 1954): 20–21; Gallup poll for

March 1954, *Los Angeles Times*, 14 January 1954; Gallup poll for April 1954, *Washington Post*, 4 April 1954.

8. Gallup poll No. AIPO 513, March 1953, Roper Public Opinion Research Center, Williamstown, Mass.; No. AIPO 531, May 1954, ibid.; Gallup poll for June 1954, *Washington Post*, 23 June 1954.

9. Gallup poll No. AIPO 513, March 1953, Roper Center; Gallup poll No. AIPO 524, December 1953, ibid.

10. INRA State Polls 1954, in box 591, Pre-Presidential File, John F. Kennedy Papers, John F. Kennedy Presidential Library, Waltham, Mass.

11. Gallup poll for June 1954, *Washington Post*, 23 June 1954.

12. *Los Angeles Tidings*, 9 June 1950, January–June 1954, passim.

13. Interview with Robert Goff, 23 February 1972; membership figures taken from *New York Times*, 20 August 1955, p. 18; for a Catholic War Veteran's dissent from the McCarthyite majority, see Edward Butler to *New York Times*, *New York Times*, 11 November 1954, p. 30.

14. Membership figures in Luke E. Hart (Supreme Knight) to Sherman Adams, 13 July 1954, in box 824, President's Personal File, Dwight D. Eisenhower Papers, Dwight D. Eisenhower Presidential Library, Abilene, Kans.

15. "Strange Case of O'Clavichord," p. 1; "Footnote on O'Clavichord," p. 1; "A Smile for O'Clavichord," p. 1.

16. "A Smile for O'Clavichord," p. 1.

17. *Wanderer*, 26 August 1954.

18. See for instance, *Work*, July 1954, p. 2.

19. See for instance, Seymour M. Lipset, "Three Decades of the 'Radical Right,'" in *The Radical Right*, ed. Daniel Bell, p. 407; Seymour M. Lipset and Earl Raab, *The Politics of Unreason*, pp. 224–25.

20. Nelson Polsby, "Towards an Explanation of McCarthyism,"*Political Studies* 8 (October 1960): 258–62; Michael P. Rogin, *The Intellectuals and McCarthy*, pp. 238–39.

21. Rogin, *Intellectuals*, p. 239; Polsby, "Towards an Explanation," pp. 258–62.

22. Martin A. Trow, "Right-Wing Radicalism and Political Intolerance," p. 115.

23. Ibid., p. 117.

24. Gallup poll No. AIPO 525, January 1954, Roper Center.

25. Ibid.

26. Robert Sokol, "Power Orientation and McCarthyism," p. 448.

27. Robert Sokol, "Status Inconsistency," pp. 73, 75.

28. Trow, "Right-Wing Radicalism," pp. 120, 137–38.

29. Rogin, *Intellectuals*, p. 239.

30. Trow, pp. 137–38.

31. Angus Campbell and Homer C. Cooper, *Group Differences in Attitudes and Votes*, p. 149.

32. Sokol, "Power Orientation and McCarthyism," p. 80.

33. Rogin, *Intellectuals*, pp. 238–39.

34. Lipset, "Three Decades of the 'Radical Right,'" p. 407. He repeats the same thesis in his more recent *Politics of Unreason*, p. 232.

35. Allan Nevins, *Herbet H. Lehman and His Era*, p. 334; Kevin Phillips, *The Emerging Republican Majority*, pp. 158–59.

36. Poll cited in Lipset, "Three Decades," p. 407.

37. Ibid., p. 406.

38. Ibid., p. 420.

39. Ibid., p. 406. For another criticism of Lipset's interpretation, see Louis Harris, *Is There a Republican Majority?*, p. 90.

40. *Catholic Digest* 18 (February 1954): 1–2.

41. Hadley Cantril, ed., *Public Opinion, 1935–1946,* pp. 807–8; Ralph Lord Roy, *Communism and the Churches,* p. 112.

42. Robert Bellah, "Civil Religion in America," pp. 3–23; Robert Bellah, *Beyond Belief*; Robert Bellah, *Broken Covenant*.

Bibliography

Manuscript Collections

Abilene, Kans.
  Dwight D. Eisenhower Presidential Library
    Dwight D. Eisenhower Papers
Boston.
  Archives of Catholic Archdiocese of Boston
    Richard M. Cushing Papers
  Boston Public Library
    Joseph N. Welch Papers
Chicago.
  Chicago Historical Society
    Catholic Interracial Council of Chicago Papers
    Paul H. Douglas Papers
    Friendship House Papers
    Joseph T. Meek Papers
    Bernard J. Sheil Papers
Dunwoodie, N.Y.
  St. Joseph's Seminary
    Francis Cardinal Spellman Papers
Independence, Mo.
  Harry S. Truman Presidential Library
    Stephen Mitchell Papers
    Stephen Spingarn Papers
    Harry S. Truman Papers
Madison, Wis.
  State Historical Society of Wisconsin
    American Federation of Labor–C.I.O. Committee on Political Action
    Papers, 1946–1959
    Americans for Democratic Action Papers
    William Benton Papers
    Robert Fleming Papers
    Joe Must Go Club Papers
    William A. Roberts Papers

Bibliography

Richard Rovere Papers
Alexander Wiley Papers
New York
America House
John LaFarge Papers
Columbia University
Herbert H. Lehman Papers
Encyclopedia Britannica Offices
William Benton Papers
Fordham University
Jesuit Archives
National Conference of Christians and Jews
National Conference of Christians and Jews Papers
Religious News Service Papers
Woodstock College
John Courtney Murray Papers
Oakland, Calif.
College of the Holy Names
Patrick McCarran Papers
Princeton, N.J.
Princeton University
John Foster Dulles Papers
South Bend, Ind.
University of Notre Dame
George N. Shuster Papers
Waltham, Mass.
John F. Kennedy Presidential Library
John F. Kennedy Papers
Washington, D.C.
Georgetown University
Wilfred Parsons Papers
Edmund A. Walsh Papers
Library of Congress
G. Bromley Oxnam Papers
National Archives
Maurice J. Tobin Papers
National Council of Catholic Laity
National Council of Catholic Laity Papers
National Committee for an Effective Congress
National Committee for an Effective Congress Papers

Bibliography

United States Catholic Conference
National Conference of Catholic Bishops Papers
Williamstown, Mass.
Roper Public Opinion Research Center

Government Documents

U.S. Congress, Senate and House. *Congressional Record*, vols. 96–103, 1950–57.

U.S. Congress, Senate. Committee on Foreign Relations, Subcommittee of the Committee. *Employees in the State Department Disloyal to the United States: Hearings.* 81st. Cong., 2d. sess., March–May 1950.

————. Committee on Government Operations, Permanent Subcommittee on Investigations. *Security–Government Printing Office: Hearings . . . on S. R. 40.* 83d. Cong., 1st. sess., August 1953.

————. Committee on Government Operations, Permanent Subcommittee on Investigations. *Security–United Nations: Hearings . . . on S. R. 40.* 83d. Cong., 1st. sess., September 1953.

————. Committee on Government Operations, Permanent Subcommittee on Investigations. *State Department Information Program–Information Centers: Hearings . . . on S. R. 40.* 83d. Cong., 1st. sess., March–August 1953.

————. Committee on Government Operations, Permanent Subcommittee on Investigations. *State Department Information Program–Voice of America: Hearings . . . on S. R. 40.* 83d. Cong., 1st. sess., February 1953.

————. Committee on Government Operations, Permanent Subcommittee on Investigations. *Transfer of Occupation Currency Plates–Espionage Phase, Interim Report 837.* 83d. Cong., 1st. sess., 1953.

————. Committee on Government Operations, Special Subcommittee on Investigations. *Special Senate Investigation of Charges and Counter-Charges Involving: Secretary of the Army Robert T. Stevens, John G. Adams, H. Struve Hensel and Senator Joe McCarthy, Roy M. Cohn, and Francis P. Carr: Hearings.* 83d. Cong., 2d sess., March–June 1954.

————. Committee on Government Operations, Subcommittee on Reorganization. *Commission on Government Security: Hearing . . . on S. R. 21.* 84th Cong., 1st sess., March 1955.

————. Committee on the Judiciary, Subcommittee to Investigate the Administration of the Internal Security Act. *The Institute of Pacific Relations: Hearings.* 82d. Cong., 1st. and 2d. sess., July 1951–June 1952.

————. Committee on Rules and Administration, Subcommittee on Privileges and Elections. *Investigation of Senator Joseph R. McCarthy: Hearings. . . . On S. R. 187.* 82d. Cong., 2d. sess., September 1951–May 1952.

Bibliography

_____. Committee on Rules and Administration, Subcommittee on Privileges and Elections. *The Maryland Senatorial Election of 1950: Hearings . . . on S. R. 250.* 82d. Cong., 1st sess., February–April 1951.

_____. Committee on Rules and Administration, Subcommittee on Privileges and Elections. *Maryland Senatorial Election of 1950.* Report 647. 82d. Cong., 1st. sess., 1951.

_____. Committee on Rules and Administration, Subcommittee on Privileges and Elections. *Select Committee to Study Censure Charges: Hearings . . . on S. R. 301.* 83d. Cong., 2d. sess., September 1954.

_____. Committee on Rules and Administration, Subcommittee on Privileges and Elections. *Select Committee to Study Censure Charges.* Report 2508. 83d. Congs., 2nd. sess., 1954.

U.S. Congress, Senate and House. *Memorial Services Held in the Senate and House of Representatives of the United States, together with Remarks Presented in Eulogy of Joseph Raymond McCarthy.* 85th Cong., 1st. sess., 1957.

Books, Articles, and Dissertations

Abell, Aaron I. *American Catholicism and Social Action: A Search for Social Justice, 1865–1950.* Notre Dame, Ind.: University of Notre Dame Press, 1963.

Alinsky, Saul D. "The Bishop and the Senator." *Progressive* 18 (July 1954): 5–9.

Anderson, Jack, and May, Ronald W. *McCarthy: The Man, the Senator, the Ism.* Boston: Beacon Press, 1953.

Aratari, Anthony. "And Pilate Wondered . . . " *Catholic Worker* 20 (May 1954): 3, 7.

Bean, Louis. *Influences in the 1954 Mid-Term Elections.* Washington, D.C.: Public Affairs Institute, 1954.

Bechtel, William R. "Protestants and Catholics." *New Republic* 128 (27 July 1953): 11–12.

Bell, Daniel. *The New American Right.* New York: Criterion Books, 1955.

_____, ed. *The Radical Right.* New York: Anchor Books, Doubleday & Co., 1964.

Bellah, Robert. *Beyond Belief.* New York: Harper and Row, 1970.

_____. *Broken Covenant.* New York: Seabury Press, 1975.

_____. "Civil Religion in America." In *Religion in America*, edited by William C. McLoughlin and Robert Bellah, pp. 3–23. Boston: Beacon Press, 1966.

"Bishop Sheil's Resignation." *Commonweal* 60 (17 September 1954): 573–74.

Blanshard, Paul. *Communism, Democracy, and Catholic Power.* Boston: Beacon Press, 1951.

Bibliography

"The Bohlen Affair." *Nation* 176 (4 April 1953): 279.

" 'Book-Burning': Smoke Without Light." *America* 89 (11 July 1953): 371.

Breslow, Paul E. "The Relationship Between Ideology and Socio-Economic Background in a Group of McCarthyite Leaders." Master's thesis, University of Chicago, 1956.

"The Broken Record: Geneva." *Commonweal* 62 (11 August 1955): 484.

Buckley, William F., Jr., and Bozell, L. Brent. *McCarthy and His Enemies.* Chicago: Henry Regnery Co., 1954.

Budenz, Louis F. *The Bolshevik Invasion of the West: An Account of the Great Political War for a Soviet America.* Linden, N.J.: Bookmailer, 1966.

_____. "McCarthyism Vindicated." *American Mercury* 81 (October 1955): 19–21.

_____. *Techniques of Communism.* Chicago: Henry Regnery Co., 1954.

_____. *This Is My Story.* New York: McGraw-Hill, 1947.

"The Budenz Testimony." *America* 83 (6 May 1950): 129.

Burns, James M. *John Kennedy: A Political Profile.* New York: Harcourt Brace & Co., 1959.

Campbell, Angus, and Cooper, Homer C. *Group Differences in Attitudes and Votes.* Ann Arbor, Mich.: Survey Research Center, University of Michigan, 1956.

Campbell, Angus; Converse, Philip E.; Miller, Warren E.; and Stokes, Donald E. *The American Voter.* New York: John Wiley & Sons, 1960.

Campbell, Angus; Gurin, Gerald; and Miller, Warren E. *The Voter Decides.* Evanston, Ill.: Row, Peterson & Co., 1954.

Campbell, Angus, and Kahn, Robert L. *The People Elect a President.* Ann Arbor, Mich.: Survey Research Center, University of Michigan, 1952.

Cantril, Hadley, ed. *Public Opinion, 1935–1946.* Princeton, N.J.: Princeton University Press, 1951.

Carroll, Mary Elizabeth. "Bishop Sheil: Prophet Without Honor." *Harper's* 211 (November 1955): 45–51.

"Catholic Police Cheer for McCarthy; Catholic Bishop Sheil Denounces McCarthy." *Christian Century* 71 (21 April 1954): 483–84.

"Catholics and McCarthy." *Commonweal* 61 (10 December 1954): 276.

"Catholics, Non-Catholics, and Senator McCarthy." *Commonweal* 59 (2 April 1954): 639–40.

"Chavez Muddies the Waters." *America* 83 (27 May 1950): 229.

"Christianity and Politics." *Life* 37 (27 December 1954): 18.

"The Church and Politics." *Newsweek* 42 (19 October 1953): 100.

"Civil Liberties and Mundt-Nixon." *Commonweal* 48 (9 July 1948): 306–307, 354, 423; 13 August 1948, p. 23.

Bibliography

Cogley, John. "Behind the Many Faces." *Commonweal* 62 (20 May 1955): 182.

_____. "Death of Joe McCarthy." *Commonweal* 66 (24 May 1957): 206.

_____. "Two Images of One Man." *Commonweal* 62 (3 June 1955): 233.

Cohn, Roy. *McCarthy*. New York: New American Library, 1968.

"Congress Looking for Facts." *Commonweal* 52 (14 April 1950): 6–7.

Cook, Fred J. *The Nightmare Decade: The Life and Times of Senator Joe McCarthy*. New York: Random House, 1971.

Cort, John C. "Mundt-Nixon Bill." *Commonweal* 48 (2 July 1948): 285–86.

Crawford, Kenneth G. "McCarthy Goes Home, and He's a Martyr There." *Newsweek* 49 (13 May 1957): 35.

Crosby, Donald. "Boston's Catholics and the Spanish Civil War." *New England Quarterly* 44 (March 1971): 82–100.

Curry, Lerond. *Protestant-Catholic Relations in America: World War I through Vatican II*. Lexington, Ky.: University Press of Kentucky, 1972.

Davis, Elmer. *But We Were Born Free*. Indianapolis: Bobbs-Merrill Co., 1954.

Day, Dorothy. "Theophane Venard and Ho Chi Minh." *Catholic Worker* 20 (May 1954): 1, 6.

"The Decline of McCarthy." *Commonweal* 61 (25 December 1954): 324–25.

DeFerrari, Roy J. *The Sources of Catholic Dogma, Translated by Roy J. DeFerrari from the 30th Ed. of Henry Denziger's Enchiridon Symbolorum*. St. Louis, Mo.: B. Herder Book Co., 1957.

DeSantis, Vincent P. "American Catholics and McCarthyism." *Catholic Historical Review* 51 (April 1965): 1–30.

_____. "A Catholic View of McCarthy." *New Republic* 130 (7 June 1954): 22.

"Detecting Subversives." *America* 88 (3 January 1953): 370.

Dever, Joseph. *Cushing of Boston: A Candid Portrait*. Boston: Bruce Humphries, 1965.

Dineen, Joseph F. *The Kennedy Family*. Boston: Little, Brown & Co., 1959.

Donovan, Robert J. *Eisenhower: The Inside Story*. New York: Harper & Brothers, 1956.

Downing, Francis. " 'Patriots' and 'Controversial' Figures." *Commonweal* 55 (7 November 1951): 90–91.

"Draw Your Own Conclusions." *Commonweal* 59 (16 October 1953): 29–30.

"Drs. Pike and Sayre Refuted." *Ave Maria* 79 (1 May 1954): 5.

Emmet, Christopher. "The McCarthy Muddle." *Commonweal* 51 (7 April 1950): 673–75.

_____. "Mundt-Nixon Bill." *Commonweal* 48 (25 June 1948): 253–56.

"Fighting Communism: The Scope of 'Opinion' " *America* 91 (10 April 1954): 34–35.

Bibliography

"Footnote on O'Clavichord." *Columbia* 33 (September 1953): 1.

Ford, George. *A Degree of Difference*. New York: Farrar, Strauss & Giroux, 1969.

"Fortieth Anniversary Symposium." *Commonweal* 81 (20 November 1964): 261–80.

"Freedom of Catholic Opinion." *America* 91 (5 June 1954): 261.

Fried, Richard M. *Men against McCarthy*. New York: Columbia University Press, 1976.

Fuchs, Lawrence. *John F. Kennedy and American Catholicism*. New York: Meredith Press, 1967.

Gannon, Robert I. *The Cardinal Spellman Story*. Garden City, N.Y.: Doubleday & Co., 1962.

Gibney, Frank. "After the Ball: The Cohn Dinner." *Commonweal* 60 (3 September 1954): 531–35.

Ginder, Richard. "The Matthews Case." *The Priest* 9 (September 1953): 659–63.

────. "Twenty Years of Coincidence?" *The Priest* 10 (August 1954): 677–82.

Goldman, Eric. *The Crucial Decade–and After: America, 1945–1960*. New York: Alfred A. Knopf, 1960.

Gore, Leroy. *Joe Must Go*. New York: Julian Messner, 1954.

Griffith, Robert. *The Politics of Fear: Joseph R. McCarthy and the Senate*. Lexington, Ky.: University Press of Kentucky, 1970.

Guthman, Edwin. *We Band of Brothers*. New York: Harper & Row, [1971].

Halberstam, David. *The Best and the Brightest*. New York: Random House, 1972.

Hanley, T. O. "McCarthy, Joseph Raymond." *New Catholic Encyclopedia* 9 (New York: McGraw-Hill, 1967): 6.

Harper, Alan D. *The Politics of Loyalty: The White House and the Communist Issue, 1946–1952*. Westport, Conn.: Greenwood Press, 1969.

Harris, Louis. *Is There a Republican Majority?* New York: Harper & Brothers, 1954.

Hartnett, Robert C. "Benton-McCarthy Show Down?" *America* 86 (22 March 1952): 660.

────. "Congress, Communists and the Common Good." *America* 90 (27 March 1954): 677–79.

────. "Daily Worker on Stevenson." *America* 88 (20 December 1952): 301–303.

────. "Documents and Innuendoes." *America* 88 (20 December 1952): 326–28.

Bibliography

_____. "Pattern of GOP Victory." *America* 88 (22 November 1952): 208–10.

_____. "Presidential Leadership vs. Senate Hegemony." *America* 90 (13 March 1954): 621–23.

Healey, Paul F. "Galahad in the House." *Sign* 29 (July 1950): 11.

"The [Army-McCarthy] Hearings." *Commonweal* 90 (14 May 1954): 133–34.

Hirschfeld, Burt. *Freedom in Jeopardy: The Story of the McCarthy Years.* New York: Julian Messner, 1969.

Hoving, John. "My Friend McCarthy." *Reporter* 2 (25 April 1950): 28–31.

Hughes, Emmet John. *The Ordeal of Power.* New York: Atheneum Publishers, 1963.

Hyman, Sidney. *The Lives of William Benton.* Chicago: University of Chicago Press, 1969.

Irons, Peter H. "America's Cold War Crusade: Domestic Politics and Foreign Policy, 1942–1948." Ph.D. dissertation, Boston University, 1972.

Janowitz, Morris, and Marvick, Dwaine. "Competitive Pressure and Democratic Consent: An Interpretation of the 1952 Presidential Election." *Public Opinion Quarterly* 19 (Winter 1955–56): 381–400.

"Joe Must Go." *New Statesman and Nation.* 47 (3 April 1954): 427.

"Joseph R. McCarthy." *Commonweal* 66 (17 May 1957): 174.

Kearney, Vincent S. "Wedemeyer versus McCarthy." *America* 85 (30 June 1951): 323.

Keenan, Francis J. "Censure of Senator McCarthy." *Commonweal* 61 (31 December 1954): 356–58.

Kennedy, Robert F. *The Enemy Within.* New York: Harper & Row, 1964.

Kenny, Herbert A. "Senator McCarthy: A Summing Up." *Catholic World* 185 (September 1957): 440–51.

Laing, Margaret. *The Next Kennedy.* New York: Coward-McCann, 1968.

Lapomarda, Vincent A. "Maurice Joseph Tobin, 1901–1953: A Political Profile and an Edition of Selected Public Papers." Ph.D. dissertation, Boston University, 1968.

Lattimore, Owen. *Ordeal by Slander.* Boston: Little, Brown & Co., 1950.

Lawrence, David. "Keep the Churches Out of Politics." *U.S. News and World Report* 36 (2 April 1954): 132.

Lipset, Seymour M., and Raab, Earl. *The Politics of Unreason: Right-Wing Extremism in America, 1790–1970.* New York: Harper & Row, 1970.

"Loss of the South." *Ave Maria* 80 (11 September 1954): 6.

"McCarthy and the Catholics." *Christian Century* 67 (31 May 1950): 667.

"McCarthy Censure." *America* 92 (8 December 1954): 309.

Bibliography

"The McCarthy Committee." *Commonweal* 60 (20 August 1954): 477.

"McCarthy in the White House?" *Ave Maria* 77 (30 May 1953): 675.

"McCarthy, Matthews, and the Protestant Clergy." *Commonweal* 58 (24 July 1953): 383–84.

"The McCarthy Question." *Commonweal* 60 (26 October 1951): 53–54.

"McCarthy Resorts to Religious Test." *Christian Century* 70 (18 November 1953): 311.

"McCarthy's Ten Days." *New Republic* 131 (6 December 1954): 3.

Mallan, John. "Massachusetts: Liberal and Corrupt." *New Republic* 127 (13 October 1952): 10–12.

Martin, Ralph, and Plaut, Ed. *Front Runner, Dark Horse*. Garden City, N.Y.: Doubleday & Co., 1960.

Matthews, Joseph B. "Reds and Our Churches." *American Mercury* 453 (July 1953): 3–13.

"Matthews Will Return." *Commonweal* 68 (14 August 1953): 455–56.

Matusow, Allen J., ed. *Joseph R. McCarthy*. Englewood Cliffs, N.J.: Prentice-Hall, 1970.

Meyer, Karl Ernest. "The Politics of Loyalty: From La Follette to McCarthy in Wisconsin: 1918–1952." Ph.D. dissertation, Princeton University, 1956.

National Catholic Almanac, 1942–1950. Paterson, N.J.: St. Anthony's Guild Press, 1943–51.

Nevins, Allan. *Herbert H. Lehman and His Era*. New York: Charles Scribner's Sons, 1963.

Newfield, Jack. *Robert Kennedy: A Memoir*. New York: E. P. Dutton & Co., 1969.

Oakes, John B. "Report on McCarthy and McCarthyism." *New York Times Magazine* (2 November 1952): 12, 26–30.

O'Brien, David. *American Catholics and Social Reform: The New Deal Years*. New York: Oxford University Press, 1968.

O'Brien, Michael J. "Senator Joseph McCarthy and Wisconsin: 1946–1957." Ph.D. dissertation, University of Wisconsin, 1971.

O'Neill, James M. *Catholics in Controversy*. New York: Declan X. McMullen Co., 1954.

Oshinsky, David. "Joe McCarthy (Revisited)." *Commentary* 52 (October 1971): 116–19.

———. "Senator Joseph McCarthy and the American Labor Movement." Ph.D. dissertation, Brandeis University, 1971.

"The Passing of Senator McCarthy." *America* 97 (18 May 1957): 223.

"'Peaceful Overthrow' of the U.S. Presidency." *America* 91 (22 May 1954): 210–11.

Bibliography

Pfeffer, Leo. *Creeds in Competition: A Creative Force in American Culture*. New York: Harper & Brothers, 1958.

Phillips, Cabell. *The Truman Presidency: The History of a Triumphant Succession*. New York: Macmillan, 1966.

Phillips, Kevin. *The Emerging Republican Majority*. New Rochelle, N.Y.: Arlington House, 1969.

Potter, Charles E. *Days of Shame*. New York: Coward-McCann, 1965.

"The Present Danger: McCarthy's Tactics." *Nation* 176 (13 June 1953): 495.

"The Purloined Letter." *Commonweal* 60 (21 May 1954): 165–66.

"Raising False Issues: Senator McCarthy and the Catholic Church." *Nation* 179 (27 November 1954): 454.

Rogin, Michael P. *The Intellectuals and McCarthy: The Radical Specter*. Cambridge, Mass.: M.I.T. Press, 1967.

Rovere, Richard H. "The Last Days of Joe McCarthy." *Esquire* 50 (August 1958): 29–34.

_____. *Senator Joe McCarthy*. New York: Harcourt, Brace & Co., 1959.

Roy, Ralph Lord. *Communism and the Churches*. New York: Harcourt, Brace & Co., 1960.

Schlesinger, Arthur M., Jr. *A Thousand Days: John F. Kennedy in the White House*. Boston: Houghton Mifflin Co., 1965.

"Senator McCarthy Replies." *Commonweal* 59 (27 November 1953): 190.

"Senator McCarthy's Big Show." *Commonweal* 52 (28 July 1950): 381.

"Senator McCarthy's New Critics." *New Republic* 129 (3 August 1953): 3.

"Senator McCarthy's Refund." *Commonweal* 62 (6 May 1955): 117–18.

Shannon, William V. *The Heir Apparent: Robert Kennedy and the Struggle for Power*. New York: Macmillan, 1967.

_____. "The Strange Case of Louis Budenz." *New Republic* 125 (22 October 1951): 9–10.

Sheen, Fulton J. *Communism and the Conscience of the West*. Indianapolis: Bobbs-Merrill Co., 1948.

_____. *Philosophy of Religion*. New York: Appleton-Century-Crofts, 1948.

Sheerin, John B. "Senator McCarthy." *Catholic World* 180 (November 1954): iii.

"Should a Clergyman Stay Out of Politics?" *Look* 18 (10 August 1954): 66–69.

"Should Catholics Approve McCarthy for President?" *Christian Century* 70 (6 May 1953): 531.

"A Smile for O'Clavichord." *Columbia* 33 (November 1953): 1.

Smith, Alson J. "The McCarthy Falange: Rally at Madison Square Garden." *Christian Century* 71 (29 December 1954): 1580.

Bibliography

Sokol, Robert. "Power Orientation and McCarthyism." *American Journal of Sociology* 73 (January 1968): 443–52.

_____. "Status Inconsistency: Specification of a Theory." Ph.D. dissertation, Columbia University, 1961.

Sorenson, Theodore C. *Kennedy*. New York: Harper & Row , 1965.

_____. *The Kennedy Legacy*. New York: Macmillan, 1969.

Stein, Jean. *American Journey: The Times of Robert F. Kennedy*. Interviews edited by George Plimpton. New York: Harcourt Brace Jovanovich, 1970.

Stouffer, Samuel A. *Communism, Conformity, and Civil Liberties*. Garden City, N.Y.: Doubleday & Co., 1955.

Straight, Michael. "To Our Readers: McCarthyism and Catholicism." *New Republic* 128 (25 May 1953): 2.

_____. *Trial by Television*. Boston: Beacon Press, 1954.

"Strange Case of O'Clavichord." *Columbia* 32 (June 1953): 1.

Theoharis, Athan. *Seeds of Repression: Harry S. Truman and the Origins of McCarthyism*. Chicago: Quadrangle Books, 1971.

Thimmesch, Nick. "Senator McCarthy's Catholic Opposition." *Nation* 180 (5 February 1955): i.

_____., and Johnson, William. *Robert Kennedy at 40*. New York: W. W. Norton & Co., 1965.

Thompson, Robert, and Myers, Hortense. *Robert F. Kennedy: The Brother Within*. New York: Macmillan, 1962.

Trow, Martin A. "Right-Wing Radicalism and Political Intolerance: A Study of Support for McCarthy in a New England Town." Ph.D. dissertation, Columbia University, 1957.

_____. "Small Businessmen, Political Intolerance, and Support for McCarthy." *American Journal of Sociology* 64 (November 1958): 270–81.

"Trying to Make McCarthy a Catholic Martyr." *Christian Century* 71 (24 November 1954): 1420.

Vinz, Warren. "Protestant Fundamentalism and McCarthy." *Continuum* 6 (Fall 1968): 314–25.

"Voice of America." *Commonweal* 62 (13 March 1953): 567–68.

Walsh, Edmund A. *Total Empire: The Roots and Progress of World Communism*. Milwaukee: Bruce Publishing Co., 1951.

"Watchman of the Citadel." *Columbia* 37 (June 1957): 22.

"The Watkins Report." *Commonweal* 61 (8 October 1954): 4.

"We Can Do Better Than This." *America* 90 (6 March 1954): 585.

Whalen, Richard J. *The Founding Father: The Story of Joseph P. Kennedy*. New York: New American Library, 1964.

Bibliography

"What Are the Facts?" *Ave Maria* 78 (26 December 1953): 5.

"'Who Promoted Belsky?'" *Commonweal* 61 (18 February 1955): 516–17.

Williams, Helen. "Never Sound Retreat!" *Catholic World* 176 (November 1952): 86–91.

Oral-History Memoirs and Personal Interviews

Saul D. Alinsky. Personal interview. 21 December 1971.

William F. Benton Oral History Interview. John F. Kennedy Presidential Library, Waltham, Mass.

William F. Benton. Personal interview. 25 February 1972.

Kenneth M. Birkhead Oral History Interview. John F. Kennedy Presidential Library, Waltham, Mass.

Kenneth M. Birkhead. Personal interview. 2 February 1972.

William F. Buckley, Jr. Personal interview. 16 May 1972.

Louis F. Budenz. Personal interview. 14 April 1972.

James M. Burns. Oral History Interview. John F. Kennedy Presidential Library, Waltham, Mass.

John J. Cavanaugh. Personal interview. 6 January 1972.

Eugene V. Clarke. Personal interview. 28 February 1972.

John Cogley. Personal interview. 4 August 1971.

John C. Cort. Personal interview. 1 November 1971.

John F. Cronin. Personal interview. 7 February 1972.

Thurston N. Davis. Personal interview. 21 February 1972.

Vincent DeSantis. Personal interview. 6 January 1972.

William F. Douglas. Oral History Interview. John F. Kennedy Presidential Library, Waltham, Mass.

James Doyle. Personal interview. 17 November 1971.

Honorable James E. Doyle. Personal interview. 30 November 1971.

John Foster Dulles. Oral History Interview. Princeton University Library, Princeton, N.J.

James M. Eagan. Personal interview. 29 February 1972.

John Egan. Personal interview. 5 January 1972.

George B. Ford. Personal interview. 18 February 1972.

Robert Goff. Personal interview. 23 February 1972.

Robert C. Hartnett. Personal interview. 9 September 1971.

Theodore Hesburgh. Personal interview. 6 January 1972.

George M. Higgins. Personal interview. 11 February 1972.

Emmet J. Hughes. Personal interview. 20 April 1972.

Charles J. Kersten. Personal interview. 15 November 1971.

Bibliography

Francis J. Lally. Personal interview. 27 October 1971.

Patrick Lucey. Oral History Interview. John F. Kennedy Presidential Library, Waltham, Mass.

Patrick Lucey. Personal interview. 2 December 1971.

Eugene McCarthy. Personal interview. 3 February 1972.

John W. McCormack. Personal interview. 15 December 1972.

Brian McGrath. Personal interview. 8 February 1972.

Arlo McKinnon. Personal interview. 16 November 1971.

Miles McMillin. Personal interview. 22 November 1971.

Joseph P. B. McMurray. Personal interview. 2 March 1972.

Clarence E. Manion. Personal interview. 5 January 1972.

Edward A. Marciniak. Personal interview. 20 December 1971.

Harold C. Miller. Personal interview. 10 February 1972.

Patrick Mulkern. Oral History Interview. John F. Kennedy Presidential Library, Waltham, Mass.

Robert Nelson. Oral History Interview. John F. Kennedy Presidential Library, Waltham, Mass.

John A. O'Brien. Personal interview. 5 January 1972.

James O'Gara. Personal interview. 17 February 1972.

James Orford. Personal interview. 15 November 1971.

Daniel Power. Personal interview. 4 February 1972.

David F. Powers. Personal interview. 3 March 1972.

John S. Randall. Personal interview. 25 February 1972.

Cyrus Rice. Oral History Interview. John F. Kennedy Presidential Library, Waltham, Mass.

Maurice Rosenblatt. Personal interview. 1 February 1972.

Robert G. Sampon. Personal interview. 17 November 1971.

Patrick F. Scanlan. Personal interview. 28 February 1972.

George N. Shuster. Personal interview. 4 January 1972.

Edward S. Skillin. Personal interview. 17 February 1972.

George Smathers. Oral History Interview. John F. Kennedy Presidential Library, Waltham, Mass.

Arthur V. Watkins. Oral History Interview. Dwight D. Eisenhower Presidential Library, Abilene, Kans.

Clement Zablocki. Personal interview. 10 February 1972.

Index

Index

Index

Catholicism influences his politics, 59; controversy among Catholics over, 59–62; testimony before Tydings Committee condemned, 60–61; McCarthy defends, 64

Burns, James M., 210, 229; on John Kennedy and McCarthy, 105, 110, 212, 213

Buseby, Fred E., 199

Butler, John Marshall: defeats Millard Tydings, 71–73. *See also* Election of 1950

Byrnes, James F., 10

C

California: Catholics in, 234

Cartwright, John K., 221

Catholic Bishops, 6, 8–9, 63; condemn immorality in politics, 83–84; varying reaction in press, 84–85; interpretation of document, 85–86. *See also* Sheil, Bernard J.; Spellman, Francis

Catholic Boy Scouts, 12

Catholic Church: extent of assimilation, ix, xi, 172, 246; on communism, 4; "Holy Office" and Knights of Labor, 5; warns against communism in 1938, 6; anticommunism of in World War II, 8; anticommunism becomes obsession in 1945, 8–25; opposes trial of Stepinac, 10–11; continued anticommunism after 1950, 13; influence on Louis Budenz, 59

Catholic Congressmen: liberal voting of, 24

Catholic Conservatives: strength of, 23–24; share common beliefs with Catholic liberals, 22–23; and support of McCarthy, 39–40; sources of inspiration, 170–71, 246; support Roy Cohn, 190; votes of conservative Catholic senators, 217; attack Rovere, 226

Catholic Democrats: leaders on

McCarthy, 76–78. *See also* Catholic liberals; Democratic party

Catholic Information Society, 19

Catholic Institute of the Press, 204

Catholic issue, 30; McCarthy attempts to rise above, 66

Catholic labor opposes McCarthy, 235–36. *See also* Association of Catholic Trade Unionists; Labor unions

Catholic liberals: embarrassed by McCarthy's Catholicism, 40; favor Democrats, 55, 246; critical of Pike-Sayre statements asking Catholics to condemn McCarthy, 137–38; and New York Catholic police, 162; reaction to Sheil's resignation from Chicago CYO, 168, 170–73; on Catholic belief, 248; help form foundation of Catholic renaissance, 251

"Catholic Power," 122

Catholic press: on persecution of church in Iron Curtain countries, 13; division over McCarthy, 55; on McCarthy's charges against State Department, 60–62; praised by Roy Cohn, 204; influence, 247. See also *America; Ave Maria; Boston Pilot; Brooklyn Tablet; Catholic World; Columbia; Commonweal; Wage Earner; Wanderer; Work*

Catholic Press Association: McCarthy address to (May 1950), 63–67

Catholic Republicans, 217

Catholic schools: federal aid to, 122, 132–33, 246–47

Catholic vote, ix, 70–117 *passim;* myth of "Catholic Bloc" supporting McCarthy, x; and Democratic party, xi, 24, 77; and McCarthy, 29–30; in Maryland (1950), 73–75; Democrats and, 77; in McCarthy victory over Schmitt (1952), 93–95; in McCarthy's

Index

1952 victory over Fairchild, 96–97; in Benton loss in Connecticut (1952), 103; and John F. Kennedy, 106–7; and 1952 Senate campaign in Mass., 112–13; and 1952 election, 114–16; and 1952 Senate campaign in W. Va., 114; and elections of 1954, 193–94; in Chicago 1954, 198; and Senate condemnation of McCarthy, 216; party preference as factor in, 240–41. *See also* Elections of 1946, 1948, 1950, 1952, 1954, 1972; German-Americans; Irish; Italian-Americans; Polish-Americans

Catholic War Veterans, 16, 17, 176, 220; on Stepinac, 10, 11; oppose Cultural and Scientific Conference for World Peace, 16; campaign vs. Communist fifth column, 18; give McCarthy "Americanism" award, 150; and NYC Catholic support for McCarthy, 160–61; support Roy Cohn, 190; oppose McCarthy censure, 190, 200–202; and McCarthy death, 221–23; subsequent support for McCarthy, 224, 234–35

Catholic Worker Movement, 44, 172, 177. *See also* Day, Dorothy

Catholic World, 93, 223–24

Catholic Youth Organization (CYO), 12, 167–69

Catholics, American: historical role of xi; vote for Republican president in 1972, ix; voting pattern, ix; and support for McCarthy, x-xii; role of masses and leaders in McCarthy controversy, xii, 243, 247–48; conservatives in, xii–xiii; liberals in, xii–xiii; and anti-Communist impulse, 1850 to 1950, 4–25; and Spanish Civil War, 7; and Poland, 9–10; on Mindszenty, 13; anticommunism of *Commonweal*, 19; in labor movement, 21–22; liberals and conservatives in, compared,

22–23; faithful to Truman and Democrats, 24; liberals and conservatives differ in theology, 55–56; assimilation of in America, ix, 116, 171–72, 246–47; come to see communism as "their" issue, 123; and Army-McCarthy hearings, 148–92 *passim;* Catholic liberals in Senate vote for McCarthy condemnation, 216–17; opinion polls and election results show opinion on McCarthy, 228–51 *passim*; follow Democrats, support New Deal, Fair Deal, 246; role of church leadership on McCarthy, 247–48; reading habits of, 247

Catholics and Protestants, 118–46; fundamentalist support for Catholic McCarthy, 41; Tydings Committee controversy deepens split between 68–69; Protestant praise for Catholic bishops, 85; history of conflicts between prior to McCarthy, 121–22; McCarthy as cause for increased tensions between, 122–23, 245; Paul Blanchard intensifies conflict, 123–24; possibility of McCarthy running for president increases tensions between, 125–26; controversy over J. B. Matthews increases tensions between, 126–32; congressional investigations as "inquisition," 130, 135, 136; Spellman as source of conflict, 132–33; and absence of ecumenism, 133; nascent ecumenism, 139–40, 145; conflict over McCarthy strained relations between liberal Catholics and liberal Protestants, 143; beliefs both groups held in common, 144–45. *See also* Catholic Press Association; Muelder, Walter G.

Chamberlain, William H., 19

Chambers, Whittaker, 251; and Alger Hiss, 45–46

Chavez, Dennis: condemns Budenz

Index

testimony to Tydings Committee, 60–61; liberals support, 62; condemns McCarthy, 77

Chiang Kai-shek, 46

Chicago: Catholics in, 155–56, 198, 232. *See also* Cogley, John; Sheil, Bernard J.; Stritch, Samuel

Chicago Tribune, 134

China Lobby, 57, 79

Christian Century, The, 124, 126, 162, 201, 203–4

Christian Family Movement, 155

Christian Science Monitor, The, 91, 112, 245

Christoffel, Harold, 107, 109

"Citizens for the Censure of McCarthy": collect McCarthy censure petitions, 140–41

Civil liberties, xiv, 109, 134, 164–65, 170, 178–79, 183, 192, 210, 212–13, 249. *See also* American Civil Liberties Union (ACLU)

Civil religion, 172, 249–51

Clardy, Kit, 199

Clark, Mark, 122

Cogley, John, 37, 78, 164, 223, 229, 249 See also *Commonweal*

Cohn, Roy, 38, 105, 106, 147, 157, 175, 186, 189–90, 204, 210

Coleman, Thomas, 30

Colgate University, 200

Colony Restaurant Story, 47–48, 50–52

Columbia, 138, 223, 235. *See also* Knights of Columbus

Columbia University, 133

Committee for the Liberation of Archbishop Stepinac, 11

Commonweal, 6, 24, 120–21, 131, 137, 154, 158, 160, 245; anticommunism of, 19, 20–21; liberalism of, 19–20; on civil liberties, 20; condemns McCarthy, 54–55; on Tydings Committee, 54, 67; on Maryland campaign, 72; and McCarthy attack on Marshall, 81; and Benton, 83; conflict

with *Nation*, 143; and Bernard Sheil, 163–64, 167, 168; on Army-McCarthy hearings, 174, 176, 178; on Roy Cohn, 189–90; on Watkins Committee, 191–92; and McCarthy censure, 218; on McCarthy death, 223. *See also* Cogley, John; O'Gara, James; Shuster, George N.

Communism: Catholic thought on, xi-xii, 7, 8; in Iron Curtain countries, 9; and Yalta conference, 9; in Poland, 9–10; as anti-Christian, 24; and liberals, 44; and conservatives, 44; "loyalty risks" and "security risks," 45; and fall of China, 46; and John F. Kennedy, 107; Protestants and Catholics battle over, 122; and J. B. Matthews, 126–32; and Protestant clergy, 131–32; and Spellman, 133–34; Sheil on, 164–65; and Richard Cushing, 188; and George Ford, 200; McCarthy on, 202, 216–17; and Jean McCarthy, 222; and true Catholicism, 245

Communist Manifesto, 123

Communist party, U.S.A., 45, 47, 186

Congress of Industrial Organizations (C.I.O.) *See* Labor unions

Connecticut: Catholics in, 83, 102. *See also* Benton, William; McMahon, Brien; Purtell, William

Cook County Democratic party, 152

Cook, Fred, 228

Corpus Christi parish, 133

Cort, John C., 141

Coughlin, Charles, 6

Cronin, John, 56–57, 86, 199–200

"Crusade for Christian Democracy," 6

Cultural and Scientific Conference for World Peace, 16

Curley, James M., 113

Curran, Edward Lodge, 166, 222–23

Cushing, Richard, 113, 205; on Flanders speech against McCarthy, 187–88

Index

Index

Index

Index

Index

McCarthy, Timothy, 26
McClellan, James, 175
McCormack, John, 10, 81, 111
McCracken, Robert, 136, 142–43, 153
McDonald, Donald, 93, 131, 136, 229
McGinley, Lawrence, J., 61
McIntyre, Carl, 41, 142
McIntyre, James Francis, 234
MacKay, John A., 130; believes Catholics
  using congressional investigating
  committees to damage Protestants,
  135
McKeldin, Theodore R., 73–74
McKinnon, Arlo, 27–28, 30, 36
McLeod, Scott, 208
McMahon, Brien, 102–3, 112
McMahon, John, 100, 181
McMillin, Miles, 37, 91–92
McMurray, Howard, 30
McMurray, Joseph P. B., 256n
Madison Capital Times, 49, 84, 120,
  165–66. *See also* Evjue, William B.;
  McMillin, Miles
Madison State Journal, 126
Maine, Catholics in, 197
Manion, Clarence, 33, 189
Mao Tse-tung: forces of defeat
  Nationalists of Chiang Kai-shek, 46
Marcantonio, Vito, 105
Marquette University, 27–28, 150, 220
Marshall, George C., 78–82, 216
Martin, Edward R., 200–201
Marx, Karl, 159
Maryland: Catholics in, 71, 74–75.
  See also Election of 1950; Tydings,
  Millard E.
Massachusetts: Catholics in, 113, 194,
  197–98, 214, 224–25, 232. *See also*
  Catholic vote; Cushing, Richard;
  Irish; Kennedy, John F.; Kennedy,
  Joseph P., Sr.; Kennedy, Robert;
  Saltonstall, Leverett; Spellman,
  Francis
Matthews, J. B.: conflict over, 126–32

Meek, Joseph, 198
Methodist Church. *See* Matthews, J. B.
Meyer, Agnes, 150
Michigan: Catholics in, 193
Midwest: Catholics in, 233
Milwaukee Herald Citizen, 65
Milwaukee Journal, 91
Mindszenty, Joseph, 11–12
"Mindszenty Circles," 13
Minnesota: Catholics in, 193
Mission to Moscow (1943), 8
Mitchell, Stephen, 77; concern for
  Catholic vote, 151; attacks McCarthy,
  151–54; debates about McCarthy,
  156–57
Mitty, John J., 9
Mooney, Edward, 85–86
Morse, Wayne, 209
Muelder, Walter G., 66
Mulkern, Patrick, 110
Mundelein, George, 155
Mundt-Nixon Bill, 20, 24
Murray, John C., 185
Myers, Francis J., 10

N
Nation, xi, 49, 120, 143, 189, 245
National Catholic Welfare Conference
  (NCWC), 8, 13, 18–19, 56, 62, 129,
  199–200
National Committee for an Effective
  Congress (NCEC), 39, 62, 199. *See
  also* Rosenblatt, Maurice N.
National Conference of Christians and
  Jews (NCCJ), 127–28, 133
National Council of Catholic Women, 10
Nelson, Reuben, 134
New Deal, xiii, 5, 75
New England: Catholics in, 151. *See also*
  Boston, Catholics in; Kennedy, John F.
New Jersey: Catholics in, 195
New Masses, 226
New Mexico: Catholics in, 193
New Orleans, 233

-302-

Index

Index

Index

Index

Index

A Note on the Author

Donald F. Crosby, assistant professor of history and religious studies at the University of Santa Clara, is a member of the Jesuit order. He is the author of a chapter in *The Specter: Original Essays on the Cold War and the Origins of McCarthyism*, edited by Robert Griffith and Athan Theoharis, and has contributed articles to the *New England Quarterly* and *Woodstock Letters*.

A Note on the Book

Composed by The University of North Carolina Press in Mergenthaler VIP Bembo

Printed on sixty-pound Warren's Olde Style

Cover stock, Holliston Mills Roxite B-51545

Printing and binding by Kingsport Press

Published by The University of North Carolina Press